The Therapist's INTERNET HANDBOOK

The Therapist's INTERNET HANDBOOK

ROBERT F. STAMPS

PETER M. BARACH

W. W. Norton & Company
New York • London

For information about permission to reproduce selections from this book,
write to Permissions, W. W. Norton & Company, Inc.,
500 Fifth Avenue, New York, NY 10110

The text of this book is composed in Palatino
with the display set in Myriad
Manufacturing by Courier Westford
Composition and book design by Silvers Design

Library of Congress Cataloging-in-Publication Data

Stamps, Robert F., 1950–
   The therapist's internet handbook/Robert F. Stamps, Peter M. Barach.
      p.   cm.
   "Norton professional book."
   ISBN 0-393-70342-8
   1. Internet in psychotherapy—Handbooks, manuals, etc. I. Barach, Peter. II. Title.

RC489.I54 S73 2001
025.06′6168914—dc21   00-066213

W. W. Norton & Company, Inc., 500 Fifth Avenue, New York, N.Y. 10110
www.wwnorton.com
W. W. Norton & Company Ltd., Castle House, 75/76 Wells St., London W1T 3QT
1 2 3 4 5 6 7 8 9 0

CONTENTS AT A GLANCE

CONTENTS

ACKNOWLEDGMENTS

I wish to acknowledge my colleague Peter Barach for his diligence and love of the discipline, and I thank my family for their encouragement and love.

—Robert F. Stamps

Thanks to some of my early clinical supervisors, who taught me how to relate to patients as people rather than as disorders, and always to question The Accepted Wisdom: Sybille Anbar, Ph.D.; Terry Cornbleth, Ph.D.; Christine Courtois, Ph.D.; Arnold Freedman, Ph.D.; Larry V. Pacoe, Ph.D.; and Charles Vaughan, Ph.D. Also, thanks to Ben Goldhagen, who first got me connected to the Internet.

Thanks to friends and family who have both tolerated and supported my involvement in this project: Daniel Barach, David Barach, Francis Chiappa, Ph.D.; Christine M. Comstock, Ph.D.; Martha Langenbahn, Ed.D.; and Ruth Mendelsohn. Finally, I am grateful to Robert Stamps not only for conceiving of this book and inviting me to join him in writing it, but also for his continual optimism that there was a light at the end of the tunnel.

—Peter M. Barach, Ph.D.

INTRODUCTION

We are pleased to present this collection of Web sites and mailing lists to mental health professionals. We hope to generate the enthusiasm we feel for the Internet in others because we believe that both information and dialogue are what move our disciplines forward.

The Web can enhance the therapeutic process in several ways:

➤ It encourages the client to become involved and to take responsibility for change and growth. The Web sites listed in this book are not just for the immediate benefit of the clinician; many are aimed specifically at the general population.

➤ The Internet accelerates and facilitates the dissemination of ideas and research from those who study and analyze the human condition to those who labor to improve it. There is something to be said for the enforced deliberation that has always been inherent in the print process, but there are also advantages to both the broad scope, democratic nature, and instant temperament of online publishing.

➤ The cyberspace environment builds a community among therapists. E-mail, chat rooms, and mailing lists facilitate the sharing of clinical vignettes and experiences (disguised to maintain confidentiality) among professionals who otherwise would never meet. All of these things connect clinicians around the world to each other in a marvelous way. No longer do practicing therapists have to wait for a staff meeting or supervision to share the ups and the downs of therapist-client interaction with each other.

➤ The Internet empowers everyone involved in the therapeutic process: the client, his or her significant others, and the therapist. It does not, of course, help matters when a client self-diagnoses or learns that schizophrenia is caused by aliens or power lines, but new technologies have advantages and disadvantages, and the Web is no exception. All therapists should aspire to have clients who place the locus for change at least partly within themselves and within families who are educated and enthusiastic. To those ends, the Web is tailor made. Clients and their loved ones can learn the specifics of particular emotional afflictions. Clients and families facing similar issues can communicate by using e-mail, chat rooms, and mailing lists to create online support systems. It's encouraging and rehabilitative for clients and their loved ones to know that people with similar challenges can successfully weather storms and get better.

Therapists who visit the Web sites profiled in this book will quickly see that there is a staggering amount of research and advice on everything from the causes of autism to the clinical applications of Zen philosophy. With a few exceptions—family therapy and paraphilias being two of them—virtually the entire spectrum of mental health treatment is adequately represented in cyberspace. To be sure, there is nonsense on the Internet, but the therapist should remember that there is baloney for sale at the local bookstore—even in (and sometimes especially in) the psychology section. Both the social and the natural scientist must filter everything through critical eyes, even the double-blind study financed by impartial sponsors, reviewed by respected colleagues and published in the most prestigious journals. There are Web sites listed in chapter 5 to help the reader evaluate the quality of information found on the Internet; in addition to those helpful hints, the best filters are an application of the scientific method, good common sense, and the experience that years of working in the field brings to the seasoned clinician.

With respect to basic knowledge, the Web has several strong entry points for the therapist. Web sites like the one sponsored by The National Library of Medicine make it easy to access large amounts of conventional research; the online version is now a virtual representation of their entire holdings.

Information about alternative therapies, which often takes years to make its way into print, seems to spring up on the Web daily. Many of these approaches find a home on the Internet before they find much (if any) empirical support. We would never discount the weight of such validation, but the discipline as a whole benefits from a broad exposure to and a robust discussion of all methods of treatment. We have tried to be particularly inclusive with respect to non-traditional modalities even if we can offer no endorsement of any of them. Therapists who face the realities of managed care on a daily basis may discover methods to add to their repertoire that will make their work both more effective and financially viable, and clients who have been searching the Web for answers may ask for alternative treatments as well.

The Web is just as valuable a communications device as it is as a voluminous e-book. The bread and butter of this book is its listing of individual Web sites, but no therapist should neglect or underestimate the Web's ability to expedite exchanges of a professional nature between clinicians, researchers, or academicians. There are hundreds of mailing lists and e-groups that deal with mental health; more than 200 of them are listed alphabetically by subject in chapter 5. Many of the Web sites featured in the other chapters encourage postings or have contact information for the sponsor. People who establish Web sites appreciate feedback; it is the rule and not the exception for someone who submits a comment to receive a reply fairly promptly. Web publishers are especially appreciative of thank-you notes when a reader has gotten something of value, but those who use the Web should not hesitate to make constructive suggestions. Please read the advice in chapter 5 concerning subscription to any forums before subscribing, and always be especially solicitous when sending e-mail—it's easy to misinterpret electronic communication and unintentionally bruise feelings.

Therapists who are aware of Web sites, chat rooms, or mailing lists for clients might consider making a printed list of them to distribute at the appropriate time. Clients who are not yet connected at home may find Internet access at their local library or place of employment.

We have included Web sites that we consider informative and stable. We expect the overwhelming majority included in this book to be online and functional several years from the book's publication date. Don't be surprised, however, to find an occasional site unavailable—and remember that any Web site may be down at any given time for maintenance or due to a server problem. Don't assume that a Web site has gone permanently offline just because it's not immediately at hand.

In order to help readers evaluate the authoritativeness of Web sites listed here, we have included the sponsor or sponsors of each site. In some cases, the listed sponsor is the person or organization who actually supplied the information found at the site; however, sometimes the sponsor is the person or organization who designed the Web site but did not actually contribute the material that is posted on the site.

Readers will notice the Greek character Ψ (psi) displayed with some Web site reviews. This is how we highlight sites with particularly useful or extensive content. Every site reviewed in this book has something to offer, and readers should not infer that sites not given this "award" are secondary in quality or value in any way.

Although most organizations, institutions, and schools related to mental health have already established an online presence, new and helpful Web sites will appear after this book is published. Perhaps the majority of future mental health Web sites will be developed by individuals and entrepreneurs. A good starting place to find new Web sites is to use the mental health "megasites" that comprise chapter 2. There are several dozen of them, and most are continually searching cyberspace in order to update their content.

In certain places, we have included Web sites that feature products or services. As this book is intended to be a full-service resource for mental health professionals, we have noted these items when they appear to be central to the treatment process. Web sites that are exclusively and blatantly commercial or that have little or no expository information have been left out. We have also excluded the many commercial inpatient and outpatient treatment centers and clinics that have a presence on the Internet; however, search engines like Yahoo! have listings of them.

It's also important to mention that there are high-quality Web sites that have not been included. In compiling this book, we used multiple search engines and expended hundreds of hours in research, but no amount of time or diligence will be successful in locating each and every site available on the Web. The Internet is an electronic haystack with hundreds of millions of needles, and Web road maps are works in progress.

The Internet is an evolving technology that has numerous kinks begging to be ironed out. All in all, however, it's a fabulous new tool for therapists. It's true that it proliferated quickly from out of the blue, but that should not discourage a clinician from using it. The modern therapist should consider it an integral part of the treatment process, not a fad or something only to be turned to in a pinch. We were delighted with both the quality and the quantity of what we found in assembling this volume, and we share it with you eagerly. The Web is for everyone; we hope you turn to this book frequently and enthusiastically.

Peter Barach
Robert Stamps

CHAPTER 1
The *DSM* Disorders

INTRODUCTION

Web sites give valuable information with respect to virtually every disorder found in the *Diagnostic and Statistic Manual* and the ICD-10 Codes from the World Health Organization. Commonly occurring disorders, of course, have more material available than those that are infrequently seen by therapists or researchers.

There is one megasite in particular that the reader may wish to bookmark, for it contains helpful knowledge about diagnosis, treatment, and research on at least 54 separate emotional disorders: Internet Mental Health, at http://www.mentalhealth.com, which is sponsored by Dr. Phillip W. Long. Although we did not list Dr. Long's Web page for every disorder, we have cited his site either when the pages were particularly useful, or when we did not find many other sites for the disorder.

Once at the home page for Dr. Long's Web site, click on the "Disorders" icon, and select the disorder you are looking for. The site includes information for patients as well as for therapists, a section on psychotropic medications, an online mental health magazine, and links to other sites.

Here is a list of the Disorders covered at Internet Mental Health:

Acute Stress	Antisocial Personality	Bulimia Nervosa
Adjustment	Attention-Deficit	Cannabis Dependence
Agoraphobia	Autistic	Cocaine Dependence
Alcohol Dependence	Avoidant Personality	Conduct
Amphetamine	Bipolar	Cyclothymic
Dependence	Borderline Personality	Delirium
Anorexia Nervosa	Brief Psychotic	Delusional

Dementia	Narcissistic Personality	Schizoaffective
Dementia (Alcoholic)	Nicotine Dependence	Schizoid Personality
Dementia (Alzheimer's)	OCD	Schizophrenia
Dependent Personality	Obsessive-Compulsive	Schizophreniform
Depression	Personality	Schizotypal Personality
Dysthymic	Opioid Dependence	Sedative Dependence
Generalized Anxiety	Oppositional Defiant	Separation Anxiety
Hallucinogen	Panic	Shared Psychotic
Dependence	Paranoid	Social Phobia
Histrionic Personality	Phencyclidine	Specific Phobia
Inhalant Dependence	Dependence	Tourette's
Multi-Infarct Dementia	PTSD	

Chapter 1, section 4 relates to substance abuse. We have listed several Web sites that may take lenient positions with respect to recreational usage of psychoactive substances. Although we do not condone the use of psychoactive substances for recreational purposes, these sites are included for the information they provide. Refer to chapter 5 for a listing of Web sites that help the reader evaluate the quality of information found on the Web.

There are certain disorders in this chapter that have sub-sections for medication-specific Web sites. Not all medications have Web sites uniquely created to address their use; information on most drugs will be found in individual monographs contained within large pharmacology and medical sites found in chapter 4. Some of the medication-specific sites included in chapter 1 are sponsored by the drug's manufacturer. Others are either unofficial or are selected monographs that we have listed because they represent a first-line medication and contain a great deal of information.

In these sub-sections we have included only those Web sites that describe the most commonly used medications; it should not be inferred that the entire spectrum of psychopharmacological treatment is represented.

CHAPTER 1
The *DSM* Disorders

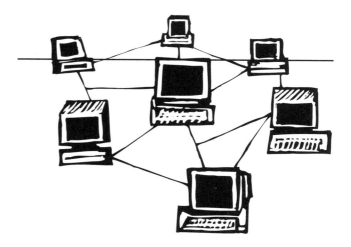

 Section 1
Disorders Usually
First Diagnosed in
Infancy, Childhood,
or Adolescence

In addition to the URLs reviewed in this chapter, the Web sites listed in the Patient Rights section of chapter 3 contain additional relevant links and resources.

This section of the *DSM-IV* includes the following disorders:

   I. Mental Retardation, which is characterized by significantly subaverage intellectual functioning.

  II. Learning Disorders, which are characterized by academic functioning below chronological age, measured intelligence, and age-appropriate educational achievement.

 III. Motor Skills Disorders, which are characterized by motor coordination substantially below expected chronological age and measured intelligence.

IV. Communication Disorders, which are characterized by difficulties in speech or language.

V. Pervasive Developmental Disorders, which are characterized by severe deficits and pervasive impairment in multiple areas of development.

VI. Attention-Deficit and Disruptive Behavior Disorders, which are characterized by prominent symptoms of inattention and/or hyperactivity impulsivity.

VII. Feeding and Eating Disorders of Infancy or Early Childhood, which are characterized by persistent disturbances in feeding or eating.

VIII. Tic Disorders, which are characterized by vocal and/or motor tics.

IX. Elimination Disorders, which are typically divided into Encopresis and Enuresis.

X. Other Disorders, including:
   A. Separation Anxiety
   B. Selective Mutism
   C. Reactive Attachment Disorder
   D. Stereotypic Movement Disorder
   E. Miscellaneous Sites of Interest

I. MENTAL RETARDATION

 ## A. GENERAL LINKS ABOUT MENTAL RETARDATION

AMERICAN ASSOCIATION ON MENTAL RETARDATION

http://www.aamr.org

Sponsor: American Association on Mental Retardation.

Information about the association and abstracts from current and back issues of its journal.

Ψ THE ARC OF THE UNITED STATES

http://thearc.org

Sponsor: The Arc of the United States, an advocacy and support organization for mentally retarded adults and children and their families.

Describes The Arc's programs and mission. Extensive directory of links to related sites.

ARTISTICAL STUDIOS

http://littlecity.org

Sponsor: Little City Foundation (IL).

Stories in pictures and words by mentally retarded adults.

BEST BUDDIES INTERNATIONAL

http://www.bestbuddies.org

Sponsor: Best Buddies International, a nonprofit organization whose programs aim to increase socialization and employment opportunities for the mentally retarded.

Describes the organization's programs and conferences. A brief FAQ section about mental retardation.

CANADIAN SPECIAL OLYMPICS

http://www.cso.on.ca

Sponsor: Canadian Special Olympics.

Information about the Canadian Special Olympics program.

Ψ COGNITIVE AND DEVELOPMENTAL DISABILITIES RESOURCES

http://www.waisman.wisc.edu/mrsites.html

Sponsor: Waisman Center, University of Wisconsin at Madison.

Extensive directory of annotated hyperlinks.

FRAXA RESEARCH FOUNDATION

http://www.fraxa.org

Sponsor: FRAXA Research Foundation.

FAQs about Fragile X Syndrome; details about current and past research.

NADD

http://www.thenadd.org

Sponsor: "NADD" (the Web site did not explain the meaning of this acronym).

FAQs on the intersection of mental health issues and mental retardation.

Information on NADD's training, educational materials catalog, and conferences.

NADD — Meeting the mental health needs of persons who have mental illness and mental retardation.

PRADER-WILLI SYNDROME FOUNDATION (USA)

http://www.pwsausa.org

Sponsor: Prader-Willi Syndrome Foundation (USA).

FAQs about PWS, along with policy statements by the Foundation.

Links to regional chapters and related organizations.

Distributes publications and booklets about PWS.

SIBLING SUPPORT PROJECT

http://www.chmc.org/departmt/sibsupp

Sponsor: Children's Hospital and Regional Medical Center (Seattle, WA).

Resources for siblings of children and adults with developmental disabilities.

The Sibling Support Project

SPECIAL OLYMPICS

http://www.specialolympics.org

Sponsor: Special Olympics, Inc.

Describes the Special Olympics and how to donate your money or time.

 ## B. DOWN SYNDROME

CANADIAN DOWN SYNDROME SOCIETY

http://www.cdss.ca

Sponsor: Canadian Down Syndrome Society.

Describes the Society's programs and conferences. Has a brief annotated list of links to other DS sites.

The Canadian Down Syndrome Society

CDSS

Building Better Tomorrows

DOWNSNET

http://www.downsnet.org

Sponsor: Down Syndrome Educational Trust (UK).

Full-text articles and books are available for a contribution; discussion forums are free.

DOWN SYNDROME: FOR NEW PARENTS

http://www.downsyn.com

Sponsors: Thomas and Michel Paul, whose son has DS.

Discussion forum for parents of DS children.

Many pages of personal stories.

Directory of DS Web sites and mailing lists.

DOWN SYNDROME ON THE INTERNET

http://www.downsyndrome.com

Sponsor: Tracey Finch (WA).

Links to national and international organizations and resources for parents of DS children and professionals.

DOWN SYNDROME WWW PAGE

http://www.nas.com/downsyn

Sponsor: Unknown.

Links to organizations and a few full-text articles. This site is not frequently updated.

DOWN'S SYNDROME ASSOCIATION (UK)

http ://www. downs-syndrome. org.uk

Sponsor: Down's Syndrome Association (UK).

FAQ section about DS and links to a few other Web sites.

MOSAIC DOWN SYNDROME ON THE WEB

http://www.mosaicdownsyndrome. com

Sponsor: National Mosaic Down Syndrome Association.

FAQs and journal articles about Mosaic DS.

NATIONAL ASSOCIATION FOR DOWN SYNDROME

http://www.nads. org

Sponsor: National Association for Down Syndrome.

Click on "Resources" for Web sites about Down Syndrome.

Ψ NATIONAL DOWN SYNDROME SOCIETY

http://www.ndss. org

Sponsor: National Down Syndrome Society.

Good FAQ section about DS.

Summaries of research on DS funded by NDSS.

Current news items.

Directory of links about DS, disability, and advocacy.

Welcome to the National Down Syndrome Society Web site — a comprehensive, on-line information source about Down syndrome.

UNO MAS! DOWN SYNDROME ONLINE
http://www.unomas21.com/index.htm
Sponsor: Michelle Mcintosh, parent of a DS child.

A support/information site for parents of DS children.

Chat room and message board.

Links to other DS Web sites.

Personal stories.

WHAT'S UP WITH DOWNS?
http ://members.ttlc.net/~Kehler/What'sUp.html
Sponsors: Michele and Jeff Kehler, parents of a DS child.

Includes personal stories about being the parent of a DS child.

Click on "DS Sources on the Web" for an annotated directory of relevant sites.

II. LEARNING DISORDERS

 A. READING DISORDERS INCLUDING DYSLEXIA

ACADEMIC LANGUAGE THERAPY ASSOCIATION
http://www.altaread.org
Sponsor: Academic Language Therapy Association, an association of professionals who treat students with dyslexia and related disorders.

FAQs about the association, with membership information.

Directory of Web sites concerning dyslexia and other learning disabilities.

BRITISH DYSLEXIA ASSOCIATION

http://www.bda-dyslexia.org.uk

Sponsor: British Dyslexia Association.

Describes BDA's programs, publications, and conferences.

DAVIS RESEARCH FOUNDATION

http://www.help-kids-read.org

Sponsor: Davis Research Foundation.

A charity that provides grants to public schools for children with dyslexia or other learning problems.

DYSLEXIA INSTITUTE

http://www.dyslexia-inst.org.uk

Sponsor: Dyslexia Institute (UK), a charity that assesses dyslexia and trains teachers to work with dyslexic people.

FAQs about assessing dyslexia and educational approaches to dyslexic children.

DYSLEXIA MAGAZINE FOR PARENTS

http://members.aol.com/dddyslexia/magazine.html

Sponsor: John Bradford, MA, an educator who conducts long-distance assessments for dyslexia.

Articles for parents helping their children cope with dyslexia.

DYSLEXIA ONLINE

http://www.dyslexiaonline.com

Sponsor: Dr. Harold Levinson, a psychiatrist and neurologist (NY).

Describes Dr. Levinson's theory that dyslexia results from an inner ear, rather than a cortical, dysfunction.

Ψ DYSLEXIA: THE GIFT

http://www.dyslexia.com

Sponsor: Davis Dyslexia Association International, which trains facilitators and markets a method of helping people cope with dyslexia.

FAQs about the Davis Method, with personal testimonials.

The excellent directory of dyslexia Web sites at http://www.dyslexia.com/links.htm is the reason why this site received a Ψ.

DYSLEXICS.NET

http://www.dyslexics.net

Sponsor: Impulse Communications.

Links to Web sites and Usenet newsgroups that provide support, information, and treatment for dyslexia.

GREENWOOD SCHOOL FOR DYSLEXIA

http://www.greenwood.org

Sponsor: Greenwood School for Dyslexia (VT).

Click on "Resources" for links about dyslexia that may be useful to parents and teachers.

INTERNATIONAL DYSLEXIA ASSOCIATION

http://www.interdys.org

Sponsor: International Dyslexia Association.

Describes IDA's programs and conferences.

FAQs about dyslexia in the form of full-text articles which address concerns of parents, college students, and educators.

Lists relevant print resources and organizations.

RECORDING FOR THE BLIND AND DYSLEXIC
http://www.rfbd.org

Sponsor: Recording for the Blind and Dyslexic, a nonprofit organization.

Records textbooks and educational materials and distributes them to eligible members for a nominal annual fee.

 ## B. MATHEMATICS DISORDER

MATHEMATICS DISORDER
http://www.adam.com/ency/article/001534.htm

Sponsor: Adam.com, an online research for health information.

Brief overview article for the general public about this disorder and its treatment.

 ## C. DISORDER OF WRITTEN EXPRESSION

MENTAL HEALTH NET: DISORDERS OF WRITTEN EXPRESSION
http://bipolar.cmhc.com/disorders/sx66.htm

Sponsors: Mark Dombeck, Ph.D.; CMHC Systems.

Summarizes *DSM-IV* criteria for this disorder.

 ## D. WEB SITES WITH RELEVANCE TO ALL LEARNING DISORDERS

INTERNET SPECIAL EDUCATION RESOURCES
http://www.iser.com

Sponsor: Internet Special Education Resources.

A directory of LD professionals, with a few articles on LD written for parents.

Ψ LD ONLINE
http://www.ldonline.org

Sponsor: WETA, a public broadcasting television station (DC).

A Web site about LD for parents, teachers, and children.

By far the most extensive collection of LD resources in a single Web site.

FAQs about LD and an online newsletter.

Numerous full-text articles by leading professionals and organizations.

Offers many opportunities for exchanging information, including bulletin boards, a chat room, and a monthly "ask the expert" feature.

First-person material, including narratives by teachers, parents, and students.

"KidZone" includes art work by LD children.

Extensive annotated hyperlinks to LD resources, lists of national and state organizations, a calendar of LD events, and a place to order PBS videotapes about learning disabilities.

® the interactive guide to learning disabilities for parents, teachers, and children

| What's New | ABCs of LD/ADD | LD In Depth | First Person | The LD Calendar | Audio Clips |
| KidZone | Finding Help | The LD Store | Talk Back | Bulletin Boards | Search |

LD RESOURCES

http://www.ldresources.com

Sponsor: Richard Wanderman, an adult with dyslexia.

Wide-ranging collection of hyperlinks about the writing process, intelligence, learning, and technological aids for dyslexic people.

LEARNING DISABILITIES ASSOCIATION OF AMERICA

http://www.ldanatl.org

Sponsor: Learning Disabilities Association of America.

Describes LDA's programs and referral network, services to parents, and advocacy resources for people with LD.

LEARNING DISABILITY RESOURCES

http://curry.edschool.virginia.edu/go/cise/ose/categories/ld.html

Sponsor: Office of Special Education, Curry School of Education, University of Virginia.

An assortment of links to Internet resources and print publications about LD.

Ψ NATIONAL CENTER FOR LEARNING DISABILITIES

http://www.ncld.org

Sponsor: National Center for Learning Disabilities.

Describes the organization and its programs.

Links to many related organizations. Full-text articles for parents and teachers of learning disabled children.

FAQs about LD.

The National Center for Learning Disabilities provides national leadership in support of children and adults with learning disabilities by providing information, resources, and referral services; developing and supporting innovative educational programs, seminars, and workshops; conducting a public awareness campaign; and advocating for more effective policies and legislation to help individuals with learning disabilities.

TEENS HELPING TEENS/TEENS VS. DYSLEXIA

http://www.ldteens.org

Sponsor: New York branch of the International Dyslexia Association.

Supportive information and study tips written mostly by dyslexic teens, for dyslexic teens.

A few links to other LD Web sites.

VSA ARTS

http://www.vsarts.org

Sponsor: VSA arts, an affiliate of the John F. Kennedy Center for the Performing Arts that offers art-based programming for the disabled.

Describes VSA's programs; online gallery of work produced by disabled people in the programs.

Click on "Resources" for links to other Web sites about disabilities and the arts.

III. MOTOR SKILLS DISORDERS (SEE ALSO COMMUNICATION DISORDERS)

DYSPRAXIA FOUNDATION

http://www.emmbrook.demon.co.uk/dysprax/homepage.htm

Sponsor: Dyspraxia Foundation (UK).

FAQs about this Developmental Coordination Disorder, links to other sites, and a summary of recent research.

DYSPRAXIA HOME PAGE

http://www.geocities.com/HotSprings/2538/nmain.htm

Sponsor: Dyspraxia Foundation (UK).

Lists publications available from the Foundation.

IV. COMMUNICATION DISORDERS

 ### A. EXPRESSIVE LANGUAGE DISORDER, MIXED RECEPTIVE-EXPRESSIVE LANGUAGE DISORDER, PHONOLOGICAL DISORDER

APRAXIA OF SPEECH (DYSPRAXIA) CITATIONS

http://www.labmed.umn.edu/~john/apraxiarefs.html

Sponsor: John G. Faughnan.

Links to abstracts of journal articles and books.

Ψ QUESTIONS AND ANSWERS ABOUT PHONOLOGICAL DISORDERS, ARTICULATION DISORDERS, DEVELOPMENTAL DYSPRAXIA, AND THE DYSARTHRIAS

http://members.tripod.com/Caroline_Bowen/phonol-and-artic.htm

Sponsor: Caroline Bowen, Ph.D., speech and language pathologist.

FAQs about phonological disorder.

Many links to Web sites for parents and professionals dealing with speech and language pathology.

Click on "Home Page" to get to the site map.

SPEECH LANGUAGE PATHOLOGY WEB SITES

http://www.herring.org/speech.html

Sponsor: Sandy Herring.

Autism-related links for organizations, treatment programs, and commercial sites.

SPEECH THERAPY WEBRING

http://nav.webring.org/cgi-bin/navcgi?ring=slp1;list

Sponsor: Unknown.

Professional and commercial Web sites about speech therapy and aphasia.

▪ B. STUTTERING

BILL PARRY'S STUTTERING LINKS

http://hometown.aol.com/wdparry/index.htm

Sponsor: Bill Parry, an attorney who founded the Philadelphia chapter of the National Stuttering Association.

Links to stuttering treatment programs and FAQs.

BRITISH STAMMERING ASSOCIATION

http://www.stammer.demon.co.uk

Sponsor: British Stammering Association.

Small but useful collection of hyperlinks for adults and children who stutter; for their significant others, and for speech therapists.

EUROPEAN LEAGUE OF STUTTERING ASSOCIATIONS

http://www.europe.is/elsa

Sponsor: European League of Stuttering Associations.

Contact information for member associations.

FRIENDS: THE ASSOCIATION OF YOUNG PEOPLE WHO STUTTER

http://www.friendswhostutter.org

Sponsor: Friends: The Association of Young People who Stutter.

Order forms for posters and publications about stuttering.

NATIONAL CENTER FOR STUTTERING

http://www.stuttering.com

Sponsor: National Center for Stuttering.

Describes this organization's theory of stuttering as "laryngeal spasm" and their treatment approach.

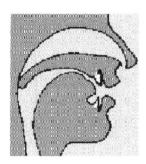

Welcome to the Home Page of
The National Center For Stuttering

NATIONAL STUTTERING ASSOCIATION

http://www.nspstutter.org

Sponsor: National Stuttering Association, a self-help and advocacy organization.

Lists support groups, activities, and publications of NSA.
FAQs about stuttering.

SPEAK EASY, INC.

http://www.vibrate.net/speakeasy

Sponsor: Speak Easy, Inc., a Canadian information and charitable organization for stutterers.

A single page with contact information; no links.

STUTTERING FOUNDATION OF AMERICA

http://www.stuttersfa.org

Sponsor: Stuttering Foundation of America.

FAQs about stuttering.

An article about how to obtain insurance reimbursement for speech therapy.

Referral lists and a directory of relevant Web sites.

Ψ THE STUTTERING HOME PAGE

http://www.mankato.msus.edu/dept/comdis/kuster/stutter.html

Sponsor: Judith Kuster, Associate Professor at Minnesota State University.

Wide-ranging and extensive megasite about stuttering.

Hyperlinks to Web sites for professionals and the general public.

Personal narratives, chat rooms, mailing lists, and information about treatment programs.

Includes links to non-English materials.

The Stuttering Homepage

STUTTERING PREVENTION

http://www.prevent-stuttering.com

Sponsor: J. Anthony Wray, a speech and language pathologist in Ontario, Canada.

FAQs about stuttering prevention and treatment.

Links for speech pathologists and parents.

STUTTERING SCIENCE & THERAPY WEB SITE

http://www.casafuturatech.com

Sponsor: Casa Futura Technologies.

Describes this company's electronic stuttering therapy devices and summarizes research on their effectiveness.

FAQs about stuttering and links to other Web sites.

V. PERVASIVE DEVELOPMENTAL DISORDERS

 ## A. GENERAL RESOURCES FOR PDD

Ψ **YALE CHILD STUDY CENTER DEVELOPMENTAL DISABILITIES CLINIC & RESEARCH HOME PAGE**

http://info.med.yale.edu/chldstdy/autism/index.html

Sponsor: Yale Child Study Center (CT).

Offers clinical descriptions, brief case illustrations, and diagnostic guidelines for each of the Pervasive Developmental Disorders.

Describes the Center's current research projects.

Well-chosen links to relevant Web sites with brief descriptions.

Lists print publications for each disorder, with separate lists for parents and professionals.

 ## B. AUTISTIC DISORDER

Because Autistic Disorder and Asperger's Syndrome are generally thought to be related, many sites focusing on one of these conditions will have information and links relevant to the other condition.

AUTISM AUTOIMMUNITY PROJECT

http://www.gti.net/truegrit

Sponsor: Autism Autoimmunity Project (NJ), a nonprofit charity that seeks funding for research on immune system abnormalities in autism.

A single long page with research abstracts related to its topic.

The Autism Autoimmunity Project

* ADDRESSING AUTISM *

THROUGH IMMUNOLOGY

*definition * treatment * prevention*

AUTISM RESOURCES

www.autism-resources.com

Sponsor: John Wobus, a software developer and computer network administrator.

Many categorized links to autism Web sites.

AUTISM: THE DISEASE & VACCINES

http://www.909shot.com/autismto.HTM

Sponsor: National Vaccine Information Center.

Presents the theory that autism is caused in some children by measles-mumps-rubella vaccination. The site is composed of a few press releases.

Autism: The Disease & Vaccines

Ψ AUTISM-PDD RESOURCES NETWORK

http://www.autism-pdd.net

Sponsor: Autism-PDD Resources Network.

Supportive resources for parents of autistic children and educators.

Describes legal, educational, and medical issues related to autism.

A Web site with practical advice.

Capsule descriptions of many treatment approaches.

CENTER FOR THE STUDY OF AUTISM

http://www.autism.com

Sponsor: Center for the Study of Autism, an affiliate of the Autism Research Institute.

The Institute conducts research and disseminates information about autism and treatment.

Broad-ranging directory of Web links about autism.

See also http://www.autism.org, another links page from the same organization.

Ψ CURE AUTISM NOW FOUNDATION
http://www.canfoundation.org

Sponsor: Cure Autism Now Foundation, a nonprofit organization of researchers and parents focusing on biological treatments and prevention of autism.

News releases about research and legal developments concerning autism.

Click on "Resources" for annotated links to Web sites for parents, clinicians, and scientists.

Includes many links that would be useful to therapists, in contrast to other sites that are more oriented toward parents.

FEAT
http://www.feat.org

Sponsor: Families for Early Autism Treatment, a nonprofit support organization for autism in northern California.

Describes how to advocate for what this organization considers effective autism treatment.

Links to related organizations in other locales and a collection of links about autism.

Maintains mailing lists and an online newsletter.

Families for Early Autism Treatment

FEAT is a non-profit organization dedicated to providing world class Education, Advocacy, and Support for the Northern California Autism Community. Click here for our Objectives!

LINKS2GO: AUTISM
http://www.links2go.com/topic/Autism

Sponsor: Links2Go.

Links page using a unique graphical layout.

NATIONAL ALLIANCE ON AUTISM RESEARCH
http://babydoc.home.pipeline.com/naar/naar.htm

Sponsor: National Alliance on Autism Research, a nonprofit research advocacy organization.

Describes current biomedical research about autism, with citations of recent print journal articles.

Links to autism research sites.

Ψ NATIONAL AUTISTIC SOCIETY

http://www.oneworld.org/autism_uk

Sponsor: National Autistic Society (UK), a charity and advocacy group for people with autism and Asperger's Syndrome and their families.

Fact sheets about autism and Asperger's Syndrome.

Has a well-organized directory of links, most with brief descriptions.

Maintains an Autism Research Database and conducts free searches for references on any aspect of autism.

The National Autistic Society (NAS)

THE SAVANT

http://www.bol.ucla.edu/~changc

Sponsor: Christina Chang.

Describes savant syndrome, with brief examples of cases.

Links to other relevant Web sites.

C. RETT'S DISORDER

Ψ INTERNATIONAL RETT SYNDROME ASSOCIATION

http://www.rettsyndrome.org

Sponsor: International Rett Syndrome Association.

Wide assortment of links to Web sites about Rett's Disorder, with information on its symptoms, related disabilities, treatments, and support resources.

International Rett Syndrome Association

Translate: français, deutsches, italiano, o português, español

RETT SYNDROME ASSOCIATION UK

http://www.rettsyndrome.org.uk

Sponsor: Rett Syndrome Association UK.

FAQs about Rett's Disorder, with links to similar associations around the world.

WE MOVE: RETT SYNDROME

http://www.wemove.org/rett.html

Sponsor: Worldwide Education and Awareness for Movement Disorders.

Detailed fact sheet about Rett's Disorder.

Up-to-date bibliography of journal articles.

 ## D. CHILDHOOD DISINTEGRATIVE DISORDER

CHILDHOOD DISINTEGRATIVE DISORDER NETWORK

http://www.stepstn.com/cgi-win/nord.exe?proc=GetDocument&rectype=2&recnum=1566

Sponsor: National Organization for Rare Disease, Inc., which sells articles about rare diseases.

Brief description and contact information for CDD Network, a non-profit support and informational resource.

PDD INFORMATION PAGES: CDD

http://info.med.yale.edu/chldstdy/autism/page13.html

Sponsor: Yale Child Study Center.

Criteria, clinical features, and a brief case illustration.

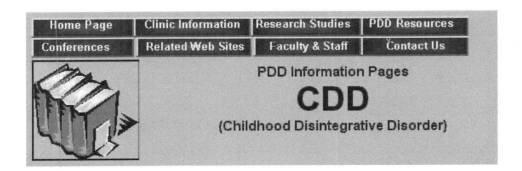

 **E. ASPERGER'S SYNDROME**

Web sites listed in this category may also have relevant information and links for Autistic Disorder.

ASPERGER'S DISORDER HOMEPAGE

http://www.ummed.edu/pub/o/ozbayrak/asperger.html

Sponsor: Kaan R. Ozbayrak, M.D., University of Massachusetts Medical School Department of Psychiatry.

Fact sheets about Asperger's.

Links to related Web sites, but without descriptions.

Lists clinicians in the U.S. and elsewhere who claim to be familiar with AS.

ASPERGER SYNDROME EDUCATION NETWORK OF AMERICA

http://www.asperger.org

Sponsor: Asperger Syndrome Education Network of America.

Links to full-text articles and Web sites about AS and related conditions The articles are summarized and evaluated.

FAMILIES OF ADULTS AFFLICTED WITH ASPERGER'S SYNDROME

http://www.faaas.org

Sponsor: FAAAS, Inc.

A few FAQs related to AS, along with a few relevant links.

Ψ ONLINE ASPERGER INFORMATION & SUPPORT

http://www.udel.edu/bkirby/asperger

Sponsor: O.A.S.I.S.

Extensive links to Web sites and articles for nonprofessionals.

Has a Kid's Corner.

Describes current research projects that seek participants.

Online Asperger Syndrome Information & Support™

"What makes the desert beautiful is that somewhere it hides a well."
— Antoine-Marie-Roger de Saint-Exupery

PDD INFORMATION PAGES: ASPERGER'S SYNDROME

http://info.med.yale.edu/chldstdy/autism/page10.html

Sponsor: Yale Child Study Center.

Detailed guidelines for assessment, making the diagnosis, and intervention in AS.

Describes current research on AS at Yale Child Study Center.

UNIVERSITY STUDENTS WITH AUTISM AND ASPERGER'S SYNDROME

http://www.users.dircon.co.uk./~cns

Sponsor: Unknown.

First-person accounts by college students with these disorders.

Fact sheets with practical information to help university students cope with autism spectrum disorders.

VI. ATTENTION-DEFICIT AND DISRUPTIVE BEHAVIOR DISORDERS

 ## A. ATTENTION-DEFICIT/HYPERACTIVITY DISORDER

Ψ ABOUT.COM: ATTENTION DEFICIT DISORDER

http://add.about.com/health/add/mbody.htm

Sponsors: About.com and the "guide" for this topic, Bob Seay, a teacher who has ADD.

Many online articles and FAQs for the nonprofessional about all aspects of ADD.

ADD CLINIC

http://www.addclinic.com

Sponsor: ADD Clinic (NV).

FAQs about ADD/ADHD for the nonprofessional.

ADD WAREHOUSE

http://www.addwarehouse.com

Sponsor: ADD WareHouse, a publisher of books, newsletters, and videos.

Online catalog and store of this publisher's products.

ADDMED

http://www.addmed.com

Sponsor: Dr. Anthony Laws, a pediatrician.

FAQs, a few links to other sites, and a description of an assessment tool developed and marketed by Dr. Laws.

ADDNET UK

http://www.btInternet.com/~black.ice/addnet

Sponsor: ADDNet UK, a volunteer organization.

Numerous full-text articles and FAQs about ADD/ADHD and treatment options.

Lists UK support groups.

ADDVANCE

http://www.addvance.com

Sponsor: ADDvance Magazine, a print publication for women and girls with ADD/ADHD.

Includes sample articles from the magazine that contain much pragmatic advice.

Lists relevant Web sites, some with brief descriptions.

ADD/ADHD ONLINE NEWSLETTER

http://www.nlci.com/nutrition

Sponsor: Laura Stevens, who has a Masters in Food and Nutrition.

Free online newsletters espousing the viewpoint that food sensitivities trigger the onset of ADD/ADHD.

ATTENTION DEFICIT HYPERACTIVITY DISORDER

http://www.med.virginia.edu/medicine/clinical/pediatrics/devbeh/adhdlin/home.html

Sponsor: Children's Medical Center University of Virginia Health Sciences Center.

Information linking basic science about ADD/ADHD with clinical practice, designed as a continuing education activity for professionals.

CHADD

http://www.chadd.org

Sponsor: CHADD (Children and Adults with Attention-Deficit/Hyperactivity Disorder), a support and advocacy group.

Describes the organization's services and local support groups.

Brief fact sheets.

A page of links to Web sites in related areas such as governmental policy, disability, and ADD/ADHD organizations.

FEINGOLD ASSOCIATION OF THE UNITED STATES

http://www.feingold.org

Sponsor: Feingold Association of the United States.

Articles, FAQs, and links to other sites concerning the hypothesis that food additives cause ADD/ADHD.

Ψ NATIONAL ATTENTION DEFICIT DISORDER ASSOCIATION

http://www.add.org

Sponsor: National Attention Deficit Disorder Association, a nonprofit volunteer organization.

Many valuable full-text articles about ADD and ADHD for nonprofessionals.

List of Web sites, with capsule descriptions and reviews.

Has a Kid's Area.

OFFICE OF SPECIAL EDUCATION: ATTENTION DEFICIT DISORDER

http://teis.virginia.edu/go/cise/ose/categories/add.html

Sponsor: Office of Special Education, Curry School of Education, University of Virginia.

A page of links to various Web sites about ADD/ADHD.

ONE ADD PLACE

http://www.oneaddplace.com

Sponsor: Great Connections, a Web site developer.

For the nonprofessional. Links to online articles, FAQS, and Web sites about ADD/ADHD and learning disorders. This site is not frequently updated.

PARENTS AGAINST RITALIN

http://www.p-a-r.org

Sponsor: Parents Against Ritalin, a nonprofit association.

Newsletter and contact information. This site is not frequently updated.

RITALIN, ADDERALL, OTHER STIMULANTS—FURTHER RESOURCES
http://www.breggin.com/ritalin.html

Sponsor: Peter R. Breggin M.D., a psychiatrist who at the time of this writing had been hired as a medical consultant for a class action suit against CHADD, the manufacturer of Ritalin, and American Psychiatric Association.

Press releases, tables of side effects, and other articles attacking stimulants. Dr. Breggin believes ADD is not a disorder but a label that is used to justify the drugging of disruptive children.

 ## B. CONDUCT AND OPPOSITIONAL DEFIANT DISORDERS

A PLACE FOR US: OPPOSITIONAL DEFIANT SUPPORT GROUP
http://www.conductdisorders.com

Sponsor: This is a companion site to a message board for parents of oppositional children.

Links to full-text articles about diagnosing ODD and conduct disorders.

Lists regional support groups and relevant governmental resources.

The Institute for the study of Antisocial behaviour in Youth

INSTITUTE FOR THE STUDY OF ANTISOCIAL BEHAVIOUR IN YOUTH
http://www.iay.org

Sponsor: Institute for the Study of Antisocial Behaviour in Youth (Canada).

Sells newsletters that summarize current research.

No specific information about antisocial behavior is available at this site.

VII. FEEDING AND EATING DISORDERS

FEEDING DISORDER PROGRAM

http://www.clevelandclinic.org/childrensrehab/programs/feed_disorder

Sponsor: Cleveland Clinic Foundation.

Brief description of this hospital's inpatient and day treatment programs for children.

MENTAL HEALTH NET: PICA SYMPTOMS

http://mentalhelp.net/disorders/sx74.htm

Sponsor: Mental Health Net.

A single page summary of *DSM-IV* criteria for Pica.

RUMINATION DISORDER

http://www.adam.com/ency/article/001539trt.htm

Sponsor: Adam.com.

Brief encyclopedia article about symptoms and treatment.

VIII. TIC DISORDERS

TOURETTE SYNDROME ASSOCIATION, INC.

http://tsa.mgh.harvard.edu

Sponsor: Tourette Syndrome Association, Inc.

Fact sheets about Tourette, back issues of TSA's newsletter, organization information about TSA's support activities. This site is not frequently updated.

TOURETTE SPECTRUM DISORDER ASSOCIATION, INC.

http://www.tourettesyndrome.org

Sponsor: Tourette Spectrum Disorder Association, Inc.

Full-text scientific articles about Tourette; a thorough and very useful chart describing medications used to treat Tourette, ADHD, and OCD; and a few annotated links to other relevant sites.

Tourette Spectrum Disorder Association, Inc.

TOURETTE SYNDROME FOUNDATION OF CANADA
http://www.tourette.ca
Sponsor: Tourette Syndrome Foundation of Canada.
FAQs about Tourette.
Lists local affiliate chapters throughout Canada.
There is a French version of this site.

Ψ TOURETTE SYNDROME SUPPORT IN THE UK
http://www.tourettesyndrome.co.uk
Sponsor: Unknown; "I am simply a mum who wanted to provide info about TS in the UK."
Has good FAQs about Tourette and comorbid conditions.
Links to over 300 related sites.
Lists links to alternative therapies.

TOURETTE-SYNDROME.COM
http://www.tourette-syndrome.com
Sponsor: S. Craig Whitley, father of a child with Tourette.
Fact sheets for the nonprofessional.
Lists more than 150 links to relevant Web sites.

Tourette-Syndrome.com

| Home | Contact | Bookstore | FAQ | Search | Contents |

IX. ELIMINATION DISORDERS

CHILDHOOD INCONTINENCE
http://village.ios.com/~tis/child.html

Sponsor: Tri-State Incontinence Support Group.

Practical information about bedwetting and treatment approaches.

DRI SLEEPER
http://www.dri-sleeper.com

Sponsor: Alpha Consultants, manufacturer of a bedwetting alarm.

Sells the alarm. FAQs about bedwetting, with a rationale for this type of product.

ENURESIS RESEARCH AND INFORMATION CENTRE
http://www.enuresis.org.uk

Sponsor: Enuresis Research and Information Centre (UK).

FAQs on enuresis for parents and teenagers, a few links to relevant sites, and products and publications sold by this Centre to nonprofessionals.

INTERNATIONAL BEDWETTING CLINIC
http://www.bedwettingcures.com

Sponsor: International Bedwetting Clinic.

Describes the Clinic's treatment program, which uses a bedwetting alarm.

FAQs about enuresis.

NATIONAL ASSOCIATION FOR CONTINENCE

http://www.nafc.org

Sponsor: National Association for Continence, an advocacy and support group.

FAQs about incontinence, along with a few links to Web sites on related topics.

NATIONAL ENURESIS SOCIETY

http://www.peds.umn.edu/Centers/NES

Sponsor: National Enuresis Society.

A thorough FAQ section about enuresis in children and its treatment. This site is not frequently updated.

TRY FOR DRY

http://www.tryfordry.com

Sponsor: Try for Dry Clinic, Childrens Memorial Hospital (Chicago).

Describes the Clinic's treatment program, which uses a bedwetting alarm; sells a book for use by parents who want to help their child stop bedwetting.

X. OTHER DISORDERS

 ## A. SEPARATION ANXIETY DISORDER

THE SEPARATION ANXIETY PAGE

http://www2.mc.duke.edu/depts/psychiatry/pcaad/sepanx.html

Sponsor: Program in Child and Adolescent Anxiety Disorder, Duke University(NC).

A summary of diagnostic criteria and differential diagnostic issues; a few links to related sites.

 **B. SELECTIVE MUTISM**

SELECTIVE MUTISM FOUNDATION, INC.

http://personal.mia.bellsouth.net/mia/g/a/garden/garden/index.htm

Sponsor: Selective Mutism Foundation, Inc., which promotes research and dissemination of knowledge about the disorder.

Describes the Foundation's services.

FAQs about the disorder.

Links to relevant Web sites.

SELECTIVE MUTISM GROUP

http://selectivemutism.org

Sponsor: Selective Mutism Group, which was started by parents of a child with selective mutism.

The site is a support resource for parents and teachers of children with selective mutism.

Click at the bottom of the page for site index.

Has an area where questions can be answered, but does not say who answers them.

Bibliography of journal articles.

Selective Mutism Group

 **C. REACTIVE ATTACHMENT DISORDER**

ATTACH

http://www.attach.org

Sponsor: Association for Treatment and Training in the Attachment of Children.

Describes attachment therapy and its rationale.

A few articles summarizing research findings.

Lists relevant Web sites.

Ψ ATTACHMENT: THEORY AND RESEARCH @ STONY BROOK

http://www.psychology.sunysb.edu/ewaters or http://www.johnbowlby.com

Sponsors: Everett Waters, Ph.D., and Judith Crowell, M.D.; State University of New York Stony Brook.

Full-text articles from scientific journals concerning attachment theory.

The site is not clinically oriented but is an invaluable resource for clinicians wanting to understand the role of attachment in child development and adult relationships.

Includes a library of attachment measures.

THE ATTACHMENT CENTER AT EVERGREEN

http://www.attachmentcenter.org

Sponsor: The Attachment Center at Evergreen (CO), a treatment center for attachment disordered children.

Describes the Center's treatment philosophy and research program.

Articles from their newsletter.

Links to Web sites about attachment and adoption issues.

The
Attachment Center
at Evergreen

ATTACHMENT DISORDER SUPPORT GROUP

http://www.syix.com/adsg

Sponsor: Attachment Disorder Support Group.

Information for nonprofessionals, listing of treatment centers and support resources, and testimonials.

ATTACHMENT HOME PAGE

http://www.attach-bond.com

Sponsor: Attachment Associates (UT).

FAQ section about attachment disorder, and links to Web sites about parenting children with attachment issues.

HEAL THE HEARTS FOUNDATION

http://www.healtheheart.org

Sponsor: Heal the Hearts Foundation, a nonprofit organization whose mission is to promote education about attachment disorder, to provide charitable support for training therapists in attachment therapy, and to provide charitable support for the cost of treatment.

Lists contact information and Web sites for treatment centers and attachment therapists.

 ## D. STEREOTYPIC MOVEMENT DISORDER

THE MOVEMENT DISORDER SOCIETY

http://www.movementdisorders.org

Sponsor: The Movement Disorder Society.

Describes the Society's meetings and training videotapes.

WE MOVE

http://www.wemove.org

Sponsor: Worldwide Awareness and Education for Movement Disorders.

Helpful fact sheets about Parkinson's Disease, Dystonia, and other movement disorders.

Links for government agencies and support/advocacy organizations.

XI. MISCELLANEOUS SITES OF INTEREST

A MINOR CONSIDERATION

http://www.minorcon.org

Sponsor: A Minor Consideration, a nonprofit association to support child actors.

Articles on the dilemmas faced by child actors and celebrities.

ADMINISTRATION ON DEVELOPMENTAL DISABILITIES

http://www.acf.dhhs.gov/programs/add

Sponsor: Administration on Developmental Disabilities, U.S. Department of Health and Human Services.

Describes the agency's programs, regulations, and outcomes; links to other Web sites concerning developmental disabilities.

AMERICAN HYPERLEXIA ASSOCIATION

http://www.hyperlexia.org

Sponsor: American Hyperlexia Association.

Full-text articles describing the disorder and remediation approaches; a few first-person accounts are included.

THE BEHAVIOR HOME PAGE

http://www.state.ky.us/agencies/behave/homepage.html

Sponsors: Kentucky Department of Education; University of Kentucky Department of Special Education and Rehabilitation Counseling.

Detailed descriptions of behavioral interventions for classroom teachers to use when dealing with children's behavior problems. Discussion forum.

DEVELOPMENTAL DISABILITIES RESOURCES

http://www.mcare.net/resourcA.htm

Sponsor: National Clearinghouse on Managed Care and Long Term Services and Support for Adults with Developmental Disabilities and their Families.

Links to about ten Web sites.

DROOLINGINFO.ORG

http://www.droolinginfo.org

Sponsor: Pinnacle Communications Group.

Information about causes of and treatments for drooling.

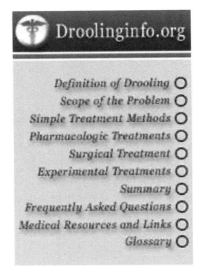

ᴪ FAMILY VILLAGE

http://www.familyvillage.wisc.edu

Sponsor: Family Village.

Extensive fact sheets and hyperlinks for specific disabilities.

Internet links to general information about disabilities. This site is not frequently updated.

NATIONAL ASSOCIATION OF DEVELOPMENTAL DISABILITIES COUNCILS
http://www.igc.apc.org/NADDC

Sponsor: National Association of Developmental Disabilities Councils.

Describes the association.

Click on "Resources File" for a list of printed materials and a few hyperlinks concerning developmental disabilities and the Americans with Disabilities Act.

OFFICE OF SPECIAL EDUCATION PROGRAMS
http://www.ed.gov/offices/OSERS

Sponsor: U.S. Department of Education.

Lists current projects, funding opportunities, and updates to Federal regulations.

A few online brochures about general topics such as safe schools.

SHAKEN BABY ALLIANCE
http://shakenbaby.com

Sponsor: Shaken Baby Alliance, which provides support to families of Shaken Baby Syndrome victims.

Victim advocacy and family support information.

Bibliography of medical articles and books.

SHAKEN BABY SYNDROME RESOURCES CENTRE
http://www.geocities.com/HotSprings/Spa/4069

Sponsor: Shaken Baby Syndrome Resources Centre.

Links to relevant Web sites; newspaper articles about SBS.

WILLIAMS SYNDROME ASSOCIATION

http://www.williams-syndrome.org

Sponsor: Williams Syndrome Association, an information and support resource.

Describes Williams Syndrome and criteria for diagnosis.

Links to resources, related Web sites, educational approaches, and professional and parent conferences.

WILLIAMS SYNDROME COMPREHENSIVE WEB SITE

http://www.wsf.org

Sponsor: Williams Syndrome Foundation, which promotes training in the arts and music for people with Williams Syndrome.

Detailed descriptions of camps for children with WS. FAQs about the disorder and many links for parents and professionals.

WILLIAMS SYNDROME FOUNDATION (UK)

http://www.williams-syndrome.org.uk

Sponsor: Williams Syndrome Foundation (UK), which promotes research and provides advocacy services.

FAQs on the disorder.

Summaries of recent research.

Detailed online versions of booklets concerning children and adults with WS.

Ψ WRIGHTSLAW: SPECIAL EDUCATION LAW AND ADVOCACY

http://www.wrightslaw.com

Sponsors: Pete Wright, an attorney with learning disabilities of his own who represents children with disabilities; Pam Wright, a psychotherapist who edits an online newsletter, The Special Ed Advocate.

Specific and highly useful information on how to advocate for the educational requirements of children with special needs.

Summaries of recent news items.

Includes links to statutes and case law decisions.

Section 2
Delirium, Dementia,
Amnestic, and Other
Cognitive Disorders

The disorders listed here represent a clinically significant deficit in cognition or memory that indicates a major change from a previous level of functioning. The disorders are:

I. Delirium, which is a disturbance of consciousness and a change in cognition developing over a short period of time.

II. Dementia, characterized by multiple cognitive deficits, including impairment in memory.

III. Amnestic Disorder, which is a memory impairment in the absence of other significant cognitive impairments.

IV. Miscellaneous Resources

I. DELIRIUM

YAHOO! HEALTH: DELIRIUM

http://health.yahoo.com/health/Diseases_and_Conditions/Disease_Feed_Data/Delirium

Sponsor: Yahoo!

A fact sheet describing signs and diagnostic tests, symptoms, causes, and treatment.

II. DEMENTIA

 ## A. ALZHEIMER'S TYPE

ALZHEIMER EUROPE

http://www.alzheimer-europe.org

Sponsor: Alzheimer Europe.

Multilingual site with annotated reviews of other sites.

FAQs for the nonprofessional.

Had not been updated in over a year at the time of our visit.

This site exists in English, French, Greek, Italian, Spanish, Dutch, Portuguese, Swedish, Danish and Finnish.
It will be soon available in German.

THE ALZHEIMER PAGE

http://www.adrc.wustl.edu/alzheimer

Sponsor: Washington University (St. Louis) Alzheimer Disease Research Center.

Companion site to a mailing list for anyone interested in Alzheimer's Disease.

Archives of the mailing list going back to 1994.

Well-organized links, with brief descriptions, to other Web sites dealing with aging and dementia.

ALZHEIMER RESEARCH FORUM

http://www.alzforum.org

Sponsor: Alzheimer Research Forum.

Up-to-date information about AD research.

Different entry points for physicians, researchers, and others. The latter leads to annotated links to pages within this and other sites.

ALZHEIMER SOCIETY OF CANADA

http://www.alzheimer.ca

Sponsor: Alzheimer Society of Canada, which has a mirror site in French.

Nice graphics, with links (some annotated) to other Web sites.

FAQs about Alzheimer's Disease and about research on its causes.

Contains links to personal stories of Alzheimer's Disease.

Many pages are useful to caretakers of people with Alzheimer's.

ALZHEIMER WEB

http://www.alzweb.org, which forwards to http://home.mira.net/~dhs

Sponsor: David Small.

Focuses on Alzheimer-related research.

Automatically searches for Alzheimer research that has been added to the MEDLINE database in the last week.

ALZHEIMER'S ASSOCIATION

http://www.alz.org

Sponsor: Alzheimer's Association.

FAQs for caregivers and professionals.

Small selection of links to other Alzheimer's Web sites.

Ψ ALZHEIMERS.COM

http://www.alzheimers.com

Sponsor: PlanetRx.

A well-organized site with fact sheets about symptoms, diagnosis, and treatment.

Current news stories on Alzheimer's research.

Links to other Web sites are described and reviewed in detail.

ALZHEIMER'S DISEASE EDUCATION AND REFERRAL CENTER

http://www.alzheimers.org

Sponsor: Alzheimer's Disease Education and Referral Center of the National Institutes of Health.

Link to a database of articles on Alzheimer's.

Lists Alzheimer's Centers in various states, all funded by the National Institute on Aging.

Database of clinical trials.

ALZHEIMER'S DISEASE INTERNATIONAL

http://www.alz.co.uk

Sponsor: Alzheimer's Disease International, an umbrella organization of Alzheimer's associations.

This hierarchically constructed Web site contains much information that is several clicks away from the home page.

Annotated links to Web sites of Alzheimer's associations and other information resources around the world.

Information for caregivers.

Describes a research program known as "10/66 Group."

Ψ ALZWELL CAREGIVER PAGE

http://www.alzwell.com

Sponsor: Susan, who was a full-time caregiver for her mother-in-law for three years.

Extensive resources, both emotional and informational in nature, for those caring for people with Alzheimer's Disease.

You can browse at random through the varied areas of this site, or click on "Resource Links" for a more organized way to search the site.

Has an "Anger Wall," where caregivers have entered their personal narratives.

 **B. VASCULAR DEMENTIA**

VASCULAR DEMENTIA
http://www.alznsw.asn.au/library/vasclar.htm

Sponsor: Alzheimer's Association NSW (Australia).

FAQs on vascular dementia.

This site is not frequently updated.

 C. DEMENTIA DUE TO OTHER MEDICAL CONDITIONS

1. HIV

See also the AIDS Web sites listed in chapter 4, section E.

PSYCHOSOCIAL INTERVENTIONS IN PERSONS WITH HIV-ASSOCIATED NEUROPSYCHIATRIC COMPROMISE
http://www.thebody.com/shernoff/neuro.html

Sponsor: Body Health Resources Corporation.

A 1998 book chapter by Stephen L. Buckingham and Michael Shernoff.

Psychosocial Interventions in Persons with HIV-Associated Neuropsychiatric Compromise

2. HEAD TRAUMA

Ψ BRAIN INJURY ASSOCIATION USA
http://www.biausa.org

Sponsor: Brain Injury Association USA, a support organization for brain-injured people and their families.

Extensive resource of online information, both technical and general, about brain injury and rehabilitation.

Links to state associations.

Nice graphics.

Many links to other Web sites for professionals and the general public, often with brief descriptions.

NATIONAL RESOURCE CENTER FOR TRAUMATIC BRAIN INJURY

http://www.neuro.pmr.vcu.edu

Sponsor: Medical College of Virginia, Virginia Commonwealth University.

Brief FAQs and links (with brief descriptions) to relevant Web sites.

3. PARKINSON'S DISEASE

NATIONAL PARKINSON FOUNDATION, INC.

http://www.parkinson.org

Sponsor: National Parkinson Foundation, Inc.

Surgical options.

Features self-assessment questionnaires for Parkinson patients to track the progress of the disease; the Web site notes that these instruments have not been validated.

Lists surgical centers for Parkinson, including contact information and hyperlinks.

Has a "Caregiver's Site."

Blazing Towards A Cure

NATIONAL PARKINSON FOUNDATION, INC.

PARKINSON FOUNDATION OF CANADA

http://www.parkinson.ca

Sponsor: Parkinson Foundation of Canada.

Brief fact sheets about the disease and basic patient care.

Links to regional Canadian associations and their fundraising events.

PARKINSON'S DISEASE FOUNDATION, INC.

http://www.pdf.org

Sponsor: Parkinson's Disease Foundation, Inc., a nonprofit organization that funds research grants.

Describes the Foundation's work.

PARKINSON'S DISEASE INDEX

http://www.bgsm.edu/bgsm/surg-sci/ns/pd.html

Sponsor: Wake Forest University School of Medicine.

Focus on surgical treatment for Parkinson's.

Articles for medical professionals and the general public.

Links to other Parkinson's information and support Web sites.

THE PARKINSON'S WEB

http://neuro-chief-e.mgh.harvard.edu/parkinsonsweb/Main/PDmain.html

Sponsor: Massachusetts General Hospital Department of Neurology.

Small number of links to Parkinson's organizations and treatment resources.

4. HUNTINGTON'S DISEASE

CARING FOR PEOPLE WITH HUNTINGTON'S DISEASE

http://www.kumc.edu/hospital/huntingtons

Sponsor: Department of Neurology, University of Kansas Medical Center; Huntington's Disease Support Groups.

Detailed FAQs about Huntington's Disease and specific issues associated with caring for them.

Links to relevant Web sites.

FACING HUNTINGTON'S DISEASE: A HANDBOOK FOR FAMILIES AND FRIENDS

http://neuro-chief-e.mgh.harvard.edu/mcmenemy/facinghd.html

Sponsor: Huntington's Disease Association (UK).

Online book, written in 1996, for caregivers and other important people in the lives of people with Huntington's Disease.

FACING HUNTINGTON'S DISEASE

A Handbook for Families and Friends

Ψ HUNTINGTON'S DISEASE INFORMATION

http://www.lib.uchicago.edu/~rd13/hd

Sponsor: Renette Davis, a librarian at University of Chicago.

A graphically plain site with many valuable links to information about HD.

Click on "Electronic Resources on Huntington's Disease" for a long single page with links for the professional and the general public.

Lists treatments of HD in fiction, many with capsule descriptions.

HUNTINGTON'S DISEASE LIGHTHOUSE

http://table.jps.net/~wuf

Sponsor: Jerry Lampson, whose wife died from Huntington's Disease.

Idiosyncratic assembly of information about the disease and its effects.

HUNTINGTON'S DISEASE SOCIETY OF AMERICA

http://www.hdsa.org

Sponsor: Huntington's Disease Society of America, which sponsors research and functions as a supportive resource.

Abstracts of recent research.

Lists genetic testing centers, long-term care facilities, and self-help groups.

Sells videotapes about caring for people with HD.

Huntington Society of Canada

Société Huntington du Canada

HUNTINGTON SOCIETY OF CANADA

http://www.hsc-ca.org

Sponsor: Huntington Society of Canada, an organization of volunteers and professionals that sponsors research on HD.

Lists meetings and publications of the Society.

FAQs about HD.

Has mirror sites in English and French.

5. PICK'S DISEASE

EUROPEAN CONCERTED ACTION ON PICK'S DISEASE
http://193.62.68.10/ecapd

Sponsor: Dementia Research Group, National Hospital for Neurology and Neurosurgery, The Institute of Neurology, University Hospital (London).

Describes a project to develop diagnostic criteria.

This site is not frequently updated.

PICK'S DISEASE SUPPORT GROUP ONLINE
http://www.pdsg.org.uk

Sponsor: Pick's Disease Support Group, which serves caregivers in Europe and North America.

Archive of newsletters and message board posts.

Personal narratives of caregivers.

Links to sites on Pick's and
Alzheimer's Diseases.

PICK'S INFORMATION PAGE
http://www.bhoffcomp.com/coping/picks.html

Sponsor: Bob Hoffmann.

Links to fact sheets, personal narratives, and support groups.

6. CREUTZFELDT-JACOB DISEASE

CREUTZFELDT-JACOB DISEASE FOUNDATION, INC.
http://www.cjdfoundation.org

Sponsor: Creutzfeldt-Jacob Disease Foundation, Inc.

Creutzfeldt-Jakob Disease Foundation, Inc.

FAQs about the disease.

Lists recent headlines concerning the disease, but without links to the articles themselves.

Lengthy article about different theories concerning the disease agent.

Links to upcoming conferences.

THE UK CREUZTFELDT-JACOB DISEASE SURVEILLANCE UNIT

http://www.cjd.ed.ac.uk

Sponsor: Western General Hospital (Edinburgh).

Describes research being done by this facility, with a bibliography of their print publications. This site is not frequently updated.

OFFICIAL MAD COW DISEASE HOME PAGE

http://mad-cow.org

Sponsor: Sperling Biomedical Foundation.

A collection of articles on this disease, with summaries of the scientific literature. The Webmaster's opinions and newspaper articles are liberally interspersed.

The Web site lists very brief titles for many articles on this site; a search engine would make it much easier to locate desired information.

III. AMNESTIC DISORDERS

AMNESIA AND COGNITION UNIT

http://www.u.arizona.edu/~pdavidso/amcog.html

Sponsor: Department of Psychology, University of Arizona.

Brief description of projects within the department and a few links to other sites.

This site is not frequently updated.

IV. MISCELLANEOUS RESOURCES

NATIONAL ACADEMY OF ELDER LAW ATTORNEYS

http://www.naela.com

Sponsor: National Academy of Elder Law Attorneys.

Most areas of the site are for members only, but there is an extensive collection of links, with capsule descriptions, about aging and related legal issues.

NATIONAL GUARDIANSHIP ASSOCIATION

http://www.guardianship.org

Sponsor: National Guardianship Association.

Online brochure about legal guardianship.

Sample copy of the Association's newsletter.

Links to a compact smorgasbord of Web sites about health care and aging.

NURSING HOME INFO

http://www.nursinghomeinfo.com

Sponsor: Nelson & Wallery, Ltd., an Internet marketing and consulting firm.

Help in choosing a nursing home, with information about payment options and selection tips.

Has a search engine that selects by special needs and/or geographical location.

NURSING HOMES REGISTRY (UK)

http://www.nursinghomes.co.uk

Sponsor: Nursing Homes Registry.

Brief descriptions and photographs of selected nursing homes in the UK.

NURSINGHOMEREPORTS.COM

http://www.nursinghomereports.com

Sponsor: National Eldercare Referral Systems, an independent company that claims to provide unbiased evaluations.

Sells rankings of the best nursing homes in a specific geographical area or for special situations.

Section 3
Mental Disorders Due to a General Medical Condition

The mental disorders in this section of *DSM-IV* are secondary to the medical conditions that cause them. Although we could not locate any Web sites specific to any of these mental disorders, the general medical sites listed in chapter 4 will be helpful in finding information about psychiatric symptoms that are caused by medical conditions.

Section 4
Substance-Related Disorders

This section contains Web sites that refer to abuse of a drug, a medication, or a toxin. Although a few sites support substance abuse or the use of illegal substances, these "enthusiast sites" are included here because they contain information useful to therapists, not because we share their viewpoint. Readers should be careful to evaluate how authoritative such information is before relying upon it.

Web sites in this section are placed into eleven classes:

    I. Alcohol-Related Disorders
       A. Support and Self-Help Organizations and Groups (dealing primarily or exclusively with alcoholism)
       B. Alcoholism Diagnosis, Research, Treatment, and Prevention
   II. Amphetamine-Related Disorders
  III. Caffeine-Related Disorders
  IV. Cannabis-Related Disorders
    V. Cocaine-Related Disorders
  VI. Hallucinogen-Related Disorders
 VII. Inhalant-Related Disorders
VIII. Nicotine-Related Disorders
  IX. Opioid-Related Disorders
   X. Phencyclidine-Related Disorders
  XI. Sedative-Related Disorders
 XII. Miscellaneous Web Sites with General Relevance to Substance Disorders

I. ALCOHOL-RELATED DISORDERS

 ## A. SUPPORT AND SELF-HELP ORGANIZATIONS AND GROUPS (DEALING PRIMARILY OR EXCLUSIVELY WITH ALCOHOLISM)

ADULT CHILDREN OF ALCOHOLICS WORLD SERVICE ORGANIZATION

http://www.adultchildren.org

Sponsor: ACA.

Describes ACA groups (not part of Alcoholics Anonymous).

Lists ACA meetings that have registered with this Web site.

Sells pamphlets and other publications.

ALANON/ALATEEN

http://www.al-anon.org

Sponsor: AlAnon Family Group Headquarters.

Describes the purposes of AlAnon and Alateen.

Contact information for AlAnon offices in North America and elsewhere.

Has mirror sites in French and Spanish.

Lists AlAnon pamphlets and other publications that may be purchased and then freely published on other Web sites.

ALCOHOLICS ANONYMOUS

http://www.alcoholics-anonymous.org

Sponsor: Alcoholics Anonymous for U.S. and Canada.

FAQs and online pamphlets about the AA program.

Lists contact information for offices throughout North America.

Has mirror sites in Spanish and French.

Full-text of current and past issues of AA's magazine, *AA Grapevine.*

ALCOHOLICS ANONYMOUS (UK)

http://www.alcoholics-anonymous.org.uk

Sponsor: General Service Office of AA Great Britain.

FAQs and online pamphlets about the AA program.

Lists contact information for offices throughout Great Britain.

ALCOHOLICS FOR CHRIST

http://www.alcoholicsforchrist.com

Sponsor: Alcoholics for Christ, which operates Christian support groups for substance abusers and their families using a rewritten version of AA's 12 steps.

Explains this organization's version of the 12 steps, with excerpts from the Bible.

Lists meetings of the organization's support groups in the U.S.

ALCOHOLICS VICTORIOUS

http://av.iugm.org

Sponsor: Alcoholics Victorious, a 12-step program for alcoholics and other addicts where members recognize Jesus Christ as their "Higher Power."

Lists AV groups across the United States.

FAQs concerning the organization's principles and mission.

ALCOHOLISM AND ALCOHOL ABUSE RESOURCES GUIDE

http://open-mind.org/Alcohol.htm

Sponsor: Open-Mind.Org (CA).

Links to mostly AA-related Web sites.

ALCOHOLISM KILLS

http://www.alcoholismkills.com

Sponsor: Recovering alcoholics who started the site because of their father's death from alcoholism.

Personal narratives about the effects of alcoholism.

Lists books and movies about alcoholism for the nonprofessional.

AMERICAN COUNCIL ON ALCOHOLISM

http://www.aca-usa.org

Sponsor: American Council on Alcoholism.

Brief FAQ section about alcoholism, brief bibliography of 12-step-related books, and links to other sites.

ANONYMOUS ONE

http://www.anonymousone.com/main.htm

Sponsor: Anonymous One.

Articles and FAQs for the nonprofessional concerning the disease model of alcoholism.

A handy database (not limited to alcoholism) of 12-step meetings, treatment centers, and hospitals/clinics.

CHRISTIANS IN RECOVERY

http://www.christians-in-recovery.org

Sponsor: Christians in Recovery, a fee-based membership organization.

Many links to Web sites with both Christian and secular information about substance abuse, recovery, and related issues.

JEWISH ALCOHOLICS, CHEMICALLY DEPENDENT PERSONS, AND SIGNIFICANT OTHERS

http://www.jacsweb.org/index_ie.html

Sponsor: JACS.

Explains how the AA program is compatible with Judaism and discusses Judaism's past tendency to deny that alcoholism is a significant problem among Jews.

Click on "Links," then "Links Home Page," for extensive links to recovery and treatment Web sites (not limited to Judaism).

JUST FOR TODAY

http://nav.webring.org/cgi-bin/navcgi?ring=russell;list

Sponsor: Unknown.

Web sites for codependents as well as families of alcohol abusers.

Ψ LIFERING SECULAR RECOVERY

http://www.unhooked.com

Sponsor: LifeRing Secular Recovery.

Describes a program of meetings to teach inner dialogues that are claimed to prevent or reduce the incidence of relapse.

Lists local meetings.

Very specific suggestions on how to deal with various stages of recovery while maintaining sobriety. Some of them could be useful as part of any relapse prevention program.

Links to alcoholism organizations and other secular recovery Web sites.

MODERATION MANAGEMENT

http://www.moderation.org

Sponsor: Moderation Management, a "recovery program and national support group for people who have made the healthy decision to reduce their drinking." States that the program is "not for alcoholics."

Information about the program and its tenets; contact information for local and online groups.

Guide book on how to start a Moderation Management group.

NATIONAL ASSOCIATION OF CHILDREN OF ALCOHOLICS

http://www.health.org/nacoa

Sponsor: National Association of Children of Alcoholics.

Articles for the nonprofessional about being the child of an alcoholic.

Has a "Just for Kids" section.

Links to sites for a number of organizations dealing with addictions.

RECOVERED ALCOHOLIC CLERGY ASSOCIATION

http://www.geocities.com/HotSprings/8872

Sponsor: Recovered Alcoholic Clergy Association, a fellowship of Episcopal clergy.

Describes the organization and its newsletter.

Has a page of basic information on "How to Help an Alcoholic."

RECOVERING COUPLES ANONYMOUS
http://www.recovering-couples.org

Sponsor: Recovering Couples Anonymous, which uses a 12-step model to help couples recover from their dysfunctional relationships.

Contains 12-step guides and other online pamphlets.

Contact information for local meetings.

Chat room.

SOBERVOICES.COM
http://www.sobervoices.com

Sponsor: Sobervoices.com.

Operates online AA meetings via voice chat rooms.

Live Voice 12 Step Meetings

WOMEN FOR SOBRIETY WEB RING
http://nav.webring.org/cgi-bin/navcgi?ring=soberwomyn;list

Sponsor: SoberDykes (see http://www.soberdykes.org), a group of recovering women.

Lists Web sites for women in recovery.

WOMEN FOR SOBRIETY, INC.
http://www.womenforsobriety.org

Sponsor: Women for Sobriety, Inc., a national self-help program for alcoholic women.

Contact information for local meetings.

Articles written for women who are alcoholic.

WORLDWIDE WEB RATIONAL RECOVERY CENTER
http://www.rational.org/recovery

Sponsor: Rational Recovery.

Describes "Planned Abstinence" as an alternative to 12-step programs for alcohol abuse; as one of its founders wrote: "AA is the drinking and drug cultures of America, gathered together to build social tolerance toward their immoral conduct."

 **B. ALCOHOLISM DIAGNOSIS, RESEARCH, TREATMENT, AND PREVENTION**

ALCOWEB

http://www.alcoweb.com

Sponsor: Lipha (France).

Fact sheets about alcoholism diagnosis, intervention, and epidemiology.

Information for the general public is separate from information for professionals.

Includes interactive versions of alcoholism screening questionnaires, but these are only within the section of the site intended for professionals.

Not updated frequently.

Ψ ABOUT.COM: ALCOHOLISM

http://alcoholism.about.com/health/alcoholism/library/blpro.htm

Sponsor: About.com.

Well-organized topical directory of articles and Web sites related to alcoholism and codependency.

Geographical directory of some treatment centers.

Frequently updated news articles on alcoholism (click on "all articles on this topic").

ALCOHOL CONCERN

http://www.alcoholconcern.org.uk

Sponsor: Alcohol Concern, "the UK national body on alcohol misuse."

Fact sheets on alcohol and its effects.

Links to many sites for alcohol treatment facilities in the UK, and to sites of alcoholism organizations.

ALCOHOL▲CONCERN

ALCOHOL RESEARCH GROUP

http://www.arg.org

Sponsor: Alcohol Research Group (CA) a National Alcohol Research Center supported by National Institute on Alcohol Abuse and Alcoholism.

Lists current researchers at ARG, their projects and grants, and past publications of ARG researchers.

Links to other centers of alcoholism research.

ALCOHOLIC LIVER DISEASE

http://cpmcnet.columbia.edu/dept/gi/alcohol.html

Sponsor: Columbia Presbyterian Medical Center.

An online article by Howard Worman, M.D.

ALCOHOLISM/TREATMENT

http://www.alcoholismtreatment.org

Sponsor: Dr. Robert Perkinson, a psychologist and drug counselor.

FAQs about how to know if someone has an alcohol problem and how to get that person into treatment.

Links to a few treatment centers.

BINGE DRINKING

http://www.drugs.indiana.edu/drug_info/binge.html

Sponsor: Indiana Prevention Resource Center, Indiana University.

Fact sheets and links about binge drinking and blood alcohol levels. The site is not frequently updated.

BINGE DRINKING PREVENTION RESOURCES

http://campussafety.org/resources/binge/index.html

Sponsor: Security on Campus, Inc., a nonprofit that focuses on prevention of campus violence and victim rights.

Links to online articles and other Web sites about binge drinking.

Recent news articles.

CENTER OF ALCOHOL STUDIES

http://www.rci.rutgers.edu/~cas2

Sponsor: Rutgers University.

Useful fact sheets on alcohol use and alcoholism.

Describes the Center's training programs in alcohol studies.

Lists the Center's publications, with recent tables of contents from *Journal of Studies on Alcohol.*

THE CENTURY COUNCIL

http://www.centurycouncil.org

Sponsor: "Funded by America's leading distillers."

Describes the Council's programs to prevent alcohol abuse and underage drinking.

Has "The Blood Alcohol Educator," an interactive page for estimating one's own blood alcohol level.

Click on "Jumplist" for a directory of Web sites for alcohol abuse prevention and transportation-related organizations.

FACE—TRUTH AND CLARITY ON ALCOHOL

http://www.faceproject.org

Sponsor: FACE, a nonprofit organization advocating for policy change on alcohol and on prevention of alcohol-related health problems.

Links and contact information related to the deleterious effects of alcohol and underage drinking.

Sells brochures and other publications.

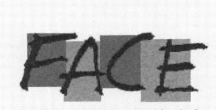
Truth and Clarity on Alcohol

INSTITUTE OF ALCOHOL STUDIES (UK)
http://www.ias.org.uk

Sponsor: Institute of Alcohol Studies (UK).

Fact sheets about alcohol use and its consequences.

Has a directory of alcohol-related Web sites, but it does not appear to be frequently updated.

INTERNET ALCOHOL RECOVERY CENTER
http://www.med.upenn.edu/~recovery

Sponsor: University of Pennsylvania Health System Department of Psychiatry.

Information about naltrexone treatment for alcoholism. Also see another Web site (which seems to be updated more frequently) from the same sponsoring organization: http://www.recovery2000.com.

INTERVENTION CENTER
http://www.intervention.com

Sponsor: Vaughn J. Howland, Intervention Center (DC and MD).

Clear descriptions and FAQs on family and executive interventions for alcohol abusers.

Links to treatment centers and substance abuse public policy Web sites.

MADD ONLINE
http://www.madd.org

Sponsor: Mothers Against Drunk Driving.

Describes the organization's programs to prevent drunk driving.

Statistics concerning alcoholism, DUI arrests, and related data.

Links (with brief descriptions) to sites dealing with alcoholism policy, prevention, and treatment.

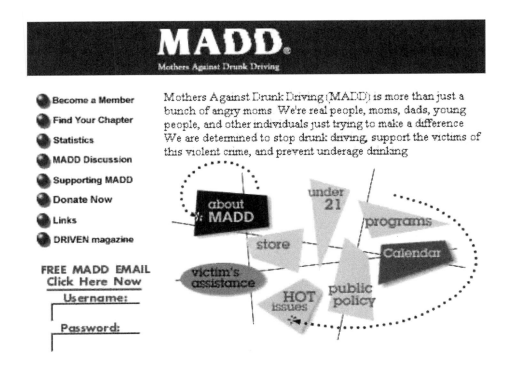

Mothers Against Drunk Driving (MADD) is more than just a bunch of angry moms. We're real people, moms, dads, young people, and other individuals just trying to make a difference. We are determined to stop drunk driving, support the victims of this violent crime, and prevent underage drinking.

MEDICAL COUNCIL ON ALCOHOLISM
http://www.medicouncilalcol.demon.co.uk

Sponsor: Medical Council on Alcoholism (UK).

Has a brief list of "useful links" to European and UK Web sites concerning addiction and alcoholism.

NATIONAL ASSOCIATION OF STATE ALCOHOL AND DRUG ABUSE DIRECTORS
http://www.nasadad.org

Sponsor: National Association of State Alcohol and Drug Abuse Directors.

Full-text articles on NASSAD's research programs and results.

Lists Web sites for substance abuse prevention and treatment organizations, with a single paragraph per link.

Ψ NATIONAL COUNCIL ON ALCOHOLISM AND DRUG DEPENDENCE, INC.

http://www.ncadd.org

Sponsor: National Council on Alcoholism and Drug Dependence, Inc.

Describes the Council's programs to disseminate information about alcoholism.

Displays JAMA's 1992 definition of alcoholism, which is handy to show to clients who insist they aren't alcoholic because they still retain (impaired) functionality.

Pamphlets for the general public, such as "What to tell your children about drinking."

Lists a number of treatment programs.

Click on "Resources and Referrals" at the bottom of the home page for extensive links to Web sites dealing with alcoholism and substance abuse.

Current media articles about substance abuse.

Ψ NATIONAL INSTITUTE ON ALCOHOL ABUSE AND ALCOHOLISM

http://www.niaaa.nih.gov

Sponsor: National Institutes of Health.

Extensive collection of fact sheets and online articles for health care professionals as well as the general public.

The "ETOH Database" is an up-to-date searchable index of more than 100,000 abstracts on alcoholism/alcohol abuse.

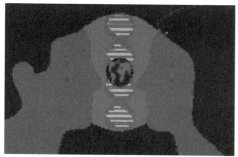

PITTSBURGH ADOLESCENT ALCOHOL RESEARCH CENTER

http://www.pitt.edu/~paarc/paarc.html

Sponsor: University of Pittsburgh Medical Center.

Description of the Center's research programs.

Abstracts of the Center's publications.

Extensive bibliography of print publications on adolescent alcohol use and abuse.

II. AMPHETAMINE-RELATED DISORDERS

AMPHETAMINES.COM

http://www.amphetamines.com

Sponsor: BLTC Research (UK), a company that promotes "paradise engineering."

Brief slide show about amphetamines and their effects.

CRYSTAL METH ANONYMOUS

http://www.crystalmeth.org

Sponsor: Crystal Meth Anonymous.

Contact information and a meeting schedule.

Links to Web sites on related topics.

FACTLINE ON METHCATHINONE

http://www.drugs.indiana.edu/pubs/factline/cat.html

Sponsor: Indiana Prevention Resource Center, Indiana University.

Information sheet about this home-brewed drug known as "Cat."

Ψ FACTS ABOUT MDMA (ECSTASY)

http://165.112.78.61/NIDA_Notes/NNVol14N4/tearoff.html

Sponsor: National Institute on Drug Abuse.

Fact sheet on this drug and its effects.

A link at the bottom of this page goes to a directory of other authoritative information about this drug.

KOCH CRIME INSTITUTE METHAMPHETAMINE LINKS AND METH INFORMATION

http://www.kci.org/meth_info/links.htm

Sponsor: Koch Crime Institute.

Information for the nonprofessional about methamphetamine abuse and meth labs.

LIFE OR METH

http://www.lifeormeth.org

Sponsor: Counterdrug Task Force, Iowa National Guard.

Brief fact sheets for the nonprofessional about methamphetamine abuse.

Ψ MEDLINEPLUS HEALTH INFORMATION: AMPHETAMINE ABUSE

http://medlineplus.nlm.nih.gov/medlineplus/amphetamineabuse.html

Sponsor: National Library of Medicine.

A portal to government-operated Web sites about amphetamine abuse.

METHAMPHETAMINE TREATMENT PROJECT

http://www.medsch.ucla.edu/som/npi/DARC/mtcc/mtcc.htm

Sponsor: UCLA Drug Abuse Research Center, Matrix Institute on Addictions.

Information about a multicenter outcome study of an outpatient methamphetamine treatment program.

Full-length articles and slide shows about the treatment model.

Directory of other drug research centers and Web sites about meth abuse and substance abuse in general.

RXLIST: AMPHETAMINE MIXED SALTS

http://www.rxlist.com/cgi/weight/amphet.htm

Sponsor: RxList.

Information about clinical use, side effects, and adverse reactions to this medication.

Amphetamine Mixed Salts

III. CAFFEINE-RELATED DISORDERS

CAFFEINE CONTENT OF DRUGS AND FOODS

http://www.cspinet.org/new/cafchart.htm

Sponsor: Center for Science in the Public Interest.

A chart of branded products and their caffeine content.

COFFEE SCIENCE SOURCE

http://www.coffeescience.org

Sponsor: National Coffee Association, a trade association.

Presents literature summaries and news items concerning the effects of coffee on health.

IV. CANNABIS-RELATED DISORDERS

CANNABIS AMOTIVATIONAL SYNDROME

http://www.druglibrary.org/schaffer/hemp/medical/canb1.htm

Sponsor: Schaffer Library of Drug Policy.

An article by Peter Nelson, Ph.D., reconceptualizing the "amotivational syndrome" as a reflection of the cognitive state of absorption that occurs in the context of depression.

INFORMATION ON DRUGS OF ABUSE: MARIJUANA

http://165.112.78.61/DrugPages/Marijuana.html

Sponsor: National Institute on Drug Abuse.

Lists NIDA publications and news releases about marijuana and its effects.

INTERNATIONAL CANNABINOID RESEARCH SOCIETY

http://cannabinoidsociety.org

Sponsor: International Cannabinoid Research Society.

Describes the Association's annual meetings.

Includes links to recent relevant articles in online journals.

MARIJUANA ANONYMOUS WORLD SERVICES

http://www.marijuana-anonymous.org

Sponsor: Marijuana Anonymous World Services.

A 12-step program in the AA tradition.

Lists local meetings.

MARIJUANA POLICY PROJECT

http://www.mpp.org

Sponsor: Marijuana Policy Project, which advocates legalization of marijuana for medical purposes.

Recent news releases about the medical uses of marijuana and its legal status.

MEDLINEPLUS HEALTH INFORMATION: MARIJUANA ABUSE

http://medlineplus.nlm.nih.gov/medlineplus/marijuanaabuse.html

Sponsor: National Library of Medicine.

A portal site for government Web sites about marijuana.

Lists sites for adults and teens.

Ψ UK CANNABIS INTERNET ACTIVISTS

http://www.ukcia.org

Sponsor: UK Cannabis Internet Activists, who promote the legalization of marijuana.

Click on "Medical Uses" for many links relating to the medical use of marijuana, government policy, and statements on this issue by medical associations.

V. COCAINE-RELATED DISORDERS

CO-ANON FAMILY GROUPS

http://www.co-anon.org

Sponsor: Co-Anon.

Sponsors 12-step meetings for family members and friends of cocaine abusers.

Description of the program, with some online pamphlets and FAQs.

Directory of local meetings.

CO-ANON FAMILY GROUPS

FOR FRIENDS AND FAMILY OF COCAINE ADDICTS

COCAINE AND REINFORCEMENT

http://www.uaf.edu/psych/psyc345/exam3/Lecture_28/sld001.htm

Sponsor: Chris Lott, Department of Psychology, University of Alaska at Fairbanks.

Slide show outlining the idea that cocaine is a powerful reinforcer.

COCAINE ANONYMOUS UK WEB SITE

http://www.cauk.org.uk

Sponsor: Cocaine Anonymous UK.

Describes CA's 12-step program, with contact information for UK meetings.

COCAINE ANONYMOUS WORLD SERVICES ONLINE

http://www.ca.org

Sponsor: Cocaine Anonymous.

A 12-step program for cocaine (including crack) users.

Contact numbers and Web sites for local meeting information.

Online pamphlets about the program.

Cocaine Anonymous World Services
"We're Here and We're Free"
Email: cawso@ca.org

COCAINE USER HELPING HAND

http://www.angelfire.com/co/Cocaine

Sponsor: Unknown.

A number of useful links to information about cocaine abuse and treatment.

INFORMATION ON DRUGS OF ABUSE: COCAINE

http://165.112.78.61/drugpages/cocaine.html

Sponsor: National Institute on Drug Abuse.

Fact sheets on crack and cocaine.

Recent and relevant news articles from NIDA.

Ψ MEDLINEPLUS HEALTH INFORMATION: COCAINE ABUSE

http://medlineplus.nlm.nih.gov/medlineplus/cocaineabuse.html

Sponsor: National Library of Medicine.

Portal page with links to U.S. Government Web sites about cocaine abuse and treatment.

VI. HALLUCINOGEN-RELATED DISORDERS

HEFFTER RESEARCH INSTITUTE

http://www.heffter.org

Sponsor: Heffter Research Institute, which awards grants for new research concerning hallucinogenic drugs.

Bibliography of research recently sponsored by the Institute.

Links to other Web sites concerning hallucinogenic drugs.

MULTIDISCIPLINARY ASSOCIATION FOR PSYCHEDELIC STUDIES

http://www.maps.org

Sponsor: Multidisciplinary Association for Psychedelic Studies, which assists in the design and funding of studies on MDMA (Ecstasy), psychedelic drugs, and marijuana.

Abstracts (sometimes with Web links) for ongoing research on psychedelics, medical use of marijuana, and MDMA.

Back issues of MAPS' newsletter.

PSYCHEDELIC

http://www.links.co.nz/culture/drugs/psychedelic.htm

Sponsor: Unknown.

Links to Web sites about psychedelic drugs.

PSYCHEDELIC LIBRARY

http://www.psychedelic-library.org

Sponsor: Peter Webster (France).

Links to book chapters and popular articles about psychedelic drugs.

THE SHROOMERY

http://www.shroomery.org

Sponsor: The Shroomery (VA).

Information about hallucinogenic mushrooms (psilocybin).

Links to other sites about hallucinogens.

The information on this site describes the hazards of using hallucinogens and often continues with information on how to use them "safely." Caveat lector.

THIRD PLATEAU

http://third-plateau.lycaeum.org

Sponsor: Kykeon Visions (WA).

Information about the cough syrup ingredient dextromethorphan. Describes the alleged hallucinogenic properties of this chemical, its risks of brain damage, and recommended dosages.

Although this is an "enthusiast site" and it is difficult to determine whether the content is authoritative, we include it as a starting place for therapists whose clients abuse this substance.

VII. INHALANT-RELATED DISORDERS

ABOUT.COM PARENTING OF ADOLESCENTS: INHALANT ABUSE

http://parentingteens.about.com/parenting/parentingteens/msub44.htm?once=true&

Sponsor: About.com.

Warning signs, risks, and other information about inhalant abuse.

ALCOHOL, TOBACCO, AND OTHER DRUGS RESOURCE GUIDE: INHALANTS

http://www.health.org/pubs/resguide/inhalan.htm

Sponsor: National Clearinghouse for Alcohol and Drug Information, U.S. Department of Health and Human Services.

A single long page listing available pamphlets and abstracts from the scientific literature with contact information.

NATIONAL INHALANT PREVENTION COALITION

http://www.inhalants.org

Sponsor: National Inhalant Prevention Coalition.

Information for the nonprofessional about inhalants and how to prevent their use.

Links to drug abuse prevention sites.

NIDA RESEARCH REPORT: INHALANT ABUSE

http://165.112.78.61/ResearchReports/Inhalants/Inhalants.html

Sponsor: National Institute on Drug Abuse.

Summary for general audiences about the prevalence and risks of inhalant abuse.

VIII. NICOTINE-RELATED DISORDERS

ACTION ON SMOKING AND HEALTH

http://www.ash.org

Sponsor: Action on Smoking and Health, a nonprofit antismoking organization.

Describes information about how to sue tobacco companies, why medical Web sites are not trustworthy, and the dangers of smoking. Access to this information requires an ASH membership.

Ψ CDC'S TIPS: TOBACCO INFORMATION AND PREVENTION SOURCE

http://www.cdc.gov/tobacco

Sponsor: Centers for Disease Control.

Information on tobacco use and its effects.

Online pamphlets on how to stop using tobacco.

Summaries of the CDC's research reports on tobacco use and its effects.

Links to governmental and nongovernmental organizations concerning tobacco use.

GREAT AMERICAN SMOKEOUT

http://www.cancer.org/smokeout

Sponsor: American Cancer Society.

Information for teens about organizing a stop-smoking day at a high school.

FAQs about the dangers of tobacco use.

NATIONAL CLEARINGHOUSE ON TOBACCO AND HEALTH

http://www.cctc.ca/ncth/index.html

Sponsor: National Clearinghouse on Tobacco and Health (Canada).

Fact sheets, charts, and bibliographies of the harmful effects of smoking.

Directory of Web links for antismoking sites and government agencies in the U.S. and Canada that deal with tobacco control.

NICOTINE ANONYMOUS
http://nicotine-anonymous.org

Sponsor: Nicotine Anonymous.

Information about a 12-step program for nicotine addicts, with lists of U.S. and international meetings.

NOTOBACCO.ORG
http://www.notobacco.org

Sponsor: Foundation for a Smokefree America.

Information for teens on how to stop smoking.

Links to other antismoking Web sites of interest to teens and children.

ONCOLINK: SMOKING AND CANCER
http://www.oncolink.upenn.edu/causeprevent/smoking

Sponsor: University of Pennsylvania Cancer Center.

Links to Web sites and recent news items concerning cancer and smoking.

OUT & FREE
http://outfree.com

Sponsor: Out & Free (WA), a stop-smoking program for gay men, lesbians, and bisexuals.

Gives a contact phone number but does not explain what is involved in the program or if there is a cost.

About the Program
Queers and Tobacco
Out & Free
Chat Room
Feedback

PHYSICIANS FOR A SMOKE-FREE CANADA

http://www.smoke-free.ca

Sponsor: Physicians for a Smoke-Free Canada.

Fact sheets concerning the harmful effects of smoking.

Documents efforts of tobacco companies to manipulate nicotine levels in cigarettes.

QUITNET

http://www.quitnet.org

Sponsor: Boston University School of Public Health.

Handy tips and guides for smoking cessation.

Links to Web resources on smoking cessation and treatment programs.

Software tools to aid in the quitting process.

Ψ QUITSMOKINGSUPPORT.COM

http://www.quitsmokingsupport.com

Sponsor: Chris Cor Webdesign.

Lists Web sites about quitting smoking.

Articles about the risks of smoking and how to quit.

Much valuable information despite ubiquitous ads.

Newsletter, chat room, and e-mail list on quitting.

QUITSMOKINGUK.COM

http://www.quitsmokinguk.com

Sponsor: Kara Miller (UK).

Fact sheets about smoking.

Specific suggestions for successful smoking cessation and how to avoid weight gain with a capsule description of cessation treatments.

| Home | Chat | Discussion Groups | Search this site | E-mail |

The UK's online community *for* quitting smokers *by* quitting smokers

RESEARCH NETWORK ON THE ETIOLOGY OF TOBACCO DEPENDENCE

http://www.tern.org

Sponsor: Robert Wood Johnson Foundation.

Describes the Network's research program.

SMOKELESS TOBACCO EDUCATION BASICS

http://www.quittobacco.com

Sponsor: A manufacturer of mint snuff non-tobacco pouches.

Describes the risks of chewing tobacco and surveys intervention techniques.

SOCIETY FOR RESEARCH ON NICOTINE AND TOBACCO

http://www.srnt.org

Sponsor: Society for Research on Nicotine and Tobacco.

Research abstracts from recent conferences of the Society. Downloadable presentation on how to write grants.

ZYBAN

http://www.zyban.com

Sponsor: Glaxo Wellcome U.S.A.

Drug manufacturer's site concerning a prescription medication that aids in smoking cessation.

IX. OPIOID-RELATED DISORDERS

ADDICTION TREATMENT CENTRES OF CANADA

http://www.detoxnow.com

Sponsor: Addiction Treatment Centres of Canada.

Describes the procedure of rapid opiate detoxification used by this clinic.

ANESTHESIA-ASSISTED OPIATE DETOXIFICATION

http://www.heroin-detox.com

Sponsor: Heroin Detox, Inc. (MA).

FAQs and abstracts of the research literature on using naltrexone on anesthetized patients as a detoxification procedure for heroin, methadone, and pain medication.

METHADONE WATCHDOG

http://www.geocities.com/HotSprings/Bath/9774

Sponsor: Unknown.

Focuses on detailing and describing ways to fight against "the humiliating, degrading and dehumanizing treatment that some of us have to endure to obtain our life-saving medication, methadone."

METHADONE INFORMATION EXCHANGE

http://methinfex.home.mindspring.com/

Sponsor: Unknown.

Information about methadone treatment.

Message board.

Directory of outpatient methadone treatment programs in the U.S.

Links with capsule descriptions to other Web sites about opioid addiction and treatment.

NATIONAL ALLIANCE OF METHADONE ADVOCATES

http://www.methadone.org

Sponsor: National Alliance of Methadone Advocates.

FAQs on methadone treatment for heroin addiction.

Links for sites dealing with methadone, drug policy, and the chemistry of opioids.

The National Alliance Of Methadone Advocates

Together We Can Make A Difference

NIDA RESEARCH REPORT: HEROIN ABUSE AND ADDICTION

http://www.nida.nih.gov/ResearchReports/Heroin/Heroin.html

Sponsor: National Institute on Drug Abuse.

FAQs on heroin, its effects, and treatment options.

NORTH AMERICAN SYRINGE EXCHANGE NETWORK

http://www.nasen.org/NASEN_II

Sponsor: North American Syringe Exchange Network.

Links to research articles and Web sites about syringe exchange, AIDS, and safe sex practices.

PROJECT SERO: SYRINGE EXCHANGE RESOURCES ONLINE

http://projectsero.org

Sponsor: Drug Reform Coordination Network.

FAQs about syringe exchange.

Links to online full-text scientific articles and news releases concerning syringe exchange.

State-by-state legislation.

X. PHENCYCLIDINE-RELATED DISORDERS

Ψ INTERNET MENTAL HEALTH: PHENCYCLIDINE DEPENDENCE

http://www.mentalhealth.com/dis/p20-sb09.html

Sponsor: Vancouver Mental Health Support.

Informative articles about effects, diagnosis, and treatment of PCP abuse.

Click on "Research" to conduct a MEDLINE search for abstracts of PCP-related articles.

NIDA INFOFAX: PCP (PHENCYCLIDINE)

http://165.112.78.61/Infofax/pcp.html

Sponsor: National Institute on Drug Abuse.

Fact sheet about PCP and its effects.

XI. SEDATIVE-RELATED DISORDERS

Ψ INTERNET MENTAL HEALTH: SEDATIVE DEPENDENCE

http://www.mentalhealth.com/dis/p20-sb10.html

Sponsor: Vancouver Mental Health Support.

Informative articles about effects, diagnosis, and treatment of sedative abuse.

Click on "Research" to conduct a MEDLINE search for abstracts of related articles.

NIDA INFOFAX: ROHYPNOL AND GHB

http://165.112.78.61/Infofax/RohypnolGHB.html

Sponsor: National Institute on Drug Abuse.

Fact sheet on Rohypnol.

PRESCRIPTIONABUSE.ORG

http://www.prescriptionabuse.org

Sponsor: David Nielson (UT).

Information source for prescription drug abusers and their families.

Links to information about commonly abused medications.

Directory of Web sites about addiction.

Inspirational songs, poetry, and personal narratives.

prescriptionabuse.org
an online resource for prescription drug abusers and their families

Ψ SITE OF DEPENDENCE

http://www.benzodiazepines.net

Sponsor: Dag Zetterberg (Sweden).

Overview of the medical literature on benzodiazepine side effects, with bibliographies.

Personal narratives concerning benzodiazepine dependence.

XII. MISCELLANEOUS WEB SITES WITH GENERAL RELEVANCE TO SUBSTANCE DISORDERS

ADDICTION RESEARCH FOUNDATION

http://www.arf.org

Sponsor: Centre for Addiction and Mental Health (Toronto, Canada).

Links and research papers.

This site is not updated frequently.

ADDICTION TREATMENT FORUM

http://www.atforum.com

Sponsor: Landmark, Inc.

Complete text for current and back issues of *A.T. Forum*, a monthly newsletter.

News releases about addiction treatment.

AMERICAN ACADEMY OF ADDICTION PSYCHIATRY

http://www.aaap.org

Sponsor: American Academy of Addiction Psychiatry.

Information about the Academy and its annual meeting.

Sells tapes of annual meetings.

AMERICAN SOCIETY OF ADDICTION MEDICINE
http://www.asam.org

Sponsor: American Society of Addiction Medicine.

Information about the Society, its publications, and conferences. Abstracts from the current issue of *Journal of Addictive Diseases.*

CENTER FOR THE NEUROBIOLOGICAL INVESTIGATION OF DRUG ABUSE
http://www.bgsm.edu/physpharm/cnida/cnidahome.html

Sponsor: Center for the Neurobiological Investigation of Drug Abuse, Wake Forest University.

Describes publications and current research projects at the Center.

COLLEGE ON PROBLEMS OF DRUG DEPENDENCE
http://views.vcu.edu/cpdd

Sponsor: College on Problems of Drug Dependence.

Policy statements on drug abuse research and treatment.

Fact sheets on behavioral, psychosocial, and pharmaceutical treatment approaches to drug use.

DATOS: DRUG ABUSE TREATMENT OUTCOME STUDIES

http://www.datos.org

Sponsor: National Institute on Drug Abuse and four collaborating drug abuse research centers.

Summarizes a research project on outcomes of treatment provided to a sample of over 10,000 drug abuser clients who received treatment in community-based treatment programs, with long-term follow-up.

DRUG AND ALCOHOL SERVICES INFORMATION SYSTEM

http://wwwdasis.samhsa.gov/ows-bin/owa/DASIS$.startup

Sponsor: Substance Abuse and Mental Health Administration, U.S. Department of Health and Human Services.

Lists state-approved substance abuse facilities

DRUGTEXT

http://www.drugtext.org

Sponsor: International Foundation for Drug Policy and Human Rights.

Extensive collection of news articles and reports on drug abuse as a social and policy problem; this site is not clinically oriented.

EUROPEAN ASSOCIATION FOR THE TREATMENT OF ADDICTION

http://www.box-1.freeserve.co.uk

Sponsor: European Association for the Treatment of Addiction.

Links to European Web sites on addiction research and treatment.

Ψ IBOGAINE DOSSIER

http://www.ibogaine.org

Sponsor: NDA International (NY).

Collection of links to abstracts and articles presenting scientific research about this drug, its hallucinogenic properties, and its claims to alleviate drug dependence.

References articles that are pro-, con-, or merely descriptive of the drug and its uses.

Good collection of Web sites about drug abuse.

Ψ INTERNET MENTAL HEALTH: DISORDERS

http://www.mentalhealth.com/fr20.html

Sponsor: Vancouver Mental Health Support.

Lists a number of substance use disorders, each with clinical description, diagnostic and treatment information, and a link that searches MEDLINE for abstracts concerning the substance.

We have included individual pages from this Web site in the sections for some of the substance abuse disorders discussed above.

JOIN TOGETHER ONLINE

http://www.jointogether.org

Sponsor: Boston University School of Public Health.

Tracks news items dealing with "hot issues" in substance abuse.

NARCOTICS ANONYMOUS WORLD SERVICES

http://www.wsoinc.com

Sponsor: Narcotics Anonymous.

Information about NA, a 12-step program for addicts.

Conference reports.

Current and back issues of NA's newsletter.

NATIONAL ACUPUNCTURE DETOXIFICATION ASSOCIATION

http://www.teleport.com/~acudetox/NADA/clearinghs.shtml

Sponsor: National Acupuncture Detoxification Association.

Distributes literature and provides training in using acupuncture for detoxification.

Click on "Guidepoints," then "Links," for other Web sites dealing with this topic.

Ψ NATIONAL INSTITUTE ON DRUG ABUSE

http://www.nida.nih.gov

Up-to-date information about abused drugs.

Lists scientific meetings, legislation, news releases, and publications about substance use and its treatment.

A complete textbook online: *Principles of Drug Abuse Treatment: A Research-based Guide.*

Ψ PREVLINE: PREVENTION ONLINE

http://www.health.org

Sponsor: National Clearinghouse for Alcohol and Drug Information.

Helpful collection of information and links concerning drugs and drug treatment.

Has a unique selection of drug prevention links for different ethnic and cultural groups (e.g., Hispanic/Latino, Gay/Lesbian/Bisexual, Elders).

Ψ STANTON PEELE ADDICTION WEB SITE

http://peele.sas.nl

Sponsor: Stanton Peele, J.D., Ph.D.

A nonmedical model of addiction: "Addiction is not limited to narcotics, or to drugs at all, and that addiction is a pattern of behavior and experience which is best understood by examining an individual's relationship with his/her world."

Collection of links to articles (by Peele and others) and other Web sites that oppose, criticize, or advocate for an alternative to the disease/12-step model of addiction and recovery.

STEROIDABUSE.ORG

http://steroidabuse.org

Sponsor: National Institute on Drug Abuse.

Links to research summaries and fact sheets on anabolic steroid abuse.

STOP DRUGS

http://www.stopdrugs.org

Sponsors: California Narcotics Officers' Association; U.S. Department of Justice.

Information on drug abuse treatment and prevention.

Photos for identifying commonly abused prescription drugs.

SUBSTANCE ABUSE AND MENTAL HEALTH DATA ARCHIVE

http://www.icpsr.umich.edu/SAMHDA

Sponsors: Inter-university Consortium for Social and Political Research, University of Michigan; Substance Abuse and Mental Health Administration, U.S. Department of Health and Human Services.

Abstracts and raw data from a series of studies on drug abuse and mental health topics.

Ψ SUBSTANCE ABUSE LIBRARIANS AND INFORMATION SPECIALISTS: LINKS

http://www.salis.org/resources/links.htm

Sponsor: Substance Abuse Librarians and Information Specialists.

Extensive directory of informational Web sites about addiction and substance use, but without descriptions.

Ψ WEB OF ADDICTIONS

http://www.well.com/user/woa

Sponsors: Andrew L. Homer, Ph.D.; Dick Dillon.

Valuable directory of links to fact sheets on this site and others about alcohol and many other drugs.

Links to Web sites concerning addiction and treatment.

Section 5
Schizophrenia

Psychosis is the defining feature of these disorders. The following disorders are included:

I. Schizophrenia, which is a disturbance lasting at least six months and including two or more of the following: delusions, hallucinations, disorganized speech, or grossly distorted or catatonic behavior.

II. Schizophreniform Disorder, which is similar to schizophrenia but shorter in duration, lasting from one to six months. A marked decline in functioning is not required.

III. Schizoaffective Disorder, which is a disturbance in which a mood episode and the active phase of schizophrenia occur together. Ordinarily proceeded by a two-week period of hallucinations.

IV. Delusional Disorder, which is characterized by one month of non-bizarre delusions without other active-phase symptoms of schizophrenia.

V. Brief Psychotic Disorder (formerly Brief Reactive Psychosis), which lasts from one day to one month.

VI. Shared Psychotic Disorder (formerly Induced Psychotic Disorder), which develops in an individual influenced by someone else who has an established delusion with similar context.

I. SCHIZOPHRENIA

A. ORGANIZATIONS

NATIONAL ALLIANCE FOR RESEARCH ON SCHIZOPHRENIA AND DEPRESSION
http://www.mhsource.com/narsad.html

Sponsor: National Alliance for Research on Schizophrenia and Depression.

Has an online newsletter.

Lists investigators funded by NARSAD with descriptions of their research.

Sells brochures and videotapes about schizophrenia and antipsychotic medication.

NATIONAL SCHIZOPHRENIA FELLOWSHIP
http://www.nsf.org.uk

Sponsor: National Schizophrenia Fellowship (UK).

Information for nonprofessionals about schizophrenia and treatment.

FAQs about the disorder and medications.

Includes a section about nonmedication treatments for schizophrenia, including cognitive therapy.

Ψ SCHIZOPHRENIA SOCIETY OF CANADA
http://www.schizophrenia.ca

Sponsor: Schizophrenia Society of Canada.

A support organization for people with schizophrenia and their families.

Complete online book about schizophrenia for patients and their families, which is also online at http://www.mentalhealth.com/book/p40-sc01.html.

Complete SSC Bulletin available online.

Links to provincial chapters.

WORLD FELLOWSHIP FOR SCHIZOPHRENIA AND ALLIED DISORDERS
http://www.world-schizophrenia.org

Sponsor: World Fellowship for Schizophrenia and Allied Disorders (Canada).

Publications of the fellowship, including online brochures about schizophrenia and treatment.

Click on "Resources" for links to other relevant sites.

 B. DIAGNOSIS, RESEARCH, AND TREATMENT

Where Web sites are listed for brand name medications, the sponsor of the site is the medication's manufacturer. Unless the site contained significantly more than prescribing information, we did not include a description of the site.

ANTIPSYCHOTIC
http://www.psyweb.com/Drughtm/phender.html

Sponsor: MAXsoft.

Patient information handouts concerning antipsychotic medication and side effects.

CLOZAPINE
http://www.mentalhealth.com/drug/p30-c02.html

Sponsor: Internet Mental Health.

Monograph on clozapine.

DEPARTMENT OF PSYCHIATRY, UNIVERSITY OF GRONINGEN: SCHIZOPHRENIA
http://psychiatry.ggz.edu/0012

Sponsor: Department of Psychiatry, University of Groningen (Netherlands).
FAQs about schizophrenia, with links to relevant sites.
This site is not updated frequently.

DOCTOR'S GUIDE: SCHIZOPHRENIA
http://www.pslgroup.com/SCHIZOPHR.HTM

Sponsor: P/S/L Consulting Group.
A portal site featuring recent news articles and links.

FUTUR.COM IN PSYCHIATRY: SCHIZOPHRENIA
http://www.futur.com

Sponsor: Johnson & Johnson.
Webtrack, a free monthly compendium of abstracts of recent journal articles about schizophrenia.

HEALTH-CENTER: ANTIPSYCHOTICS
http://www.health-center.com/pharmacy/antipsychotics

Sponsor: Clinical Tools, Inc.

NEUROLEPTIC MALIGNANT SYNDROME INFORMATION SERVICE
http://www.nmsis.org

Sponsor: Neuroleptic Malignant Syndrome Information Service.
Brief fact sheets about the syndrome, with a bibliography.

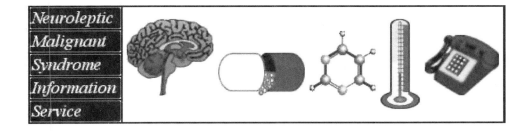

Ψ SCHIZOPHRENIA RESEARCH AT THE NATIONAL INSTITUTE OF MENTAL HEALTH
http://www.nimh.nih.gov/publicat/schizoph.htm

Sponsor: National Institute of Mental Health.

A snapshot of current schizophrenia research at NIMH, with information on ordering *Schizophrenia Bulletin*.

SCHIZOPHRENIA SUPPORT ORGANIZATIONS
http://members.aol.com/leonardjk/support.htm

Sponsor: Unknown.

Links to support organizations around the world.

SCHIZOPHRENIA.CO.UK
http://www.schizophrenia.co.uk

Sponsor: Institute of Psychiatry; Royal College of Psychiatrists (UK).

News releases and first-person accounts.

Assortment of links to various mental health sites.

Ψ SCHIZOPHRENIA.COM
http://www.schizophrenia.com

Sponsor: Brian Chiko.

This site has a large number of message boards at http://www.schizophrenia.com/discuss/Disc3.html for schizophrenics and their families.

Exceptional directory of links about the most commonly prescribed antipsychotics.

Click on "In Depth Schizophrenia Information for Researchers and Professionals" for links to research Web sites and journals.

The Schizophrenia Homepage
www.schizophrenia.com

SCHIZOPHRENIA-HELP ONLINE RESOURCE CENTER
http://www.schizophrenia-help.com

Sponsor: Brian Chiko.

Focuses on psychosocial treatment for schizophrenia, with personal accounts and articles.

SCHIZOPHRENICS ANONYMOUS
http://www.sanonymous.org

Sponsor: Schizophrenics Anonymous.

A self-help program for schizophrenia.

Contact info for obtaining brochures about the program (no specific information about the Schizophrenics Anonymous program appeared to be on the site).

Ψ SEROQUEL
http://www.seroquel.com

FAQs for nonprofessionals about schizophrenia.

Click on "Information for Providers" for "Manual of Rating Scales for the Assessment of Serious Mental Illness," which includes the actual scales as well as brief descriptions.

SHOULD THE USE OF NEUROLEPTICS BE SEVERELY LIMITED?
http://www.breggin.com/neuroleptics.html

Sponsor: Peter Breggin, M.D.

Reprint of an article by Dr. Breggin.

SIDE EFFECTS FROM NEUROLEPTICS
http://neuroland.com/psy/neurolep_se.htm#top

Sponsor: Charles Tuen, M.D. (TX).

Brief chart of neuroleptic side effect syndromes such as tardive dyskinesia and acute dystonic reaction, with treatment recommendations.

SUCCESSFUL SCHIZOPHRENIA
http://www.webcom.com/thrive/schizo

Sponsor: Al Sibert, Ph.D.

Views mental illness as an unscientific construct and references Web sites and articles about spontaneous recovery from schizophrenia.

ZYPREXA
http://www.zyprexa.com

Includes material about living with schizophrenia. The site is not updated frequently.

II-VII. (OTHER PSYCHOTIC DISORDERS)

Information on the other psychotic disorders is best found at the Internet Mental Health Web site at http://www.mentalhealth.com. (Click the "Disorders" icon at the left of the main page.)

Section 6
Mood Disorders

This section has three components:

I. Depressive Disorders

    A. Major Depressive Disorder, which lasts for a period of at least two weeks, during which there is either depressed mood or loss of interest or pleasure in nearly all activities.

        1. Research, Diagnosis, and Treatment

        2. Electro Convulsive Therapy (ECT)

    B. Dysthymic Disorder, which consists of day-long depressed mood for more than half of the days during a period of two years or more.

II. Bipolar Disorders

    A. Bipolar Disorder I, which is the presence of only one manic episode and no past major depressive episodes.

    B. Bipolar Disorder II, which is the presence of one or more major depressive episodes, a history of at least one hypomanic episode, and a history of manic or mixed episodes.

    C. Cyclothymic Disorder, which is a condition lasting at least two years with numerous periods of both hypomanic and depressive symptoms that do not meet the criteria for Major Depressive Episode.

III. Miscellaneous Mood Disorder Topics

    A. Postpartum Onset Specifier (*Postpartum Depression*), which is severe depression that begins within 4 weeks after the delivery of a child.

    B. Seasonal Onset Specifier (*Seasonal Affective Disorder*), which is severe depression at characteristic times of the year. It usually begins in fall or winter and remits in spring.

    C. Suicide

    D. Web Sites for Specific Medications

I. DEPRESSIVE DISORDERS

 ## A. MAJOR DEPRESSIVE DISORDER

1. RESEARCH, DIAGNOSIS, AND TREATMENT

Ψ DEPRESSION ALLIANCE ONLINE
http://www.depressionalliance.org

Sponsor: Depression Alliance Online (UK), a charity run by people with depression that offers support groups and information.

A collection of detailed FAQs for the public about depression and available treatments.

Good directory of Web sites on many topics related to depression and other emotional disorders.

Search engine for news stories about depression that have been posted on the Internet.

Ψ DEPRESSION AND PREGNANCY
http://www.angelfire.com/de2/depressionpregnancy

Sponsor: C. L. Cameron, Ph.D.

Frequently updated links to abstracts in the scientific literature concerning treatment of depression during pregnancy, effects of antidepressant medications on the developing fetus and during lactation, and postpartum depression.

DEPRESSION AND RELATED AFFECTIVE DISORDERS ASSOCIATION
http://www.med.jhu.edu/drada

Sponsor: Depression and Related Affective Disorders Association.

Links to FAQs on other sites about depression and bipolar disorders.

"The Reference Shelf" contains articles by psychiatrists for nonprofessionals about various affective disorders and pharmacological treatments; it also has a useful article on how to choose a therapist to treat depression.

Links to research studies seeking participants.

DEPRESSION RESOURCE CENTER

http://www.healingwell.com/depression

Depression Resource Center
@ HealingWell.com   Community, Information, Resources

Sponsor: Healingwell.com, which focuses on chronic illnesses.

News items about depression and treatment.

Small collection of links to relevant sites.

Lists message boards and Usenet newsgroups for depression support.

Quiz: Are You Depressed?

Types of Depression

Antidepressant Therapies

The Good News About Depression

Anxiety and Depression

Sex and Depression

DEPRESSION.COM

http://www.depression.com

Sponsor: PlanetRx, Inc.

Well-written articles for the nonprofessional about depression and aspects of treatment.

Articles summarizing each commonly prescribed antidepressant medication (note that the main business of the site's sponsor is online pharmaceutical sales).

A good introduction to cognitive therapy, listing the typical cognitive errors; the article would be useful for patients starting or considering cognitive therapy.

Brief descriptions of alternative treatments for depression, such as acupuncture and herbal medicines.

DOCTOR'S GUIDE: DEPRESSION

http://www.pslgroup.com/DEPRESSION.HTM

Sponsor: P\S\L Consulting Group, Inc.

A useful place to read recent news releases about depression.

Directory of Web sites about depression, but without any descriptive information.

This is a portal site that can be configured to display the user's links to favorite journals and other Web sites at each visit.

Ψ DR. IVAN'S DEPRESSION CENTRAL
http://www.psycom.net/depression.central.html

Sponsor: Ivan Goldberg, M.D.

Well-organized collection of links to journal abstracts and full-text journal articles about many aspects of depression and other mood disorders.

Directory of relevant Web sites.

NATIONAL DEPRESSIVE AND MANIC-DEPRESSIVE ASSOCIATION
http://www.ndmda.org

Sponsor: National Depressive and Manic-Depressive Association.

Focuses on the biochemical view of depression and on medication as the treatment of choice.

Online brochures for the nonprofessional about aspects of depression such as mood disorders in adolescents and suicide.

Directory of sites about depression.

Information about the Association's local support chapters throughout the U.S. and Canada.

Our Mission Statement

The mission of the National Depressive and Manic-Depressive Association is to educate patients, families, professionals, and the public concerning the nature of depressive and manic-depressive illness as treatable medical diseases; to foster self-help for patients and families; to eliminate discrimination and stigma; to improve access to care; and to advocate for research toward the elimination of these illnesses.

NATIONAL FOUNDATION FOR DEPRESSIVE ILLNESS, INC.
http://www.depression.org

Sponsor: National Foundation for Depressive Illness, Inc., which aims to disseminate information about depression to the public.

Very brief fact sheets about depression and treatment that emphasize the "chemical imbalance" theory of depression.

PSYCHOLOGY INFORMATION ONLINE: DEPRESSION
http://www.psychologyinfo.com/depression

Sponsor: Donald J. Franklin, Ph.D. (NJ).

Fact sheets for clients about mood disorders and treatment options.

Particularly good section about the history, theory, and practice of cognitive therapy.

WING OF MADNESS: A DEPRESSION GUIDE
http://www.wingofmadness.com

Sponsor: Deborah Gray.

A useful site for clients who need general information about depression.
Directories of links to other relevant sites.

2. ELECTRO CONVULSIVE THERAPY (ECT)

Ψ ECT-ON-LINE
http://www.priory.co.uk/psych/ectol.htm

Sponsor: Carl Littlejohns, MB, ChB MRCPsych (North Wales, UK).

Presents pros and cons.

Has links to other sites about ECT, as well as a bibliography of print literature.

Patient information booklets.

SHOCKED!
http://www.ect.org

Sponsor: Juli Lawrence, ECT Survivor.

Presents the case against ECT, particularly focusing on issues concerning adequacy of informed consent.

 ## B. DYSTHYMIC DISORDER

CLARKE INSTITUTE OF PSYCHIATRY: ABOUT DYSTHYMIA
http://www.camh.net/CLARKEPages/about_illnesses/dysthymia.html

Sponsor: Clarke Institute of Psychiatry (Canada).

FAQs for nonprofessionals about Dysthymic Disorder as an illness that is treatable by interpersonal psychotherapy.

II. BIPOLAR DISORDER

BIPOLAR GENETICS COLLABORATION
http://www.bipolargenes.org

Sponsor: National Bipolar Genetics Collaboration, a coalition of university research centers that look for the genetic basis of Bipolar Disorder.

Brief FAQ section about Bipolar Disorder.

Has a link to a thirty-minute video for patients and families about Bipolar Disorder, which is viewable online.

⟩⟨ BIPOLAR GENETICS COLLABORATION

Ψ CHILD & ADOLESCENT BIPOLAR FOUNDATION
http://www.bpkids.org

Sponsor: Child & Adolescent Bipolar Foundation.

An assembly of scientific journal articles for the professional and nontechnical articles for parents and other family members of children and teens with Bipolar Disorder.

Timeline of the psychiatric history of Bipolar Disorder.

Message boards, chat rooms, and online support groups; available only to members.

HARBOR OF REFUGE: BIPOLAR DISORDER
http://www.harbor-of-refuge.org

Sponsor: Harbor of Refuge Organization.

Online moderated discussion groups for people with Bipolar Disorder.

FAQs about BD and treatment options.

Useful printout of self-care strategies.

MANIC DEPRESSION WEB RING
http://nav.webring.org/cgi-bin/navcgi?ring=maniaring;list

Sponsor: Unknown.

Many personal (noninstitutional) Web pages about Bipolar Disorder.

MOODSWING.ORG
http://www.moodswing.org

Sponsor: Bipolar Disorder Online Support Group.

FAQs about Bipolar Disorder, and links to other sites about BD. This site is not updated frequently.

NIMH: BIPOLAR DISORDER
http://www.nimh.nih.gov/publicat/bipolarresfact.cfm

Sponsor: National Institute of Mental Health.

Has a link to a detailed fact sheet, with an overview of Bipolar Disorder and brief discussions of current lines of research that NIMH sponsors.

Updates on Bipolar Disorder in children and adolescents.

Ψ PENDULUM RESOURCES
http://www.pendulum.org

Sponsor: Doug Barlow, Pendulum Resources.

A superb resource, with annotated links to articles for both professionals and the general public.

Links to support and advocacy groups.

Personal narratives about Bipolar Disorder and links to the home pages of some people with BD.

Ψ SOCIETY FOR MANIC DEPRESSION
http://societymd.org

Sponsor: Society for Manic Depression.

Details a medication compliance program for Bipolar Disorder.

Click on "Library" for brief directories of related sites.

WINDS OF CHANGE
http://www.windsofchange.com

*Sponsor: Winds of Change, an online Bipolar Disorder
Support Group.*

Information for the nonprofessional about BD
and medications.

Long directory of relevant Web sites.

Message board and chat room.

III. MISCELLANEOUS MOOD DISORDER TOPICS

 ## A. POSTPARTUM ONSET SPECIFIER ("POSTPARTUM DEPRESSION ")

DEPRESSION AFTER DELIVERY
http://www.behavenet.com/dadinc

*Sponsor: Depression after Delivery, Inc., a nonprofit
organization.*

FAQs about postpartum depression.

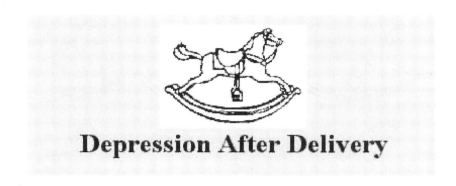

Depression After Delivery

DEPRESSION.COM: POSTPARTUM DEPRESSION
http://www.depression.com/health_library/types/types_03_postpartum.html

Sponsor: PlanetRx.

A single article that explains postpartum depression and treatment options.

ONLINE PPD SUPPORT GROUP
http://www.geocities.com/Wellesley/4665

Sponsor: Online PPD Support Group.

Links to other sites about postpartum depression; lists of other resources with contact information.

Operates an online discussion area and a mailing list.

For women with postpartum depression there is a useful page, "Reasons to live," written by members of the online support group.

Ψ POSTPARTUM DEPRESSION
http://www.chss.iup.edu/postpartum

Sponsor: Indiana University of Pennsylvania Department of Anthropology; Postpartum Support International.

FAQs for new parents about postpartum depression.

Searchable bibliography of relevant medical and cross-cultural literature.

Links to other sites.

B. SEASONAL ONSET SPECIFIER ("SEASONAL AFFECTIVE DISORDER")

Ψ CANADIAN CONSENSUS GUIDELINES FOR THE TREATMENT OF SEASONAL AFFECTIVE DISORDER

http://www.fhs.mcmaster.ca/direct/depress/sad.html

Sponsor: Reprinted from Canadian Journal of Diagnosis.

Review of the scientific literature on the diagnosis and treatment of SAD, with recommendations.

COLUMBIA UNIVERSITY CLINICAL CHRONOBIOLOGY GROUP

http://www.lightandions.org

Sponsor: Columbia University Clinical Chronobiology Group.

Describes ongoing clinical trials for light treatment.

DEPRESSION.COM: SEASONAL AFFECTIVE DISORDER

http://www.depression.com/health_library/types/types_02_seasonal.html

Sponsor: PlanetRx.

Long article about SAD for nonprofessionals.

Links to companies that sell light treatment devices.

OUTSIDE IN

http://www.outsidein.co.uk

Sponsor: Outside In (UK).

Seasonal Affective Disorder fact sheet from a company that sells light devices for treating the disorder.

Abstracts of scientific literature on SAD.

SADASSOCIATION

http://www.sada.org.uk

Sponsor: SAD Association, a support organization for Seasonal Affective Disorder.

Brief FAQ section on SAD, with information on purchasing a full information pack.

SOCIETY FOR LIGHT TREATMENT AND BIOLOGICAL RHYTHMS
http://www.sltbr.org

Sponsor: Society for Light Treatment and Biological Rhythms.

Information about the Society and its services.

FAQs for nonprofessionals about Seasonal Affective Disorder.

Links to Web sites about SAD and circadian rhythms.

SOCIETY FOR

LIGHT TREATMENT

AND

BIOLOGICAL RHYTHMS

 **C. SUICIDE**

Ψ AMERICAN ASSOCIATION OF SUICIDOLOGY
http://www.suicidology.org

Sponsor: American Association of Suicidology.

Extensive links to Web sites about suicide.

List of recommended books, with brief descriptions.

National directory of support groups for suicide survivors.

Lists crisis centers throughout the U.S.

BEFRIENDERS INTERNATIONAL ONLINE
http://www.befrienders.org

Sponsor: Befrienders International.

Lists warning signs of suicide, with suggestions on how to help.

International directory of suicide hot lines.

Befrienders International
listening, always listening

Working to prevent suicide worldwide
with 31,000 volunteers in over 40 countries

en español   en français   em português
باللغة العربية   Dansk

NIMH SUICIDE RESEARCH CONSORTIUM
http://www.nimh.nih.gov/research/suicide.htm

Sponsor: National Institute of Mental Health.

Links to information available from NIMH, including a bibliography on suicidal behavior and suicide statistics.

SUICIDE INFORMATION AND EDUCATION CENTRE
http://www.siec.ca

Sponsor: Suicide Information and Education Centre (Canada).

Describes the Centre's print library of materials on suicide and prevention.

Links to Web sites dealing with suicidology and survivor support.

YELLOW RIBBON SUICIDE PREVENTION PROGRAM
http://yellowribbon.org

Sponsor: Light for Life Foundation International.

Describes available materials for conducting an adolescent suicide prevention program.

 # D. WEB SITES FOR SPECIFIC MEDICATIONS

Each of the Web sites in this section offers a fact sheet about a single medication, usually covering indications, recommended dosages, side effects, methods of administration, and adverse reactions. We have not added an additional description unless the site offered significant original information about the disorder(s) being treated by the medication. Also, unless otherwise noted, the sponsor is the manufacturer of the medication.

CELEXA
http://www.celexa.com

Lists support and advocacy groups and chat rooms.

Useful list of books for patients and family members, with brief reviews.

Offers a separate section for health professionals with links to mental health-related Web sites and a database of pharmaceuticals (which does not appear to be updated frequently).

DEPAKOTE
http://www.rxabbott.com/dephome/dephome.htm

EFFEXOR
http://www.effexor.com

LITHIUM
http://www.fairlite.com/ocd/medications/lithium.shtml

Sponsor: Fairlight Consulting.

LITHIUM INFORMATION CENTER
http://www.healthtechsys.com/mimlithium.html

Sponsor: Madison Institute of Medicine (WI).

Collects information from the scientific literature about lithium and other treatments for Bipolar Disorder. The site provides information for contacting an information specialist by phone, but the information itself is not found on the Web site.

LUVOX
http://www.fairlite.com/ocd/medications/luvox.shtml

Sponsor: Fairlight Consulting.

MAO INHIBITORS
http://www.depression.com/health_library/anti_depressant_therapies/anti_04_mao.html

Sponsor: PlanetRx.

NEURONTIN
http://www.neurontin.com

PAXIL
http://www.paxil.com

PROZAC
http://www.prozac.com

REMERON
http://www.remeron.com

Register (free) as a medical professional to get information about this medication, including audio replay of scientific papers.

By clicking on "Visitor," the site displays only general information about depression and a single paragraph about Remeron.

SERZONE
http://www.oze-mail.com.au/~drobb/bms/serz1.htm

ST. JOHN'S WORT
http://www.primenet.com/~camilla/STJOHNS.FAQ

Sponsor: Camilla Cracchiolo.

A lengthy article on St. John's Wort, with updates referring to recent research.

ST. JOHN'S WORT: QUESTIONS AND ANSWERS
http://www.nimh.nih.gov/publicat/stjohnqa.cfm

Sponsor: National Institute of Mental Health.

THYROID HORMONE (T3)
http://www.drmirkin.com/morehealth/G171.htm

Sponsor: Gabe Mirkin, M.D.

TRAZODONE
http://www.planetrx.com/product/rx/shelf/add_info/2185_introduction.html

Sponsor: PlanetRx.

TRICYCLIC ANTIDEPRESSANTS
http://www.netwellness.org/mhc/scr/001815sc.htm

Sponsor: University of Cincinnati Medical Center Libraries.

WELLBUTRIN
http://www.planetrx.com/product/rx/shelf/add_info/714_introduction.html

Sponsor: PlanetRx.

WELLBUTRIN SR
http://www.wellbutrin-sr.com

ZOLOFT
http://www.zoloft.com

Prescribing information for professionals.

Information for nonprofessionals concerning the conditions for which Zoloft is FDA-approved.

Section 7
Anxiety Disorders

The DSM-IV lists these disorders:

I. Panic Attacks, which are characterized by the sudden onset of intense apprehension, fearfulness, or terror, often with a sense of impending doom. Physiological symptoms are often reported. Panic attacks may be part of the symptomatology of any of the anxiety disorders. Recurrent panic attacks as a primary symptomatic feature suggest that Panic Disorder should be considered as the patient's diagnosis.

II. Agoraphobia, which is characterized by anxiety about or avoidance of situations from which escape might be difficult. As is true with panic attacks, agoraphobia is a symptom that sometimes occur in the content of any of the anxiety disorders.

III. Phobias, which are characterized by irrational fears and avoidance of specific stimuli.

IV. Obsessive-Compulsive Disorder, which is characterized by obsessions and/or compulsions.

V. Posttraumatic Stress Disorder, which is a biphasic condition in which the reexperiencing of a traumatic event will alternate with withdrawal reminders of the trauma; the patient also continually experiences hyperarousal. Acute Stress Disorder is similar but lasts a maximum of four weeks and requires the presence of dissociative symptoms connected with the traumatic stimulus.

VI. Generalized Anxiety Disorder and other nonspecific forms of anxiety, which are characterized by excessive worry and often accompanied by somatic symptoms of anxiety.

We have added the following section:

VII. Web Sites for Specific Medications

I. PANIC ATTACKS

Ψ ANSWERS TO YOUR QUESTIONS ABOUT PANIC DISORDER

http://www.apa.org/pubinfo/panic.html

Sponsor: American Psychological Association.

An excellent handout that explains Panic Disorder to patients, with a description of cognitive therapy and medication.

ANXIETY NETWORK: PANIC DISORDER HOME PAGE

http://www.anxietynetwork.com/pdhome.html

Sponsor: Thomas A. Richards, Ph.D.

Useful articles for nonprofessionals describing Panic Disorder, Agoraphobia, and treatment options.

Ψ MENTAL AND EMOTIONAL HEALTH: PANIC DISORDER

http://www.queendom.com/mental.html#PD

Sponsor: Plumeus, Inc. (Canada).

Excellent literature review with a description of etiological theories and the data for and against each. However, it does not discuss treatment options and appears not to be updated frequently.

Ψ PANIC AND ANXIETY HUB

http://www.paems.com.au

Sponsor: Panic Anxiety Education Management Services (Australia).

Many useful articles about Panic Disorder and various treatment options.

For therapists who use cognitive therapy with Panic Disordered patients, this site offers a unique e-mail exchange between someone getting cognitive therapy for Panic Disorder and a therapist giving encouragement and explanation of the process (click on "Articles"). The e-mail messages will help to prepare a Panic Disorder patient for the process of cognitive therapy.

Thorough descriptions of several research projects conducted by the sponsor of this site.

PANIC DISORDERS INSTITUTE

http://www.algy.com/pdi

Sponsors: Stuart Shipko, M.D.; Panic Disorders Institute.

Explains Panic Disorder as caused by stress-related abnormalities in sleep that affect the secretion of endorphins and cholecystokinin.

The site is not updated frequently.

II. AGORAPHOBIA

ABOUT.COM: AGORAPHOBIA

http://panicdisorder.about.com/health/panicdisorder/msubmenu4.htm

Sponsor: About.com.

Diagnostic criteria and fact sheets.

Links for offline and online agoraphobia support resources.

AGORAPHOBIA RESOURCES AND INFORMATION

http://www.nursehealer.com/Agoraphobia.htm

Sponsor: Mary Catherine Miller.

Links to relevant sites, with summaries and commentary.

ANXIETY NETWORK: PANIC DISORDER HOME PAGE

http://www.anxietynetwork.com/pdhome.html

Sponsor: Thomas A. Richards, Ph.D.

Useful articles for nonprofessionals that describe Panic Disorder, Agoraphobia, and treatment options.

OPEN DIRECTORY PROJECT: AGORAPHOBIA

http://www.dmoz.org/Health/Mental_Health/Disorders/Phobias/Agoraphobia

Sponsor: Open Directory Project.

Directory of Web sites about Agoraphobia.

III. PHOBIAS

Ψ ANXIETY DISORDERS ASSOCIATION OF AMERICA

http://www.adaa.org

Sponsor: Anxiety Disorders Association of America.

For the professional, there is a description of the association, a searchable list of members, and links to treatment programs and support organizations.

For the consumer, there is a viewable video about social anxiety by Donny Osmond, message board, chat room, and helpful brochures about anxiety disorders.

Useful chart comparing pros and cons of treatment options.

CENTER FOR ADVANCED MULTIMEDIA PSYCHOTHERAPY

http://www.vrphobia.com

Sponsor: Center for Advanced Multimedia Psychotherapy, California School of Professional Psychology Research and Service Foundation.

Click on "VR Therapies" for fears of driving, flying, spiders, claustrophobia, Agoraphobia, and social phobia. Some of the sections describe treatment protocols in detail, while others have pictures of the computer equipment and treatment setting.

MCP HAHNEMANN UNIVERSITY SOCIAL ANXIETY TREATMENT PROGRAM

http://www.mcphu.edu/shp/fear

Sponsor: MCP Hahnemann University Social Anxiety Treatment Program (Philadelphia, PA).

Basic FAQs about social phobia.

Brief directory of Web sites about social phobia.

Lists anxiety disorders clinics and self-help books.

PHOBIA LINKS

http:// phobialist.com

The Phobia List ™

Sponsor: Fredd Culbertson.

Directory of links to phobia Web sites.

Lists names for specific phobias.

SOCIAL-ANXIETY.ORG

http://www.social-anxiety.org

Sponsor: Complete Medical Communications (UK), supported by a grant from SmithKline Beecham.

FAQs about social phobia.

Links for nonprofessionals to Web sites for support groups and other Web sites about social anxiety.

VIRTUAL REALITY EXPOSURE THERAPY

http://www.cc.gatech.edu/gvu/virtual/Phobia/phobia.html

Sponsor: Graphics, Visualization, and Usability Center, Georgia Tech.

Fact sheet on virtual reality treatment for phobia, accompanied by pictures of the equipment and a few virtual reality images.

IV. OBSESSIVE-COMPULSIVE DISORDER

Ψ CENTER FOR COGNITIVE-BEHAVIORAL THERAPY

http://www.hope4ocd.com

Sponsor: Center for Cognitive-Behavioral Therapy (Los Angeles).

Outline of OCD and treatment options.

Detailed outline of Dr. Jeffrey Schwartz's four-step procedure for coping with obsessive thoughts and compulsions, which is from his book *Brain Lock.*

Promises monthly summaries of a few important and recent scientific journal articles.

Ψ OBSESSIVE COMPULSIVE FOUNDATION

http://www.ocfoundation.org

Sponsor: Obsessive Compulsive Foundation.

Outstanding collection of links.

Thoughtful discussions of treatment options, with separate articles on medication for children and for adults.

- What Is OCD?
- Related Disorders
- How Is OCD Treated?
- OCD In Children
- Medication For Adults
- Medication For Children
- OCD Screening Test
- OCD Articles

Ψ OC & SPECTRUM DISORDERS ASSOCIATION

http://www.ocdhelp.org

Sponsors: Monica Terwilliger, OC & Spectrum Disorders Association.

Links to OCD treatment programs and support organizations

Detailed FAQs about OCD and treatment options.

Directory of support groups in California, with an online support group.

OCD WEB SERVER

http://www.fairlite.com/ocd

Sponsor: Fairlight Consulting.

Links to OCD Web sites.

Ψ OCDONLINE.COM

http://www.ocdonline.com

Sponsor: Dr. Stephen Phillipson.

Detailed and clearly written description of the process of cognitive therapy for OCD.

Helpful articles by Dr. Phillipson and Dr. Dean McKay describing traditional cognitive therapy and innovative variations on CBT for OCD.

Annotated links to relevant Web sites.

Detailed, thoughtful reviews of several OCD self-help books.

V. POSTTRAUMATIC STRESS DISORDER AND ACUTE STRESS DISORDER

Because peritraumatic dissociation is a strong predictor of the development of PTSD, please also see section 10 of chapter 1 for information on Dissociative Disorders.

AUSTRALIAN TRAUMA WEB

http://www2.psy.uq.edu.au/PTSD

Sponsor: Grant Devilly, Ph.D., Psychology Department, University of Queensland (Australia).

Links to online brochures and sites of special relevance to Australians.

Ψ DAVID BALDWIN'S TRAUMA INFORMATION PAGES

http://www.trauma-pages.com

Sponsor: David Baldwin, Ph.D.

Regularly updated directory of briefly annotated Web links dealing with trauma, dissociation, and psychological responses to disaster.

BREAKING THE SILENCE: A COMMUNITY OF SURVIVORS

http://nav.webring.org/cgi-bin/navcgi?ring=survivors;list

Sponsor: Unknown.

Lists sites by and for survivors of child abuse.

INTERNATIONAL CRITICAL INCIDENT STRESS FOUNDATION, INC.

http://www.icisf.org

Sponsor: International Critical Incident Stress Foundation, Inc.

Articles about Critical Incident Stress Debriefing, with links to related Web sites.

INTERNATIONAL SOCIETY FOR TRAUMATIC STRESS STUDIES

http://www.istss.org

Sponsor: International Society for Traumatic Stress Studies, which is a worldwide professional association of clinicians and researchers.

Describes the Society's publications, membership benefits, and annual conference.

Ψ NATIONAL CENTER FOR PTSD

http://www.ncptsd.org

Sponsor: U.S. Department of Veterans Affairs.

One of the most outstanding resources on the Internet.

Complete issues of *PTSD Research Quarterly.*

Link to PILOTS database, which is a searchable database of scientific journal abstracts on PTSD and trauma, updated quarterly.

Fact sheets and recommended books for nonprofessionals.

OFFICE FOR VICTIMS OF CRIME

http://www.ojp.usdoj.gov/ovc

Sponsor: U.S. Department of Justice.

Information about victims' rights.

How to access State compensation programs for victims.

Articles about various forms of victimization.

Ψ PILOTS CATALOG

http://dciswww.dartmouth.edu:50080/v3?db=105&conn=143302914&page=d

Sponsor: National Center for PTSD (VT).

Searchable international bibliography of PTSD literature.

PTSD TODAY

http://www.thegrid.net/dakaiser/today/ptsd.htm

Sponsor: David Alan Kaiser, Ph.D.

Links to mental health news sources and abstracts of recent journal articles.

PTSD.COM

http://www.ptsd.com

Sponsor: Eric Borgos.

Selected links to Web sites with general information about PTSD, as well as to support resources, professional associations, and treatment techniques. The site is not updated frequently.

Ψ SIDRAN TRAUMATIC STRESS FOUNDATION

http://www.sidran.org

Sponsor: Sidran Traumatic Stress Foundation, a nonprofit foundation that publishes and supports treatment in Dissociative Disorders and other trauma.

Handouts for clients about PTSD.

Links to trauma/dissociation Web sites.

SNAP: SURVIVORS NETWORK OF THOSE ABUSED BY PRIESTS

http://www.snap-net.org

Sponsor: SNAP, a self-help organization.

Links to news articles and relevant Web sites.

Offers an "online support group" (mailing list).

TEARS OF A COP UNDER PRESSURE

http://www.tearsofacop.com

Sponsor: Unknown.

Articles and information for nonprofessionals about PTSD among police officers.

Links to relevant sites.

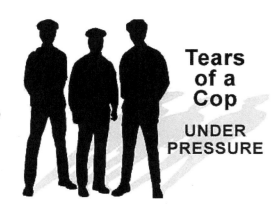

Ψ TRAUMA ARTICLES ONLINE

http://home.earthlink.net/~hopefull

Sponsor: Hope E. Morrow, M.A., M.F.T., C.S.

Regularly updated directory of articles about PTSD, dissociation, disaster response, and related topics. Most of the articles are directed to therapists.

TRAUMATOLOGYE

http://www.fsu.edu/~trauma

Sponsor: Charles Figley, Ph.D., Florida State University.

Quarterly electronic journal with cutting-edge articles concerning PTSD theory, treatment approaches, and research.

WOUNDED HEALER JOURNAL

http://twhj.com

Sponsor: Linda Chapman.

An online journal and chat room for therapists who have been victims of trauma.

VI. GENERALIZED ANXIETY DISORDER AND OTHER NONSPECIFIC FORMS OF ANXIETY

 ## A. GENERAL RESOURCES

ANXIETIES.COM

http://www.anxieties.com

Sponsor: R. Reid Wilson, Ph.D.

The site describes itself as a free self-help resource, and contains the general outline of behavioral self-treatment for Phobia, Generalized Anxiety Disorder, and Obsessive Compulsive Disorder. However, the self-treatment program requires you to purchase books and audiotapes by Dr. Wilson that are advertised on the site.

ANXIETY NETWORK INTERNATIONAL: GENERALIZED ANXIETY HOME PAGE

http://www.anxietynetwork.com/gahome.html

Sponsor: Thomas Richards, Ph.D.

Some helpful strategies for attacking anxiety, intermingled with ads for anti-anxiety audiotapes.

THE ANXIETY PANIC INTERNET RESOURCE (TAPIR)

http://www.algy.com/anxiety

Sponsor: Algy's Herbs.

A self-help resource for all of the anxiety disorders except PTSD.
Links to sites for each of the anxiety disorders.
News items.

QUEENDOM.COM: GENERALIZED ANXIETY DISORDER

http://www.queendom.com/mental.html#GAD

Sponsor: Plumeus, Inc. (Canada).

Fact sheet about Generalized Anxiety Disorder and a review of the literature about treatment options.
Links to self-help resources.

 **B. STRESS MANAGEMENT**

Please refer to section 15 of chapter 1 (Adjustment Disorders).

VII. WEB SITES FOR SPECIFIC MEDICATIONS

See also section 6 of chapter 1 (Mood Disorders), since many of the medications listed there are also effective for anxiety disorders.

ANXIETY/STRESS

http://216.94.120.154/mc/mcsite.nsf/drugdbmain?OpenForm&stressdrugindex

Sponsor: Mediconsult.com.

Useful charts of anxiolytic and sedative medications, with links to patient information handouts about each.

BENZODIAZEPINES AND OTHER DRUG TREATMENTS FOR ANXIETY

http://pharmacology.about.com/health/pharmacology/library/weekly/aa970724.hm

Sponsor: About.com.

Although this article is from 1997, it remains a good overview of this class of medications.

For information about a specific benzodiazepine, consult http://www.mentalhealth.com/fr30.html or any of the databases of prescribed medications that we have listed in part 2 of chapter 4.

BETA-ADRENERGIC BLOCKING AGENTS (SYSTEMIC)

http://www.nlm.nih.gov/medlineplus/druginfo/betaadrenergicblockingagentssy202087.html

Sponsor: National Library of Medicine.

Outline of beta blockers that unfortunately omits discussion of their utility in treating somatic anxiety symptoms.

BUSPAR

http://www.buspar.com

Sponsor: Bristol-Myers Squibb Company.

KAVA KAVA HOME PAGE

http://www.betterlivingusa.com

Sponsor: Don Ansley, Better Living Products.

Describes Kava Kava, an herb that is lauded as a treatment for anxiety and panic, with links to articles.

Section 8
Somatoform Disorders

These disorders suggest a physical problem or cluster of problems not fully explained by a general medical condition, substance, or other mental disorder. Symptoms cause significant stress and impairment in everyday functioning.

The *DSM-IV* categorizes them as follows:

I. Somatization Disorder, which begins before age 30 and is characterized by combinations of pain, gastrointestinal, sexual, and psychoneurological symptoms.

II. Conversion Disorder, which involves unexplained symptoms affecting voluntary motor or sensory function that suggest a neurological or medical condition.

III. Pain Disorder, in which pain is the major focus of clinical attention. Psychological factors may play a significant role.

IV. Hypochondriasis, which is the fear of having a serious disease based on a misinterpretation of bodily functions or symptoms.

V. Body Dysmorphic Disorder, which is a preoccupation with an imagined or exaggerated defect in physical appearance.

I AND II. SOMATIZATION DISORDER AND CONVERSION DISORDER

Reflecting the fact that this diagnosis varies considerably from patient to patient in its symptom constellation, there appear to be few or no Web sites that focused in detail on these disorders. Some have suggested that these disorders be reclassified as forms of Dissociative Disorder; please see section 10 of chapter 1 for information on Dissociative Disorders.

ADAM.COM: SOMATIZATION DISORDER

http://www.adam.com/ency/article/000955.htm

Sponsor: ADAM Software, Inc.

Information sheet about Somatization Disorder.

ADOLESCENT MEDICINE: CONVERSION AND SOMATIZATION DISORDERS

http://www.mc.vanderbilt.edu/peds/pidl/adolesc/convreac.htm

Sponsor: Vanderbilt University School of Medicine.

Overview of symptoms, proposed etiology, and management.

III. PAIN DISORDER

AMERICAN ACADEMY OF PAIN MANAGEMENT

http://www.aapainmanage.org

Sponsor: American Academy of Pain Management.

For professionals, the site displays information about the Academy and a list of available books and tapes.

For nonprofessionals, there is a directory of pain management programs.

AMERICAN ACADEMY OF PAIN MEDICINE

http://www.painmed.org

Sponsor: American Academy of Pain Medicine.

Position statements and excerpts from the Academy's publications.

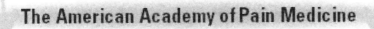
The American Academy of Pain Medicine

AMERICAN COUNCIL FOR HEADACHE EDUCATION

http://www.achenet.org

Sponsor: American Council for Headache Education.

Includes information for patients about different types of headaches and treatment options.

American Council for Headache Education

AMERICAN HEADACHE SOCIETY

http://www.ahsnet.org

Sponsor: American Headache Society, an organization for professionals.

Describes the Society's activities and scientific meetings.

Abstracts from current and back issues of the Society's journal.

Ψ AMERICAN PAIN SOCIETY

http://www.ampainsoc.org

Sponsor: American Pain Society.

Describes the Society and its activities.

Full text of the Society's bulletin is available online.

Click on "Resources" for annotated descriptions of relevant sites for patients and professionals.

CHRONIC PAIN

http://www.emerson.edu/acadepts/CS/healthcom/Resources/pain.htm

Sponsor: Emerson-Tufts Program in Health Communication.

Directory of Web sites about chronic pain, each with a descriptive paragraph.

CHRONIC PAIN ASSOCIATION OF CANADA

http://ecn.ab.ca/cpac

Sponsor: Chronic Pain Association of Canada, a support organization for people with chronic pain.

Fact sheet on chronic pain.

Ψ DICK CHAPMAN'S HOME PAGE

http://faculty.washington.edu/crc

Sponsor: C. Richard Chapman, M.D., Department of Anesthesiology, University of Washington (Seattle).

Excellent collection of links to Web sites about pain and pain management.

NATIONAL FOUNDATION FOR THE TREATMENT OF PAIN

http://www.paincare.org

Sponsor: National Foundation for the Treatment of Pain.

Brief fact sheets about intractable pain and FAQs about migraine.

PAIN NET, INC.

http://www.painnet.com

Sponsor: Pain Net, Inc.

The most useful information on this site is the newsletters that deal with practical aspects of running a pain management practice.

Ψ PAIN.COM

http://www.pain.com

Sponsor: Dannemiller Educational Memorial Foundation.

A wide variety of full-text articles for professionals about various aspects of pain and its management. The articles are usually up-to-date and well-written.

Interviews with pain management experts.

Extensive directory of sites about pain and related professional organizations.

SOCIETY FOR PAIN PRACTICE MANAGEMENT

http://www.sppm.org

Sponsor: Society for Pain Practice Management.

Describes the Society's membership benefits and annual meetings.

Links to Web sites about pain management.

News items of practical interest, such as dealing with insurance and billing issues in the treatment of chronic pain.

IV. HYPOCHONDRIASIS

HYPOCHONDRIASIS

http://www.bewell.com/sym/sym240.asp

Sponsor: HealthGate.com.

Brief fact sheet on the disorder and suggested general treatment approach.

V. BODY DYSMORPHIC DISORDER

BODY DYSMORPHIC DISORDER AND BODY IMAGE PROGRAM

http://www.butler.org/bdd.html

Sponsor: Butler Hospital (Providence, RI).

Describes the disorder and the Hospital's (currently) free treatment program.

Lists a few books and other resources for help.

DO YOU HAVE A BODY IMAGE PROBLEM?

http://homearts.com/depts/health/12bodqz1.htm

Sponsor: Hearst New Media.

An article describing Body Dysmorphic Disorder.

Do You Have a Body Image Problem?

Section 9
Factitious Disorders

Factitious Disorders are characterized by the intentional production or feigning of physical or psychological symptoms with the goal of becoming or remaining a patient. When external incentives such as economic gain or avoidance of legal responsibility are present, the condition is considered malingering rather than Factitious Disorder. Munchausen Syndrome best fits this category and Web sites for this disorder are listed below.

Ψ ARTICLES

http://www.psych9.com/Articles/articles.html

Sponsor: Stuart J. Clayman, Ph.D.

Brief review articles by Dr. Clayman on identifying malingering and faked symptoms in the forensic context.

ASHERMEADOW MUNCHAUSEN SYNDROME BY PROXY RESOURCE CENTER

http://www.ashermeadow.org

Sponsor: Unknown.

A smattering of links to online articles and news reports.
Brief descriptions of cases.

FACTITIOUS DISORDER ABSTRACTS

http://php.iupui.edu/~pcoons/factitio.html

Sponsor: Philip M. Coons, M.D., Indiana University School of Medicine.

Abstracts of articles by Dr. Coons on factitious dissociative disorders.

FACTITIOUS DISORDERS (MUNCHAUSEN SYNDROME) WITH PSYCHOLOGICAL SIGNS AND SYMPTOMS

http://perso.club-Internet.fr/andreisz/index.html

Sponsor: Andrei Szoke, M.D. (France).

Bibliography of print and online articles.

DR. MARC FELDMAN'S MUNCHAUSEN SYNDROME, FACTITIOUS DISORDER, AND MUNCHAUSEN BY PROXY PAGE

http://www.munchausen.com

Sponsor: Marc Feldman, M.D.

Links to Web sites and articles, including scientific articles, case reports, and personal accounts by people with these conditions.

MOTHERS AGAINST MUNCHAUSEN SYNDROME BY PROXY ALLEGATIONS

http://www.msbp.com

Sponsor: Mark Patrick.

Newspaper and journal articles that suggest that there is an "assault on innocent parents" by professionals who are "career building at the expense of children."

MUNCHAUSEN BY PROXY SURVIVORS NETWORK

http://www.mbpsnetwork.com

Sponsor: Munchausen by Proxy Survivors Network.

Bibliography on MSBP, with a few links to other sites.

Art and poetry by survivors.

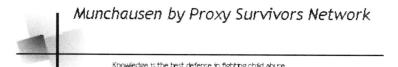

Munchausen by Proxy Survivors Network

Knowledge is the best defence in fighting child abuse.

Section 10
Dissociative Disorders

These disorders are characterized by a disruption in the usually integrated functions of consciousness, memory, identity, or perception. They are divided into:

I. Dissociative Amnesia, which is characterized by the inability to recall important personal information that is too extensive to be explained by forgetfulness.

II. Dissociative Fugue, which is characterized by sudden and unexplainable travel away from familiar places and the inability to recall one's past.

III. Depersonalization Disorder, which is characterized by a persistent feeling of being detached from one's mental process or body.

IV. Dissociative Identity Disorder (formerly Multiple Personality Disorder), which is characterized by the presence of two or more distinct identities or personalities.

V. Dissociative Disorder Not Otherwise Specified, which designates the presence of significant dissociative symptoms that do not quite fit any of the other Dissociative Disorder categories.

We have added the following topic, which is not a disorder but is relevant to the dissociative disorders:

VI. The Recovered Memory/False Memory Controversy

VII. General Resources for Dissociative Disorders

I. DISSOCIATIVE AMNESIA

II. DISSOCIATIVE FUGUE

Other than occasional case studies, there is little published literature on these conditions; we located few Web sites with information that was specifically about these conditions. However, because Dissociative Identity Disorder (DID) includes Dissociative Amnesia as one of its diagnostic criteria, and because fugue states are common in people with DID, many of the Web sites dealing with DID will provide information about Dissociative Amnesia and Fugue. See also the section below concerning the recovered memory/false memory controversy, where we have also placed Web sites in which the central focus is on the idea that DID is almost always iatrogenic.

TRAUMATIC AMNESIA BIBLIOGRAPHY

http://php.iupui.edu/~pcoons/amnesia.html

Sponsor: Philip M. Coon, M.D., Indiana University School of Medicine.

Bibliography of print publications on amnesia associated with many types of trauma.

III. DEPERSONALIZATION DISORDER

DEPERSONALIZATION AND DISSOCIATION RESEARCH PROGRAM

http://www.mssm.edu/psychiatry/deperson.html

Sponsor: Mount Sinai Department of Psychiatry (NY).

Describes the Department's ongoing research program, which has neuropsychological, medication, and psychotherapy components.

IV. DISSOCIATIVE IDENTITY DISORDER

Some people with Dissociative Identity Disorder (DID) consider their condition to be a "gift" rather than a disorder, and they oppose the idea that people with DID need therapy. A few of these sites are represented in our selection, in addition to the many sites that view DID as an emotional disorder.

ASTRAEA'S MULTIPLE PERSONALITY RESOURCES AND CONTROVERSY

http://www.astraeasweb.net/household

Sponsor: Unknown.

This nonprofessional site takes the position that multiplicity is not always caused by childhood trauma but is a form of multiple consciousness that may have a genetic component.

THE CIA AND MILITARY MIND CONTROL RESEARCH: BUILDING THE MANCHURIAN CANDIDATE

http://mindcontrolforum/MCF/ckln01.htm

http://mindcontrolforum/MCF/ckln02.htm

Sponsor: Mind Control Forum.

Transcripts of 1996 lectures by Colin Ross, M.D., describing his investigation of CIA mind control research and his conclusion that the CIA purposely created people with DID to use in undercover operations.

Ψ COLIN A. ROSS INSTITUTE FOR PSYCHOLOGICAL TRAUMA

http://www.rossinst.com

Sponsor: Colin A. Ross, M.D.

This site receives an award because of its useful information concerning the assessment of dissociation.

Includes a review of the literature concerning the Dissociative Experiences Scale.

Complete text and scoring information for Dissociative Disorders Interview Schedule, a structured interview by Dr. Ross that has been used in numerous research studies.

Ψ DISSOCIATION, TRAUMA, & RECOVERED MEMORIES

http://www.acsu.buffalo.edu/~jjhall/dissociation.html.

Sponsor: Jennifer J. Hall, CSW, State University of New York Buffalo.

More than 2,500 references to journal articles about dissociation, with abstracts. This site appears to be updated frequently.

GUIDELINES FOR TREATING DID IN ADULTS

http://www.issd.org/isdguide.htm.

Sponsor: International Society for the Study of Dissociation.

The **International Society** for the **Study** of **Dissociation**

Outline of recommended diagnosis and treatment procedures. These guidelines have been cited as a standard of care in several court cases.

HEALINGHOPES

http://www.healinghopes.org

Sponsors: Mary Ann Cox; HealingHopes, Inc.

A support forum for people with DID, including information on how to choose a therapist, message boards, and a chat room.

A HISTORY OF THE STUDY OF MPD/DID

http://incestabuse.about.com/health/incestabuse/library/weekly/aa030998.htm?pid =2791&cob=home

Sponsors: Nancy Burnett, an attorney; About.com.

A brief history of the condition, with references to scientific journals and books.

Links to other Web sites about various aspects of DID and related issues.

Some areas of this site are not frequently updated.

MPD * DID * ART

http://www.multiple-personality.com

Sponsor: Judy Castelli.

Art and writings by "an artist/survivor with MPD."

MPD/DID WEBRING

http://nav.webring.org/cgi-bin/navcgi?ring=mpd;list

Sponsor: Unknown.

Lists support Web sites by and for survivors of child abuse who have DID.

NEW YORK SOCIETY FOR THE STUDY OF MULTIPLE PERSONALITY AND DISSOCIATION

http://www.nyssmpd.org

Sponsor: New York Society for the Study of Multiple Personality and Dissociation.

Describes the Society's scientific meetings and activities.

Links to other sites dealing with dissociation.

Message board for people with DID.

RISK MANAGEMENT IN DISSOCIATIVE DISORDER AND TRAUMA THERAPY

http://www.mindcontrolforum/MSF/ckln19.htm

Sponsor: Mind Control Forum.

Transcript of a 1997 conference presentation by Alan Scheflin, a law professor, on how to protect oneself against allegations of iatrogenesis and "memory implantation" when working with DID patients.

SERVICE PLANNING GUIDELINES

http://www.hs.state.az.us/bhs/tx_did.pdf

Sponsor: Arizona Department of Health Services.

Outline of goals and recommended treatment approaches for people with DID.

Ψ SIDRAN TRAUMATIC STRESS FOUNDATION

http://www.sidran.org.

Sponsor: Sidran Traumatic Stress Foundation, a nonprofit foundation that publishes and supports treatment in dissociative disorders and other trauma.

Describes Sidran's training program, for agencies, in stress and trauma.

Articles and handouts for clients and their families concerning DID and PTSD.

Bibliography of print publications concerning dissociation; with abstracts.

Links to trauma/DID-related sites.

TRAUMA AND CHAPLAINCY

http://www.jmahoney.com/mpdindex.htm

Sponsor: Father Joseph Mahoney.

Father Mahoney's opinions on spiritual issues and healing from trauma, written from a Catholic perspective. Could be useful food for thought by both clients and therapists.

Selected bibliography of books on dissociation, with capsule evaluations.

V. DISSOCIATIVE DISORDER NOT OTHERWISE SPECIFIED

Although there are no Web sites (or print publications) specifically about this diagnostic category, the sites in IV. Dissociative Identity Disorder and VII. General Dissociative Disorder Resources will be helpful in working with patients who fall into this category.

VI. THE RECOVERED MEMORY/FALSE MEMORY CONTROVERSY

Ψ ABUSE, SCIENCE, MEMORY, ETHICS, MALPRACTICE

http://idealist.com/memories/index.shtml

Sponsor: Kenneth S. Pope, Ph.D.

Full-text articles by Pope that examine whether there is any scientific basis in the claims made by the False Memory Syndrome Foundation and their supporters concerning an "epidemic" of false memories of abuse caused by therapists.

Also includes abstracts of research by Dr. Pope and associates on therapists' sexual intimacy with clients.

BRITISH FALSE MEMORY SOCIETY

http://www.bfms.org.uk

Sponsor: British False Memory Society, British analogue of the False Memory Syndrome Foundation.

Describes the Society's concerns about alleged creation of false memories of child abuse and satanic abuse by incompetent therapists.

Includes the full text of the Society's most recent newsletter, which generally has material about recent research supporting the iatrogenic view of DID.

Links to Web sites about false allegations of abuse and false memory.

Ψ ELIZABETH F. LOFTUS HOME PAGE

http://faculty.washington.edu/eloftus

Sponsor: Elizabeth F. Loftus, Ph.D., University of Washington (Seattle).

Articles on the suggestibility of memory in research and psychotherapy by a member of the False Memory Syndrome Foundation's Scientific Advisory Board.

FALSE MEMORY SYNDROME FOUNDATION

http://www.fmsonline.org

Sponsor: False Memory Syndrome Foundation.

Describes the FMSF's point of view: Therapists have created an epidemic of family disruption by suggesting or coercing patients to believe that their parents sexually abused them as children.

Web site includes the full text of current and back issues of the FMSF newsletter.

Narratives by "retractors" (people who formerly believed that they were abused by their parents but who now believe they were led to make these false allegations by malpracticing therapists).

Includes a lengthy review article by Campbell Perry, Ph.D. on key concepts in hypnosis and the history of its therapeutic use.

FALSE MEMORY SYNDROME VS. RECOVERED MEMORIES

http://ourworld.compuserve.com/homepages/Arael_Et_Al/DID-FMS.HTM

Sponsor: Unknown.

Links, without comment, to articles and Web sites about both sides of the controversy.

"THE GREENBAUM SPEECH"; HYPNOSIS IN MPD: RITUAL ABUSE

http://mindcontrolforum/MCF/grnbaum.htm

Sponsor: Mind Control Forum.

Transcript of a 1992 conference presentation by D. Corydon Hammond, Ph.D. (a past president of the American Society of Clinical Hypnosis), alleging that the CIA used an ex-Nazi to perpetrate mind control programming on children in order to make them into "Manchurian candidates" that kill, engage in child programming, and smuggle drugs. This presentation is widely attacked by critics of "recovered memory therapy."

MULTIPLE PERSONALITY DISORDER A.K.A. DISSOCIATIVE IDENTITY DISORDER: BOTH SIDES TO THE DEBATE

http://www.religioustolerance.org/mpd_did.htm

Sponsor: Ontario Consultants on Religious Tolerance.

Despite its stated intent to be balanced, the site is highly skewed in favor of the idea that DID is almost always iatrogenic.

Includes links to Web sites that take both sides of the debate.

Ψ RECOVERED MEMORIES OF SEXUAL ABUSE: SCIENTIFIC RESEARCH & SCHOLARLY RESOURCES

http://www.jimhopper.com/memory

Sponsor: Jim Hopper, Ph.D.

Extensive and scholarly summary of research findings on the accuracy of recovered memories, concluding that delayed recall of child abuse memories is not rare, and that traumatic and nontraumatic memories have some different characteristics.

Links to other Web pages dealing with recovered memories.

Recovered Memories of Sexual Abuse:
Scientific Research & Scholarly Resources

RECOVERED MEMORY PROJECT

http://www.brown.edu/Departments/Taubman_Center/Recovmem

Sponsor: Ross E. Cheit, Ph.D., Brown University.

Describes cases collected by Dr. Cheit of corroboration for recovered memories of abuse.

The Recovered Memory Project

U-TURN ON MEMORY LANE

http://www.cjr.org/year/97/4/memory.asp

Sponsor: Mike Stanton; Columbia Journalism Review.

Stanton describes how, in his opinion, the False Memory Syndrome Foundation systematically misled the media with one-sided or inaccurate information.

VII. GENERAL RESOURCES FOR DISSOCIATIVE DISORDERS

INTERNATIONAL SOCIETY FOR THE STUDY OF DISSOCIATION

http://www.issd.org

Sponsor: International Society for the Study of Dissociation, an international organization of professionals promoting research and education in dissociation.

Describes the Society's annual conference and membership benefits.

Includes a downloadable spreadsheet for obtaining the Dissociative Experiences Scale Taxon score, which claims to enhance the specificity of the most widely used screening tool for dissociative symptoms.

Treatment guidelines for DID.

NEW ENGLAND SOCIETY FOR THE TREATMENT OF TRAUMA AND DISSOCIATION

http://www.nessd.org

Sponsor: New England Society for the Treatment of Trauma and Dissociation.

Describes the Society's meetings, with a bulletin board for local training opportunities.

Articles from present and past NESSD newsletters.

SURVIVORS LINE AROUND THE WORLD

http://nav.webring.org/cgi-bin/navcgi?ring=dhearts;list

Sponsor: Unknown.

List of support Web sites by and for survivors of abuse, including many about DID.

Section 11
Sexual and Gender Identity Disorders;
Sexual Orientation Issues

Sexual Disorders fall into three categories:

I. Sexual Dysfunctions, which are characterized by disturbances in the process of the sexual response cycle or by pain associated with sexual intercourse.

II. Paraphilias, which are characterized by recurrent and intense sexual urges, fantasies, or behaviors that involve unusual objects, activities, or situations that cause significant distress or impairment in normal functioning.

III. Gender Identity Disorders, which are characterized by strong and persistent cross-gender identification accompanied by persistent discomfort with one's assigned sex.

We add:

IV. Intersexual Issues ("Hermaphroditism")

V. Sexual Orientation Issues

VI. Miscellaneous Sites Dealing with Sexuality

I. SEXUAL DYSFUNCTIONS

DISEASES OF THE VULVA

http://www.med.umich.edu/obgyn/vulva/vulvedu.html

Sponsor: Center for Vulvar Diseases, Department of Obstetrics and Gynecology, University of Michigan Medical Center.

Description of the Center's programs.

Fact sheet about sexuality and pain, as well as others about vulvar diseases.

IMPOTENCE.ORG

http://www.impotence.org

Sponsor: American Foundation for Urologic Disease, Inc.

Site claims to provide information about diagnosis and treatment options, but a number of pages within the site did not load when we visited them.

Links to other Web sites dealing with sexual dysfunction and urology.

IMPOTENCE WORLD ASSOCIATION ONLINE

http://www.impotenceworld.org

Sponsors: Impotence World Association, an educational association and manufacturer of treatments for erectile dysfunction.

Basic facts about erectile dysfunction and brief descriptions of treatment options.

Ψ MEDBROADCAST.COM: MALE SEXUAL DYSFUNCTION

**http://www.medbroadcast.com/health_topics/mens
_health/mens_sexual_dysfunc**

Sponsor: MedBroadcast.com.

Useful FAQs about erectile dysfunction and treatment by medication.

With the aid of video and animation, our Men's Health channel provides you with up to the minute information on a host of health issues that can affect not only yourself, but also your partner and family. Get the facts on the latest diagnostic procedures and treatments available, so you can make informed choices

Ψ MEDBROADCAST.COM: FEMALE SEXUAL DYSFUNCTION

http://www.medbroadcast.com/health_topics/womens_health/f_sex_dysfunc

Sponsor: MedBroadcast.com.

Deals with lack of sexual enjoyment and pain during sex. Good FAQs with drawings and practical suggestions.

Our Women's Health channel was created to provide you with reliable, current information on a wealth of women's health issues, and to help you find the answers to questions that most of us either have or will face at some point in our adult lives

SUCCESSFULLY TREATING IMPOTENCE

http://www.impotent.com

Sponsors: Pharmacia & Upjohn.

Information about impotence for nonprofessionals, emphasizing the prostaglandin injection therapy approach that is marketed by the sponsors of this site.

VIAGRA.COM

http://www.viagra.com

Sponsor: Pfizer, Inc.

Basic information about erectile dysfunction and Viagra as a treatment option.

VULVAL PAIN SOCIETY

http://www.vul-pain.dircon.co.uk

Sponsor: Vulval Pain Society (UK).

Fact sheet about vulvar pain and its causes, with links to related mailing lists and sites.

FAQs about the problem and practical suggestions for managing it.

VULVAR PAIN FOUNDATION

http://www.vulvarpainfoundation.org

Sponsor: Vulvar Pain Foundation.

Describes symptoms and recommended treatments.

Today You Can Choose Recovery.

VULVODYNIA HOMEPAGE

http://www.vulvodynia.com

Sponsor: Howard I. Glazer, Ph.D.

Brief description of Dr. Glazer's home training package for treating vulvar pain, sold by Dr. Glazer.

II. PARAPHILIAS

It was difficult to find Web sites on this topic that informed rather than demonstrated or displayed paraphilias. We have listed sites about Transvestic Festishism under Gender Identity Disorder because all of the sites discussed the former diagnosis solely in comparison to Gender Identity Disorder.

EXHIBITIONISM AND FROTTEURISM

http://www.lifewell.com/educenter/368.cfm

Sponsor: US HealthNet, Inc.

Brief article describing these behaviors.

FREQUENTLY ASKED QUESTIONS ABOUT PEDOPHILIA

http://www.camh.net/CLARKEPages/forensic/pedophilia_faq.html

Sponsor: Clarke Institute of Psychiatry (Canada).

Just what the title implies.

IN SEARCH OF AN ETIOLOGICAL MODEL OF PEDOPHILIA

http://www.unites.uqam.ca/dsexo/Revue/Vol2no1/10_Freund~1.html

Sponsor: Sexological Review, University of Quebec.

A review of epidemiological research on pedophilia.

PARAPHILIA

http://www.intimacyinstitute.com/sex_data/topics/paraphilia.html

Sponsor: Sinclair Intimacy Institute, distributor of adult sex education videos.

Good fact sheet about the definition of paraphilia and descriptions of several varieties of paraphilia.

THERAPY FOR SEXUAL IMPULSIVITY: THE PARAPHILIAS AND PARAPHILIA-RELATED DISORDERS

http://php.iupui.edu/~flip/reading13.html

Sponsor: Martin P. Kafka, M.D., Harvard Medical School.

A lengthy, scholarly article discussing treatment options.

VOYEURISM

http://www.lifewell.com/educenter/414.cfm

Sponsor: US HealthNet, Inc.

Brief article about voyeurism.

WHAT SEXUAL SCIENTISTS KNOW ABOUT HUMAN SEXUALITY: COMPULSIVE SEXUAL BEHAVIOR

http://www.sexologica.com/Compsexua” l.html

Sponsor: Amaya Gergoff (Venezuela).

Article describing some of the basic definitional, philosophical, and treatment issues concerning paraphilic and nonparaphilic sexual compulsivity.

III. GENDER IDENTITY DISORDER

Many in the transgendered community do not wish to be thought of as having a disorder. Several of the Web sites we have listed address their concerns.

ATHEALTH.COM: GENDER IDENTITY DISORDER

http://www.athealth.com/Consumer/Disorders/GenderIden.html

Sponsor: AtHealth.com.

FAQs for nonprofessionals.

THE DISPARATE CLASSIFICATION OF GENDER AND SEXUAL ORIENTATION IN AMERICAN PSYCHIATRY

http://www.priory.com/psych/disparat.htm

Sponsor: Psychiatry On-Line; Priory Lodge Education Limited.

A scholarly article by Katherine K. Wilson that attacks the inclusion of Gender Identity Disorder and Transvestic Fetishism in the *DSM-IV*.

FTM INTERNATIONAL

http://www.ftm-intl.org

Sponsor: FTM (Female-to-Male) International.

Articles and links to Web sites about female to male transsexualism.

GLOBAL TRANSGENDERING

http://nav.webring.org/cgi-bin/navcgi?ring=tr;list

Sponsor: Unknown.

Personal Web pages of transgendered individuals, along with links to sites offering support.

Ψ INTERNATIONAL FOUNDATION FOR GENDER EDUCATION

http://www.ifge.org

Sponsor: International Foundation for Gender Education.

FAQs about gender identity and transgender issues.

Links to relevant sites.

Ψ INTERNATIONAL JOURNAL OF TRANSGENDERISM

http://www.symposion.com/ijt

Sponsor: International Journal of Transgenderism.

Full-text of the first scholarly journal on gender dysphoria and disorders.

MYTH, STEREOTYPE, AND CROSS-GENDER IDENTITY IN THE *DSM-IV*

http://www.transgender.org/tg/gic/awptext.html

Sponsor: Gender Identity Center of Colorado, Inc.

A 1996 conference presentation by Katherine K. Wilson and Barbara Hammond, Ph.D., that criticizes the *DSM-IV* for the pathologizing of transgendered people.

NATIONAL TRANSGENDER ADVOCACY COALITION

http://www.ntac.org

Sponsor: National Transgender Advocacy Coalition.

Information about transgender issues, which advocates an end to discrimination against transgendered people.

Links to relevant Web sites.

Ψ NOTES ON GENDER TRANSITION

http://www.avitale.com

Sponsor: Anne Vitale, Ph.D.

A site packed with practical information concerning the process of gender transition, with links to support and information resources. Appears to be frequently updated.

PRESS FOR CHANGE

http://www.pfc.org.uk

Sponsor: Press for Change, a lobbying and educational association aiming "to achieve equal civil rights for all transgendered people in the United Kingdom."

Describes current relevant legal issues in the UK.

Links to relevant Web sites.

THE RENAISSANCE TRANSGENDER ASSOCIATION, INC.

http://www.ren.org

Sponsor: The Renaissance Transgender Association, Inc.

Information about local support groups for transsexual people. Articles about crossdressing.

Ψ THE STANDARDS OF CARE FOR GENDER IDENTITY DISORDERS

http://www.symposion.com/ijt/ijtc0405.htm

Sponsors: International Journal of Transgenderism; Harry Benjamin International Gender Dysphoria Association.

Detailed review of current treatment standards and recommendations.

TRANSGENDER FORUM'S RESOURCE GUIDE

http://www.tgfmall.com.

Sponsor: 3-D Communications.

Links to Web sites offering support and products for transgendered people.

Extensive bibliography of relevant print publications that is not frequently updated.

Ψ TRANSSEXUAL WOMEN'S RESOURCES

http://www.annelawrence.com/twr

Sponsor: Anne Lawrence, M.D.

Extensive links, with brief descriptions, to articles about transsexualism and sex reassignment surgery.

IV. INTERSEXUAL ISSUES ("HERMAPHRODITISM")

Ψ ANDROGEN INSENSITIVITY SYNDROME SUPPORT GROUP

http://www.medhelp.org/www/ais

Sponsor: Androgen Insensitivity Syndrome Support Group (UK).

Provides information and support to people with AIS and their parents.

Well-written FAQs with references to relevant scientific publications.

Descriptions of current research studies on AIS which seek participants.

Available in Spanish, French, and German.

Extensive, annotated links to relevant Web sites.

Ψ INTERSEX SOCIETY OF NORTH AMERICA

http://www.isna.org

Sponsor: Intersex Society of North America, an advocacy, support, and educational nonprofit association "for intersex people."

Focuses on a nonpathologizing view of hermaphroditism, a term that ISNA views as stigmatizing.

FAQs about intersex, which is viewed here as a genetic variation rather than an abnormality.

Bibliography of print publications.

Links, with brief descriptions, to relevant Web sites.

INTERSEX SUPPORT GROUP INTERNATIONAL

http://www.isgi.org

Sponsor: Intersex Support Group International.

Views intersexed people from a Christian perspective.

FAQs about hermaphroditism.

KLINEFELTER'S SYNDROME CLUB (UK) HOMEPAGE

http://hometown.aol.com/kscuk/index.htm

Sponsor: Klinefelter's Syndrome Club (UK), a support group run by adults with KS.

Lengthy FAQ section about KS, with references to scientific publications.

Rather disorganized information about support resources in the UK and elsewhere.

V. SEXUAL ORIENTATION ISSUES

Homosexuality and bisexuality are not considered psychological or psychiatric disorders. Therapists who are informed about dealing with intrapsychic and societal issues encountered by lesbian, gay, and bisexual clients will be able to help such clients cope with common issues such as internalized homophobia, decisions about "coming out," and the effects of stigmatization on emotional well-being.

ASSOCIATION OF GAY AND LESBIAN PSYCHIATRISTS

http://www.aglp.org

Sponsor: Association of Gay and Lesbian Psychiatrists.

Describes the association's mission and conferences.

Full text of AGLP's current newsletter.

Online referral service (list of members).

Extensive bibliography of print publications on lesbian, gay, and bisexual parenting.

BI.ORG

http://bi.org

Sponsor: Nick Smith.

Extensive links to Web sites about bisexuality, Internet newsgroups, and mailing lists.

BISEXUAL RESOURCE CENTER

http://www.biresource.org

Sponsor: East Coast Bisexual Network, Inc., a nonprofit educational organization.

Online informational pamphlets about bisexuality.

Many links to relevant Web sites and contact information for other resources.

BISEXUAL.ORG

http://www.bisexual.org

Sponsor: American Institute of Bisexuality, a nonprofit corporation.

Links to nonpornographic Web resources about bisexuality.

E-DIRECTORY OF LESBIGAY SCHOLARS

http://newark.rutgers.edu/~lcrew/lbg_edir.html

Sponsor: Louie Crew, Department of English, Rutgers University (NJ).

Lists academics with interest in lesbian/gay/bisexual studies.

About two-thirds of the list is public; the full directory is available only to those who submit an entry form.

Directory of listees' Web pages.

E-Directory of Lesbigay Scholars

HOMORAMA

http://www.homorama.com

Sponsor: Mediapolis, Inc.

Links to gay-relevant Web sites, with detailed descriptions and evaluations.

Makes an effort to choose quality sites rather than being all-inclusive.

LESBIAN.COM

http://www.lesbian.com

Sponsor: Beckwith Technology Consulting.

General site offering a directory of resources with brief descriptions and opinions concerning the linked sites.

LESBIANATION.COM

http://www.lesbianation.com

Sponsor: Gay Wired.

Online magazine for and about lesbians and bisexual women.

Links to relevant Web sites.

Chat room and discussion board.

PLANETOUT

http://www.planetout.com

Sponsor: PlanetOut Corporation.

Online magazine for gays, lesbians, and bisexuals.

PRIDELINKS.COM

http://www.pridelinks.com

Sponsor: Catherine M. Matier, Pridelinks.com.

Extensive ad-free directory of Web sites relevant to lesbians, gay people, bisexuals, and transgendered people, categorized with brief descriptions.

QUEER RESOURCES DIRECTORY

http://www.qrd.org

Sponsor: Ron Buckmire, Occidental College (CA).

Links with brief descriptions to articles, bibliographies, Web sites, and other resources.

Queer Resources Directory

SOCIETY FOR THE PSYCHOLOGICAL STUDY OF LESBIAN, GAY, AND BISEXUAL ISSUES

http://www.apa.org/divisions/div44

Sponsor: Society for the Psychological Study of Lesbian, Gay, and Bisexual Issues (Division 44 of American Psychological Association).

Describes the Division's mission to education psychologists and the general public about lesbian, gay, and bisexual concerns and to promote relevant research.

Newsletters of the Division.

Links to relevant Web sites.

WWWOMEN SEARCH DIRECTORY: LESBIANS

http://www.wwwomen.com/category/lesbia1.html

Sponsor: WWWomen.

Links to sites about lesbianism, with brief descriptions.

VI. MISCELLANEOUS SITES

ALAN GUTTMACHER INSTITUTE

http://www.agi-usa.org

Sponsor: Alan Guttmacher Institute.

News releases and policy papers about birth control and sexually transmitted diseases.

ASSOCIATION FOR THE TREATMENT OF SEXUAL ABUSERS

http://www.atsa.com

Sponsor: Association for the Treatment of Sexual Abusers.

Describes the Association's activities and conferences. Tables of contents for the Association's journal.

AMERICAN ACADEMY OF CLINICAL SEXOLOGISTS

http://www.sexologist.org

Sponsor: American Academy of Clinical Sexologists.

Offers training programs for treating juvenile sex offenders.

FRIENDS FIRST

http://www.friendsfirst.org

Sponsor: Friends First Network.

Advocates sexual abstinence for teens, with training programs and print/video materials.

KINSEY INSTITUTE FOR RESEARCH IN SEX, GENDER, AND REPRODUCTION

http://www.indiana.edu/~kinsey

Sponsor: Kinsey Institute, Indiana University.

Bibliography of the Institute's publications, with full-text of its newsletter.

Describes training and research programs conducted at the Institute.

Links to other sexology sites.

SEXUALITY INFORMATION AND EDUCATION COUNCIL OF THE UNITED STATES (SIECUS)

http://www.siecus.org

Sponsor: Sexuality Information and Education Council of the United States.

Disseminates information about sexuality to the general public.

Online informational pamphlets about sex, sexually transmitted diseases, and birth control; for teens and adults.

Section 12
Eating Disorders

Eating Disorders are characterized by severe disturbances in eating behavior and an exaggerated concern for the role of body weight in one's self-evaluation. The disorders are usually classified as:

I. Anorexia Nervosa, which is a refusal to maintain a minimally normal body weight and a fear of gaining weight, coupled with a disturbed perception of one's body weight.

II. Bulimia Nervosa, which is characterized by repeated episodes of binge eating followed by self-induced vomiting, use of laxatives, fasting, or excessive exercise.

Therapists are often confronted with issues regarding eating that do not specifically relate to Anorexia or Bulimia. This section takes a more holistic approach than *DSM-IV,* including Web sites that deal with healthy eating, size acceptance, positive body image, and weight management.

Ψ ABOUT-FACE

http://www.about-face.org

Sponsor: Kathy Bruin.

Specific information on how women can change their attitudes towards their bodies while developing a critical awareness of destructive images and attitudes in the mass media.

Gallery of "offenders": Ads that glorify starved women.

Links to relevant Web sites.

ACADEMY FOR EATING DISORDERS

http://www.acadeatdis.org

Sponsor: Academy for Eating Disorders, a multidisciplinary professional association.

Includes membership information.

Information about the Academy's conferences.

Full-text of some of the Academy's newsletters.

AMERICAN ANOREXIA BULIMIA ASSOCIATION

http://www.aabainc.org

Sponsor: American Anorexia Bulimia Association.

FAQs about eating disorders.

Information about the Association's eating disorders screening program.

Annotated bibliography of selected books for nonprofessionals about eating disorders.

Ψ ANOREXIA NERVOSA AND RELATED EATING DISORDERS, INC.

http://www.anred.com

Sponsor: Anorexia Nervosa and Related Eating Disorders, Inc., a nonprofit organization.

Detailed, well-written FAQ section for nonprofessionals about eating disorders.

Links to related Web sites, with brief descriptions.

Ψ ASK NOAH ABOUT: EATING DISORDERS

http://www.noah.cuny.edu/wellconn/eatdisorders.html

Sponsor: Nidus Information Services.

A single long page. Excellent overview of eating disorders, presumed etiologies, comorbid conditions, and treatment options.

Links to useful and relevant Web sites.

BODY POSITIVE

http://www.bodypositive.com

Sponsor: Debora Burgard, Ph.D.

Focuses on achieving positive attitudes about one's body by defining " 'healthy weight' not from a generic height/weight chart or even arbitrary Body Mass Index cut-offs, but rather as the weight your body is when you are living a reasonable life."

Some descriptive information about the "Body Positive" approach, along with links that market workshops.

Ψ CARING ONLINE

http://caringonline.com

Sponsor: Referral Services (NY).

Extensive links to relevant Web sites, online articles, and news items, but without descriptive information about the hyperlinks.

Eating Disorders
News, Stories, Poetry

CARING ONLINE

NEWS & RESOURCES	TOPICS	PERSONAL THOUGHTS
News	Binge eating	Coping
News and headlines	*When eating takes over*	*How to cope*
People	Athletics	Friends
People in the news	*Eating disorders in athletes*	*Poems For Online friends*
Introduction	Body Image	Krista
Reviews, photos	*And eating disorders*	*Poetry and stories*
Books on EDs:	Diets & Nutrition	Poetry
Including Videos	*Eating right, food allergies*	*Over 100 insightful poems*
Treatment Centers	Insurance & HMOs	Stories
List of centers	*Visit Discussion Board*	*Personal stories about eating*
Web Sites	Infants and Eating	*disorders*
Web sites on eds	*Eating problems in infants*	
Exceptional Articles	Males	
Viewpoints & Wisdom	*Males with eating disorders*	Guestbook
Search the Net	Medications	Discussion Page
Over 100 links	*Medicinal approaches*	Pen Pals
Support	Questionnaires	
Online support	*Do you have an eating disorder?*	Kathy's Humor Pages
	Therapies	
Mary Fleming Callaghan	*Is your therapy working?*	Inspirational Stories
answers your questions		

Ψ *DIMENSIONS* MAGAZINE'S 500 TOP SIZE-ACCEPTANCE LINKS

http://www.pencomputing.com/dim/links

Sponsor: Dimensions *magazine.*

Extensive links, with brief descriptions, to mostly noncommercial sites advocating "fat acceptance."

EATING DISORDER REFERRAL AND INFORMATION CENTER

http://www.edreferral.com

Sponsor: 1-800-Therapist, a referral network that charges therapists an annual membership fee and provides prospective clients with free referrals to network members.

Information in outline format for nonprofessionals.

EATING DISORDERS ASSOCIATION

http://www.gurney.org.uk/eda

Sponsor: Eating Disorders Association (UK), a charity that offers telephone hotlines, support resources, and groups.

FAQ section about how to help a friend who has an eating disorder.

Lengthy fact sheet about the general topic of eating disorders, and about specific types of eating disorders.

EATING DISORDERS AWARENESS AND PREVENTION, INC.

http://www.edap.org

Sponsor: Eating Disorders Awareness and Prevention, Inc., a nonprofit organization that engages in educational activities and community action.

Describes educational curricula and other print/audio materials to enhance awareness and prevention of eating disorders.

FAQs about eating disorders, including guidelines to encourage more responsible coverage of eating disorders. A therapist who is interviewed by the media about eating disorders might want to print out the guidelines for the reporter's use.

Links to relevant Web sites, with brief descriptions.

FOODFIT.COM

http://www.foodfit.com

Sponsor: FoodFit.Com, a commercial organization.

Recipes and practical information concerning healthy eating and fitness.

Links to relevant Web sites.

GÜRZE BOOKS

http://www.bulimia.com

Sponsor: Gürze Books, a publisher specializing in eating disorders.

Online catalog of books and videos.

Links to Web sites concerning treatment and prevention of eating disorders.

HUGS INTERNATIONAL

http://www.hugs.com

Sponsor: HUGS International.

Offers licensed program for nondieting approaches for helping people to develop healthy eating habits.

Links, with descriptions, to Web sites with a similar philosophy.

INTERNATIONAL SIZE ACCEPTANCE ORGANIZATION

http://www.size-acceptance.org

Sponsor: International Size Acceptance Organization.

Links promoting acceptance of large-sized people.

Ψ LUCY SERPELL'S EATING DISORDER RESOURCES

http://www.serpell.com/eat.html

Sponsor: Lucy Serpell, a researcher and Ph.D. student.

Focuses especially on academic and professional online resources for eating disorders, especially those in the UK.

Links to online articles, treatment programs, newsgroups, and mailing lists.

Eating Disorders Resources

NATIONAL ASSOCIATION OF ANOREXIA NERVOSA AND RELATED DISORDERS

http://www.anad.org

Sponsor: National Association of Anorexia Nervosa and Related Disorders, a nonprofit support organization for people with eating disorders and their families.

Fact sheets about eating disorders, including one on confronting a person with an eating disorder.

NATIONAL ASSOCIATION TO ADVANCE FAT ACCEPTANCE

http://naafa.org

Sponsor: National Association to Advance Fat Acceptance, a nonprofit organization aiming to end discrimination against overweight people.

Describes events, conventions, and publications of the Association.

Policy statements on conflicts of interest among obesity researchers, weight loss drugs, and other topics.

NATIONAL EATING DISORDER INFORMATION CENTRE

http://www.nedic.on.ca/

Sponsor: National Eating Disorder Information Centre (CA).

FAQ section for nonprofessionals about eating disorders.

Brief guide for family and friends of people with eating disorders.

OVEREATERS ANONYMOUS

http://www.overeatersanonymous.org

Sponsor: Overeaters Anonymous World Service Office.

A self-help program to manage compulsive overeating, patterned after Alcoholics Anonymous.

RENFREW CENTER

http://www.renfrew.org/index.html

Sponsor: Renfrew Center, a women's mental health center specializing in eating disorders, with multiple locations on the East Coast of the U.S.

Includes articles for professionals from the Center's journal.

Offers conferences, workshops, and training materials for professionals.

SOMETHING FISHY WEB SITE ON EATING DISORDERS

http://www.something-fishy.org

Sponsor: Something Fishy Music & Publishing.

Online articles and links for nonprofessionals.

UNBINDING THE BODY BETRAYED WEBRING

http://nav.webring.org/cgi-bin/navcgi?ring=bibri;list

Sponsor: Paul Bentivegna.

Directory, with brief descriptions, for over one hundred Web sites of widely varying quality dealing with abuse, eating issues, and mental health.

Ψ WOMEN'S CAMPAIGN TO END BODY HATRED AND DIETING

http://www.overcomingovereating.com

Sponsors: Jane R. Hirschmann, M.S.W.; Carol H. Munter (NY).

Information about ending the yo-yo dieting cycle by identifying "bad body thoughts" and changing them to an empowering and positive perspective on one's appearance.

Links to treatment resources in various parts of the U.S. that teach this method to clients via workshops.

Links to Web sites that encourage "fat acceptance.

YAHOO! HEALTH: ANOREXIA NERVOSA

http://health.yahoo.com/health/Diseases_and_Conditions/Disease_Feed_Data/Anorexia_nervosa

Sponsor: Yahoo! Inc.

Summarizes symptoms (not completely the same as those in *DSM-IV*), complications, and a few links to relevant Web sites.

Section 13
Sleep Disorders

Primary sleep disorders are divided into:

I. Dyssomnias, which are abnormalities in the amount, quality, or timing of sleep. These included:
  A. Insomnia, which is characterized by difficulty initiating or maintaining sleep, or non-restful restorative sleep. The condition must last for at least one month.
  B. Hypersomnia, which is characterized by excessive sleepiness for at least one month, as evidenced by either prolonged sleep episodes or daytime sleep episodes occurring almost daily.
  C. Narcolepsy, which is characterized by irresistible attacks of refreshing sleep that occur daily over a three-month period.
  D. Breathing-related sleep disorder, which is characterized by sleep disruption leading to excessive sleepiness or insomnia.
  E. Circadian Rhythm Sleep Disorder, which is characterized by a persistent or recurrent pattern of sleep disruption that leads to excessive sleepiness or insomnia. This is due to a mismatch between the sleep-wake schedule required by someone's environment and their circadian sleep-wake pattern.
  F. Other sleep disorders, including environmental factors, sleep deprivation, Restless Legs Syndrome, and nocturnal myoclonus (brief limb jerks).

II. Parasomnias, which are abnormal behavior or psychological events occurring in association with sleep, sleep stages, or sleep-wake transition. This category includes:

    A. Nightmare Disorder, which is characterized by a repeated occurrence of frightening dreams that lead to awakenings.

    B. Sleep Terror Disorder, which is characterized by abrupt awakenings from sleep usually beginning with a panicky scream or cry.

    C. Sleepwalking Disorder, which is characterized by repeated episodes of complex motor behavior initiated during sleep, including rising from bed and walking about.

    D. Other parasomnias, including motor activity and sleep paralysis.

We add:

III. Web Sites of General Relevance to Sleep Disorders or Healthy Sleep

I. DYSSOMNIAS

CENTER FOR NARCOLEPSY RESEARCH

http://www.uic.edu/depts/cnr

Sponsor: Center for Narcolepsy Research, University of Illinois at Chicago.

FAQ section concerning narcolepsy.

Information about print publications and videos concerning narcolepsy, with separate lists for professionals and the general public.

EXCESSIVE DAYTIME SLEEPINESS INFORMATION SITE

http://www.daytimesleep.org

Sponsor: Cephalon, Inc., a pharmaceutical manufacturer.

Fact sheets about narcolepsy, sleep apnea, and other dyssomnias (with the exception of insomnia).

FATIGUE COUNTERMEASURES GROUP

http://www-afo.arc.nasa.gov/zteam

Sponsor: Ames Research Center, National Aeronautics and Space Administration.

Describes a research program on whether there is a safety program due to jet lag among air transport personnel.

Research publications available online.

Fatigue Countermeasures Program

KLEINE-LEVIN SYNDROME

http://www.klsfoundation.org

Sponsors: Cindy, Dick, and Stephen Maier.

Information about a rare disorder that causes the need for excessive amounts of sleep.

Includes a bulletin board.

Bibliography of journal articles about KLS.

Kleine-Levin Syndrome

NARCOLEPSY COMMUNICATION CENTER

http://narcolepsy.homepage.com

Sponsor: Lynn Hutchins.

Lists relevant chat rooms, message boards, and mailing lists.

NARCOLEPSY NETWORK

http://www.websciences.org/narnet

Sponsor: Narcolepsy Network, a nonprofit association for people with narcolepsy, their families and friends, and professionals.

Includes a FAQ section about narcolepsy.

Sells audiotapes and brochures.

Site is not updated frequently.

NATIONAL SLEEP FOUNDATION

http://www.sleepfoundation.org

Sponsor: National Sleep Foundation, a nonprofit educational and advocacy association.

FAQs about dyssomnias.

Links to related Web sites.

RESTLESS LEGS SYNDROME FOUNDATION

http://www.rls.org

Sponsor: Restless Legs Syndrome Foundation.

Detailed FAQs about RLS, one for the general public and one for health care professionals.

Lists international support groups.

Links to related Web sites, with annotations.

Restless Legs Syndrome Foundation

SLEEP APNEA INFORMATION CLEARINGHOUSE

http://www.pilgrimvoices.com/apnea

Sponsors: Jim and Meg Garrison.

Links to articles, sites, and news items concerning sleep apnea.

Lists online and live support resources.

SLEEP NEURAL NETWORK HOME PAGE

http://www.acsu.buffalo.edu/%7Esolh

Sponsor: PredictOnline, Inc.

Brief fact sheets about sleep apnea, with a questionnaire for determining the probability that one has sleep apnea.

SLEEPQUEST

http://www.sleepquest.com

Sponsor: SleepQuest, Inc.

FAQs about dyssomnias.

Chat area and weekly column by a leading sleep researcher.

Especially detailed FAQ section about sleep apnea and different surgical treatment options.

UNIVERSITY OF PENNSYLVANIA HEALTH SYSTEM: OBSTRUCTIVE SLEEP APNEA

http://www.med.upenn.edu/health/pf_files/penntoday/v6n1/sleep.html

Sponsor: University of Pennsylvania Health System.

MRI images of normal and sleep apneic individuals, with information about treatment options.

II. PARASOMNIAS

NIGHT TERROR RESOURCE CENTER

http://www.nightterrors.org

Sponsor: David W. Richards.

Information about sleep terror, sleep paralysis, and other parasomnias.

Information about medications for treating parasomnias.

Personal narratives.

Message board and chat area.

PARASOMNIAS

http://sleepmed.bsd.uchicago.edu/parasomnias.html

Sponsor: Mateen Ahmed, M.D.; Sleep Research Laboratory, University of Chicago.

Medical course outline concerning parasomnias.

III. WEB SITES OF GENERAL RELEVANCE TO SLEEP DISORDERS OR HEALTHY SLEEP

ABOUT.COM: SLEEP DISORDERS

http://sleepdisorders.about.com/health/sleepdisorders/mbody.htm

Sponsor: About.Com.

Links and articles for the nonprofessional.

AMERICAN ACADEMY OF SLEEP MEDICINE

http://www.asda.org

Sponsor: American Academy of Sleep Medicine.

Describes the Academy's activities.

Lists position statements and practice parameters.

Has separate areas for professionals and nonprofessionals.

BABY AND TODDLER SLEEP

http://www.babycenter.com/sleep

Sponsor: BabyCenter, Inc., a commercial site.

Specific information for nonprofessionals about normal sleep in infant and toddlers.

Strategies for helping parents manage their children's sleep difficulties.

CANADIAN SLEEP SOCIETY

http://www.css.to

Sponsor: Canadian Sleep Society.

FAQs about sleep disorders.

Lists sleep disorder facilities in Canada.

Has a mirror site in French.

KIDSHEALTH FOR PARENTS: GENERAL HEALTH

http://kidshealth.org/parent/general

Sponsor: KidsHealth.

About halfway down the page are a few links to articles for the general public on "Your Kid's Sleep," including discussions of apnea, parasomnias in general, and night terrors.

NAPS: NEW ABSTRACTS AND PAPERS IN SLEEP

http://www.websciences.org/bibliosleep/naps

Sponsor: WebSciences International.

A free service that sends weekly citations by e-mail of new articles in the field of sleep and sleep disorders.

SAN DIEGO SLEEP AND RHYTHMS SOCIETY

http://varesearch.ucsd.edu/klemfuss/sdsrs.htm

Sponsor: San Diego Sleep and Rhythms Society.

Links, mostly research-related, about sleeping disorders.

SHUTEYE ONLINE

http://www.shuteye.com

Sponsor: Searle.

Practical advice on sleep hygiene and coping with insomnia.

Ψ SLEEP HOME PAGES

http://www.sleephomepages.org

Sponsor: Web Sciences International, a Web site developer.

A portal site for professionals, with links to Web sites for publications, associations, and bibliographies.

Discussion forums concerning sleep disorders research and practice, with brief scientific articles; however, most of the actual postings are from nonprofessionals.

SLEEP MEDICINE

http://sleepmed.bsd.uchicago.edu/tableofContents.html

Sponsor: Wallace Mendelson, M.D., Director of the Sleep Research Laboratory, University of Chicago.

Outlines from medical school curricula concerning various dyssomnias and parasomnias.

Ψ SLEEP MEDICINE HOME PAGE

http://www.users.cloud9.net/~thorpy

Sponsor: Unknown.

A single long page with links to every area of sleep disorders, including mailing lists; Web sites about sleep disorders, related journals and professional associations, sleep research, medications, and many more areas.

SLEEP RESEARCH ONLINE

http://www.sro.org

Sponsor: Websciences International, a Web site developer.

Complete text for current and back issues of this online journal.

Ψ SLEEP RESEARCH SOCIETY

http://www.sleephomepages.org/srs

Sponsor: Sleep Research Society, a nonprofit association promoting education and training of professionals in the understanding of sleep and sleep disorders.

Describes the Society's activities.

Contains full-text of some of the Society's newsletters.

Links to sleep societies' Web sites around the world.

Sleep Research Society

SLEEP, DREAMS, AND WAKEFULNESS

http://sommeil.univ-lyon1.fr/index_e.html

Sponsor: Unknown.

Links, in English and French, to scientific articles on sleep mechanisms.

SLEEPNET.COM

http://www.sleepnet.com

Sponsor: Sharon Keenan School of Sleep Medicine (CA).

FAQs about normal sleep and sleep disorders, including a page on children's sleep.

Links to sleep disorder centers.

SLEEP/WAKE DISORDERS CANADA

http://www.geocities.com/HotSprings/1837

Sponsor: Sleep/Wake Disorders Canada, an association of volunteers who disseminate information about sleep disorders.

Links to online articles and Web sites about sleep disorders.

Section 14
Impulse Control Disorders Not
Elsewhere Classified

The essential feature of these disorders is the failure to resist an impulse, drive, or temptation to perform an act that is harmful to the person or others. They include:

I. Intermittent Explosive Disorder, which is characterized by a failure to resist aggressive impulses that result in serious assaults or destruction of property.

II. Kleptomania, which is characterized by a recurrent failure to resist impulses to steal objects not necessary for personal use or monetary value.

III. Pyromania, which is characterized by a pattern of setting fires for pleasure, gratification, or relief of tension.

IV. Pathological Gambling, which is characterized by recurrent and persistent maladaptive gambling behavior.

V. Trichotillomania, which is characterized by the recurrent pulling out of one's hair for pleasure, gratification, or relief of tension.

We add:

VI. Internet Addiction

The following Web site is a collection of links for a number of the impulse control disorders, not just Pathological Gambling:

HEALTHNBODY.COM: DISORDERS: GAMBLING
http://healthnbody.com/Disorders/Gambling.htm

Sponsor: WorldViewer.com, Inc.

I. INTERMITTENT EXPLOSIVE DISORDER

Although we found Web sites dealing with school, domestic, and workplace violence, none focused on the underlying disorders. We found few sites dealing specifically with Intermittent Explosive Disorder, other than those listing the *DSM-IV* criteria or mentioning the disorder in a case report as one of several comorbid conditions.

TREATING INTERMITTENT EXPLOSIVE DISORDER WITH NEUROFEEDBACK

http://www.brainwavetx.com/library/explosiv.html

Sponsors: Steven Padgitt, Ph.D.; Brain Wave Treatment Centers International (CA).

Anecdotal report about successful treatment using EEG biofeedback.

II. KLEPTOMANIA

SHOPLIFTERS ALTERNATIVE

http://www.shopliftersalternative.org

Sponsor: Shoplifters Anonymous.

Provides educational information to the public and support services to shoplifters.

Shoplifters Alternative (SA) is a national not-for-profit organization and educational division of Shoplifters Anonymous, Inc. The organization works with law enforcement, retailers and the courts, providing rehabilitation programs and ongoing support services to people with a shoplifting problem.

THEFT TALK

http://www.teleport.com/~theft/index.htm

Sponsor: Theft Talk Counseling Service, Inc. (OR), specializing in counseling for theft offenders.

Provides training for counselors who treat thieves.

III. PYROMANIA

We found no Web sites other than those describing the diagnostic criteria.

IV. PATHOLOGICAL GAMBLING

CANADIAN FOUNDATION ON COMPULSIVE GAMBLING

http://www.responsiblegambling.org

Sponsor: Canadian Foundation on Compulsive Gambling.

Contact information for the Foundation's library of information on compulsive gambling.

Links for treatment programs in Canada and other Web sites concerned with compulsive gambling.

FAQ section on responsible versus problem gambling.

Search engine for news articles and other items in the Foundation's online database.

GAM-ANON

http://www.gam-anon.org

Sponsor: Gam-Anon International Service Office.

Information about Gam-Anon's self-help program for family and friends of compulsive gamblers.

FAQs about compulsive gambling.

GAMBLERS ANONYMOUS

http://www.gamblersanonymous.org

Sponsor: Gamblers Anonymous International Service Office.

Twelve-step self-help program for compulsive gamblers.

Describes the program's philosophy and program.

Directory of GA meetings in the U.S. and other countries.

GAMCARE

http://www.gamcare.org.uk

Sponsor: GamCare (UK), a charity promoting responsible attitudes towards gambling.

Offers individual counseling and education materials.

NATIONAL CENTER FOR RESPONSIBLE GAMING

http://www.ncrg.org

Sponsor: National Center for Responsible Gaming, which funds research on under-age and problem gambling.

Describes the Center's grant program.

Lists publications by Center-funded investigators.

Links to training and certification programs in the addictive disorders.

NATIONAL CENTER FOR RESPONSIBLE GAMING

A Division of the Gaming Entertainment Research & Education Foundation

NATIONAL COUNCIL ON PROBLEM GAMBLING, INC.

http://www.ncpgambling.org

Sponsor: National Council on Problem Gambling, Inc., a nonprofit agency disseminating information about Pathological Gambling.

Describes the Council's annual conference.

"Are You a Compulsive Gambler?" quiz.

Links to Web sites on related topics.

NORTH AMERICAN TRAINING INSTITUTE

http://www.nati.org

Sponsor: North American Training Institute, a division of the Minnesota Institute on Compulsive Gambling.

Offers courses and educational materials for prevention and treatment of compulsive gambling.

PROBLEM GAMBLING: A CANADIAN PERSPECTIVE

http://icewall.vianet.on.ca/pages/gcooper/Index.htm

Sponsor: Gerry Cooper, Program Director of Sudbury, Ontario, office of Addiction Research Foundation.

Links to Canadian and non-Canadian Web sites about problem gambling, with critiques of the sites' information and utility.

PROBLEMGAMBLING.COM

http://www.problemgambling.com

Sponsor: Unknown.

FAQs and news releases about compulsive gambling.

Links to treatment centers in the U.S.

V. TRICHOTILLOMANIA

See also section 7 of chapter 1 (Obsessive Compulsive Disorder).

AMANDA'S TRICHOTILLOMANIA GUIDE

http://home.intekom.com/jly2

Sponsor: Unknown.

FAQs, links, personal stories about Trichotillomania.

TRICH WEB SERVER

http://www.fairlite.com/trich

Sponsor: Fairlight Consulting.

FAQ section on Trichotillomania.

Links to relevant Web sites.

TRICHOTILLOMANIA LEARNING CENTER, INC.

http://www.trich.org

Sponsor: Trichotillomania Learning Center, Inc., a support and resource nonprofit organization.

Brief fact sheet about the disorder.

Phone number for finding support groups.

VI. INTERNET ADDICTION

The *DSM-IV* predates the emergence of the phenomenon of "Internet addiction." Whether or not one considers Internet addiction to be a specific disorder, this clinically recognizable phenomenon is common among clients.

ABOUT.COM: NET CULTURE

http://netculture.about.com/Internet/netculture/library/weekly/msub13.htm?rnk=r2&terms=%22Internet+addiction%22

Sponsor: About.com.

Links to articles and sites, both pro and con, about the concept of Internet addiction.

CENTER FOR INTERNET STUDIES

http://www.virtual-addiction.com

Sponsor: Dr. David Greenfield (CT).

Articles about Internet addiction and its destructive effects on marriages, with hints on how to rescue one's marriage.

Links to other Web sites about Internet addiction.

CENTER FOR ONLINE ADDICTION

http://www.netaddiction.com

Sponsor: Kimberly Young, Ph.D.

Links to online journals, and to full-text articles, about computer addiction.

Offers virtual (online) counseling for Internet addiction.

Online newsletter about cyber-addiction.

Ψ INTERNET ADDICTION

http://psychcentral.com/netaddiction

Sponsors: PsychCentral.com; Dr. John Grohol.

Critical review of the concept "Internet Addiction Disorder" and associated research.

Links, with critical annotations, to online articles both endorsing and criticizing the conception of Internet addiction, and other relevant Web sites.

Section 15
Adjustment Disorders

Adjustment Disorders involve clinically significant emotional or behavioral symptoms in response to psychosocial stress. The hallmark of an adjustment disorder is experienced distress beyond what one would expect given the particular stressor.

Although we did not find many sites dealing with treatments specific to adjustment disorders, we have listed a few Web sites dealing with common stressors to enhance the awareness of therapists concerning the effects of these stressors. Any general search engine (e.g., Google, Yahoo!, AltaVista, Northernlight) would be helpful in finding Web sites about other stressors. Also, Web sites in other areas of this book provide access to many support resources for stressors such as illness, death of a significant other, pregnancy, sexual difficulties and concerns, and others. Web sites about divorce, one of the prime stressors, are included with sites on relational problems in section 17 of chapter 1.

The structure of *DSM-IV* relegates some clearly stressful events to discussions of other disorders. For example, because *DSM-IV* notes bereavement as an exclusion criterion for adjustment disorder, sites dealing with bereavement are not listed here; instead, see section 17 of chapter 1. Topics relating to clearly traumatic stressors and their effects are listed in section 7 of chapter 1.

ADJUSTMENT DISORDER

http://soe.drake.edu/nri/syllabi/reha222/psychmods/Adjustment/dafault.html

Sponsor: National Rehabilitation Institute, Drake University (IA).

This class syllabus is an outline of the disorder and its treatment, directed to rehabilitation students.

COPING WITH THE STRESS OF MOVING

http://localpartners.com/denver/welcomehome/stress.html

Sponsors: Audrey Brodt, Ph.D.; Welcome Home, the Magazine of Denver.

Brief discussion of the stresses of moving, with common sense coping tips.

DOWNSIZING AND LAYOFFS

http://fullcoverage.yahoo.com/fc/Business/Downsizing_and_Layoffs

Sponsor: Yahoo! Inc.

Current news clippings about downsizing and layoffs.

FAMILY MATTERS: MANAGING THE STRESS OF MOVING

http://www.montana.edu/wwwpb/home/moving.html

Sponsor: Steve Duncan, University of Montana-Bozeman Extension Service.

Brief article about helping family members to manage moving.

FOUR DOZEN WAYS TO STAY UNEMPLOYED

http://members.mint.net/lifework/ways48.html

Sponsor: Unknown.

Lists the reasons most commonly cited by employers for turning down job applicants. This could be helpful in counseling unemployed clients.

HEALTH INFORMATION LIBRARY: STRESS IN THE SENIOR YEARS

http://www.covenanthealth.com/features/health/aging/agin4127.htm

Sponsor: Covenant Health.

Very brief summary of stressors affecting senior citizens, with a list of solutions.

Ψ HEALTH-CENTER: ADJUSTMENT DISORDER PAGES

http://site.health-center.com/brain/adjustment/default.htm

Sponsor: Clinical Tools, Inc.

Describes adjustment disorders and lists stresses that may cause them.

Hosts an adjustment disorder bulletin board.

HEALTHCENTRAL: ADJUSTMENT DISORDERS

http://www.healthcentral.com/mhc/top/000932.cfm

Sponsor: HealthCentral.com.

Brief article about diagnostic criteria, treatment approaches, and expected prognosis.

Ψ HOW TO SURVIVE UNBEARABLE STRESS

http://www.teachhealth.com

Sponsor: Thomas Sweet.

A Web book by Steven Burns, M.D., describing what stress is and how to cope with it.

Simple to read, with concrete and highly useful ideas on reducing stress and its effects on health.

NORTH AMERICAN MENOPAUSE SOCIETY

http://www.menopause.org

Sponsor: North American Menopause Society, a scientific organization promoting the understanding of menopause.

FAQs about menopause.

Abstracts of relevant journal articles.

Sells guidebooks for nonprofessionals about menopause.

POWER SURGE

http://www.power-surge.com

Sponsors: AOL/Time Warner, Oxygen Media, Thrive.

Online menopause support group.

Interviews with experts.

Chat area and message board.

RETIREMENT PLANNING IGNORES MENTAL HEALTH

http://www.newswise.com/articles/1999/9/RETIRMNT.NCW.html

Sponsor: NewsWise.com.

News release concerning 1999 research on the psychosocial adjustment difficulties of retired persons.

SIMPLICITY RESOURCE GUIDE

http://www.gallagherpress.com/pierce/index.htm

Sponsor: Linda Breen Pierce.

Links to Web sites and bibliographies about simplifying one's life and thereby reducing stress.

Ψ STRESS MANAGEMENT FOR PATIENT AND PHYSICIAN

http://www.mentalhealth.com/mag1/p51-str.html

Sponsors: David B. Posen, M.D.; Internet Mental Health.

A 1995 journal article on stress management, with generally applicable suggestions for stress reduction such as using relaxation techniques, improving sleep, changing beliefs, etc.

Section 16
Personality Disorders

A Personality Disorder is an enduring pattern of inner experience and behavior that:

- deviates markedly from the expectations of the individual's culture
- is pervasive and inflexible
- has an onset in adolescence or early adulthood
- is stable over time, and
- leads to distress or impairment.

Personality disorders are generally divided into three clusters: Individuals who appear odd or eccentric; individuals who often appear dramatic, emotional, or erratic; and individuals who appear anxious or fearful.

Because these disorders are not easily remedied and do not generally spawn organizations or institutes to study and treat them, they are not extensively represented on the Web. The best overall reference for Personality Disorders is found at Internet Mental Health at: http://www.mentalhealth.com. We have included a listing of Web sites that relate to personality disorders either individually or collectively, and we have also included sites that concern personality and individual differences.

I. PERSONALITY DISORDERS

AGGRESSION AND TRANSFERENCE IN SEVERE PERSONALITY DISORDERS

http://www.mhsource.com/pt/p950216.html

Sponsors: Otto F. Kernberg, M.D.; Psychiatric Times.

Excerpts of a 1995 presentation by Kernberg on the effects of hatred and aggression on the treatment relationship with personality disordered patients.

ALL ABOUT PERSONALITY DISORDERS

http://personalitydisorders.mentalhelp.net

Sponsors: Mental Health Net and CMHC Systems.

Brief summary of the basics about personality disorders.

Outlines one person's view of each personality disorder and suggested treatment approaches.

ANTECEDENTS OF PERSONALITY DISORDERS IN YOUNG ADULTS

http://www.mhsource.com/pt/p960237.html

Sponsors: Joseph M. Rey, M.D.; Psychiatric Times.

Six-year follow-up study of adolescents who had been referred to a treatment unit in Australia.

Ψ AN EQUIFINALITY MODEL OF BORDERLINE PERSONALITY DISORDER

http://www.aaets.org/arts/art20.htm

Sponsors: Joseph Santoro, Ph.D., Michael Tisbe, M.D., Michael Katsarakes; American Academy of Experts in Traumatic Stress.

The authors' description of BPD as the product, either singly or in combination, of PTSD from early childhood and biological vulnerability.

APART FROM...BEING SCHIZOID

http://www.lightdarkness.com/schizoid

Sponsor: Unknown; a self-described schizoid.

Describes the inner life of a schizoid person.

Links to relevant Web sites and a bibliography of related books.

Anonymous mailing list for schizoid individuals.

AVOIDANT PERSONALITY DISORDER HOMEPAGE

http://www.geocities.com/HotSprings/3764

Sponsor: Unknown.

Support site for people with Avoidant Personality Disorder.

Brief description of the disorder with links to relevant Web sites.

Personal narratives and a link to join a mailing list.

AVOIDANT PERSONALITY DISORDER

http://watarts.uwaterloo.ca/~acheyne/courses/Avoidpd.html

Sponsors: Lorri Baier-Barth and Amanda Crawford, students of Al Cheyne at University of Waterloo's Department of Psychology (Canada).

Review article on the characteristics, etiology, and course of APD.

BEHAVIORAL TECHNOLOGY TRANSFER GROUP

http://www.dbt-seattle.com

Sponsor: Behavioraltech (WA), founded by Marsha M. Linehan, Ph.D.

Offers training and consultation in Linehan's Dialectical Behavior Therapy treatment approach to Borderline Personality Disorder.

Summary of DBT, which was written for this site by Linehan.

Links to handouts and other DBT workshop materials.

BORDERLINE AND BEYOND: A PROGRAM OF RECOVERY FROM BORDERLINE PERSONALITY DISORDER

http://www.laurapaxton.com

Sponsor: Laura Paxton, a counselor in California formerly diagnosed with BPD.

Describes the self-help program for coping with BPD sold by Paxton.

Ψ BORDERLINE PERSONALITY DISORDER SANCTUARY

http://www.mhsanctuary.com/borderline

Sponsor: Tim Pheil (OR).

Many full-text articles about BPD for the professional.

Links to related Web sites and mailing lists.

Clinicians' forum (discussion board) about BPD.

BPD CENTRAL

http://www.bpdcentral.com

Sponsor: Eggshells Press.

A support resource for family members and others associated with someone who has BPD.

FAQs about BPD, along with an explanation of myths about the diagnosis.

Links to related Web sites and mailing lists.

HEALTH-CENTER: PERSONALITY DISORDERS

http://new.healthcenter.com/db/TopicReq?SessionID=448&TopicID=68&Action=view

Sponsor: Health-Center.com.

Descriptions of each personality disorder.

MASTERSON INSTITUTE FOR PSYCHOANALYTIC PSYCHOTHERAPY

http://www.mastersoninstitute.org

Sponsor: Masterson Institute for Psychoanalytic Psychotherapy (NY).

Describes the Institute's training programs, publications, and tapes on Masterson's approach to the treatment of personality disorders.

NARCISSISTIC PERSONALITY: A STABLE DISORDER OR A STATE OF MIND?

http://www.mhsource.com/pt/p960235.html

Sponsors: Elsa Ronnington, Ph.D.; John Gunderson, M.D.; Psychiatric Times.

Summary of a prospective study of narcissistic patients.

NARCISSISTIC PERSONALITY DISORDER: HOW TO RECOGNIZE A NARCISSIST

http://www.halcyon.com/jmashmun/npd/index.html

Sponsor: Joanna M. Ashmun.

Description of the personality and traits of a narcissistic individual, from a nonprofessional perspective.

NPD CENTRAL

http://www.npd-central.org

Sponsor: Murray Kester, who describes himself as formerly married to a narcissist.

Includes information about Narcissistic Personality Disorder for "professionals, students, and victims of NPD."

Hosts a mailing list for people who have a significant other or parent who is/was a narcissist.

Although not a scholarly list, much of the material gives the reader an understanding of what it is like to be involved with someone who has this disorder.

PERSONALITY DISORDERS INSTITUTE

http://www.borderlinedisorders.com

Sponsor: Personality Disorders Institute, Weill Medical College, Cornell University.

Overview of BPD for the general public.

Descriptions of books by Institute staff.

SCHEMA THERAPY

http://www.schematherapy.com

Sponsor: Jeffrey Young, Ph.D.

An extension of cognitive therapy to the treatment of personality disorders.

Includes slide shows of basic concepts in Schema Therapy and cognitive therapy.

SECRET SHAME

http://www.palace.net/~llama/psych/injury.html

Sponsor: Unknown.

Information and hyperlinks to Web sites that provide support for self-mutilative individuals.

Site is not updated frequently.

SELF-HARM LINKS

http://www.gurlpages.com/zines/grrrlyzine/cut.html

Sponsor: iTurf, Inc.

Links to many Web pages about self-mutilation, presented in alphabetical order and with little or no annotation.

Ψ SELF PSYCHOLOGY PAGE

http://www.selfpsychology.org

Sponsor: International Council for Psychoanalytic Self Psychology.

Focus is the approach of Heinz Kohut, which gives narcissism and its vicissitudes a central role in the etiology of personality disorders.

Original papers and conference abstracts.

Many articles and lectures by well-known advocates of self psychology can be found here and nowhere else.

Links to other Web sites offering training in self psychology and psychoanalysis.

Ψ SEMINAR ON SUBSTANCE ABUSE AND AXIS II PERSONALITY DISORDERS: FULL-TEXT ARTICLES

http://www.toad.net/~arcturus/dd/ourdesk.htm

Sponsors: Bob and Sharon Ekleberry.

Detailed review articles for each of the personality disorders, with recommendations for treatment.

Useful for professionals working with any personality disordered patient, with or without concurrent substance abuse.

Ψ WITHOUT CONSCIENCE

http://www.hare.org/index.html

Sponsor: Robert D. Hare, Ph.D.

Extensive bibliography of print publications on psychopathy and Antisocial Personality Disorder, which appears to be frequently updated.

Abstracts of recent articles.

Describes Hare's psychological instrument, the Psychopathy Checklist.

II. PERSONALITY AND INDIVIDUAL DIFFERENCES

EUROPEAN ASSOCIATION OF PERSONALITY PSYCHOLOGY

http://allserv.rug.ac.be/~fdefruyt/eapp.html

Sponsor: European Association of Personality Psychology.

News of the Association and information about past conferences. The site is not updated frequently.

INSTITUTE FOR ADVANCED STUDIES IN PERSONALITY AND PSYCHOPATHOLOGY

http://millon.net

Sponsor: Theodore Millon, Ph.D.

Outline of Millon's taxonomy of personality styles and their relationship to psychopathology.

Descriptions of Millon's tests.

INTERNATIONAL PERSONALITY ITEM POOL

http://ipip.ori.org/ipip

Sponsor: Lewis R. Goldberg, Ph.D., a professor at the University of Oregon.

Scales and items for a public domain personality inventory.

INTERNATIONAL SOCIETY FOR THE STUDY OF INDIVIDUAL DIFFERENCES

http://www.issid.org

Sponsor: International Society for the Study of Individual Differences.

Information about the Society's publications and conferences.

Links to personality research Web sites.

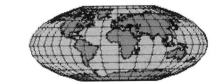

Ψ THE PERSONALITY PROJECT

http://personality-project.org/personality.html

Sponsor: William Revelle, Director of the Graduate Program in Personality, Department of Psychology, Northwestern University.

Review of current trends in personality theory, with annotated links to important publications.

The site is an excellent way to update one's knowledge of personality theory.

Many useful links to Web sites related to academic psychology and personality research.

SOCIETY FOR PERSONALITY AND SOCIAL PSYCHOLOGY

http://www.spsp.org

Sponsor: Society for Personality and Social Psychology.

Describes the Society's publications and activities.

Links to relevant academic Web sites.

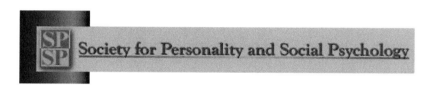

Section 17
Other Conditions That May Be the
Focus of Clinical Attention

DSM-IV suggests several conditions that may be a focus of clinical attention. They include:

I. Psychological Factors Affecting Medical Condition.

II. Medication-Induced Movement Disorders.

III. Relational Problems, which are characterized by a pattern of interaction resulting in significant impairment in functioning.

IV. Problems Related to Abuse or Neglect, which consist of severe mistreatment of one individual by another through physical abuse, sexual abuse, or child neglect.

V. Additional Conditions. The significant condition here is Bereavement, a reaction to the death of a loved one.

I. PSYCHOLOGICAL FACTORS AFFECTING MEDICAL CONDITION

We did not find Web sites specifically focused on these issues. However, many of the sites dealing with Somatoform Disorders and those dealing with physical illnesses may aid therapists in treating patients with this disorder.

II. MEDICATION-INDUCED MOVEMENT DISORDERS

Many sites describing tardive dyskinesia refer to Tardive Dyskinesia/Tardive Dystonia, 4244 University Way, N.E., P.O. Box 45732, Seattle, WA 98145-0732 (telephone 206-522-3166), but no Web site could be located for this organization.

TARDIVE DYSKINESIA

http://www.ninds.nih.gov/health_and_medical/disorders/tardive_doc.htm

Sponsor: National Institute of Neurological Disorders and Stroke, National Institutes of Health.

Fact sheet for the general public, which appears not to be frequently updated.

TARDIVE DYSKINESIA AND NEUROLEPTIC MALIGNANT SYNDROME

http://www.nami.org/about/naminyc/meds/sidefx.html

Sponsor: National Alliance for the Mentally Ill (New York City Metro Chapter).

FAQs about these conditions.

Ψ VIRTUAL HOSPITAL: CLINICAL PSYCHOPHARMACOLOGY SEMINAR: TARDIVE DYSKINESIA

http://www.vh.org/Providers/Conferences/CPS/08.html

Sponsor: University of Iowa.

A scholarly review of etiological theories and treatment options for tardive dyskinesia which, at the time of our visit, was last updated in late 1999.

III. RELATIONAL PROBLEMS

We have included sites dealing with divorce, sibling problems, and marital/relationship discord in this category.

Ψ ALTERNATIVES TO MARRIAGE PROJECT

http://www.unmarried.org

Sponsor: Alternatives to Marriage Project, a national organization for unmarried people.

Articles about alternatives to marriage for gay and straight couples.

FAQs about alternatives to marriage.

Links to relevant Web sites, intermingled with information about print publications.

Information about subscribing to the Project's e-mail newsletter, along with an archive of past issues.

Alternatives
to Marriage
Project

Ψ DIVORCE CENTRAL

http://www.divorcecentral.com

Sponsors: Pam Weintraub and Terry Hillman.

Comprehensive source of information about divorce.

Links to divorce laws, state by state.

Lists support organizations.

Practical and specific FAQs for emotional, legal, parenting, and financial issues, written by appropriate experts.

Chat areas and message boards.

Annotated links to relevant Web sites for legal, emotional, and parenting aspects of divorce.

DIVORCE ONLINE

http://www.divorceonline.com

Sponsor: Creative Communications.

Articles about legal, financial, psychological, and parenting issues in divorce.

FABER/MAZLISH WORKSHOPS

http://fabermazlish.com

Sponsors: Adele Faber and Elaine Mazlish, authors of Siblings Without Rivalry *and* How to Talk So Kids Will Listen & Listen So Kids Will Talk.

Information about the authors' workshops and publications.

Summary of research findings on their approach to improving parent-child communication.

Ψ HANDLING SIBLING RIVALRY

http://childdevelopmentinfo.com/parenting/sibling_rivalry.shtml

Sponsor: Child Development Institute (CA).

Pragmatic and specific strategies for managing sibling rivalry.

Lists helpful books and relevant Web pages on sibling rivalry and other parenting issues.

Discusses handicapped and gifted siblings.

INDEPENDENT GAY FORUM: MARRIAGE AND RELATIONSHIPS

http://www.indegayforum.org/library/marriage.html

Sponsor: Independent Gay Forum.

Opinion pieces about aspects of gay relationships and marriages.

MARRIAGE ENCOUNTER

http://www.encounter.org

Sponsor: Marriage Encounter United Methodist.

FAQs about the marriage encounter programs conducted within the principles of United Methodist Church.

Database of this program's marriage encounters, searchable by location and date.

Lists questions that may be used to generate dialogue between couples.

Lists other marriage encounter sites that are sorted by religious faith.

MILITARY DIVORCE ONLINE

http://www.militarydivorceonline.com

Sponsor: John H. Carney.

Fact sheets about divorce, with added information that is specific to military divorce.

Lists military attorneys by state.

Ψ MY CHILD IS GAY! NOW WHAT DO I DO?

http://www.pe.net/~bidstrup/parents.htm

Sponsor: Scott Bidstrup.

Detailed FAQs to help parents come to terms with learning that their child is gay, lesbian, bisexual, or transgendered.

Information on helping parents support their gay child in dealing with loneliness, isolation, and harassment.

Information about PFLAG, a support and advocacy organization for parents of gays and lesbians.

My Child is GAY! Now What Do I Do?

PARTNERS TASK FORCE FOR GAY & LESBIAN COUPLES

http://www.buddybuddy.com

Sponsor: Partners Task Force for Gay & Lesbian Couples.

Many articles on legal and emotional aspects of lesbian/gay relationships, marriages, and parenting.

PROJECT NOSPANK

http://www.nospank.org

Sponsor: PTAVE.

Links to many news articles and informational pieces about parenting without spanking.

RETROUVAILLE... A LIFELINE FOR MARRIED COUPLES

http://www.retrouvaille.org

Sponsor: Catholic Church.

Brief description of this Catholic weekend program for troubled marriages, with links to newspaper articles about the program.

Links to sites about marriage.

SINGLE DAD'S INDEX

http://www.vix.com/pub/men/single-dad.html

Sponsor: World Wide Virtual Library, Vixie Enterprises.

Links to articles and Web sites.

STRAIGHT SPOUSE NETWORK

http://www.ssnetwk.org

Sponsor: Straight Spouse Network, an organization providing support to heterosexual partners of bisexual and gay spouses who have come out of the closet.

Contact information for support groups.

Links to Web sites, mailing lists, and chat areas providing support.

Provides mailing lists for children of gay, lesbian, or bisexual parents.

Straight Spouse Network

Reaching Out, Healing, Building Bridges

WORLD WIDE MARRIAGE ENCOUNTER

http://www.wwme.org

Sponsor: World Wide Marriage Encounter.

Describes weekend enrichment programs for "ho-hum" marriages.

IV. PROBLEMS RELATED TO ABUSE OR NEGLECT

In addition to the sites listed below, the sections in chapter 1 on Reactive Attachment Disorder (section 1), Posttraumatic Stress Disorder (section 7), and Dissociative Disorders (section 10), are relevant to abuse and neglect.

AMERICAN PROFESSIONAL SOCIETY ON THE ABUSE OF CHILDREN

http://www.apsac.org

Sponsor: American Professional Society on the Abuse of Children, a multidisciplinary society disseminating information on child abuse prevention and treatment, as well as related forensic issues.

Describes the Society's conferences and publications.

CHILDHELP USA

http://www.childhelpusa.org

Sponsor: Childhelp USA, an organization promoting treatment, prevention, and research for abused children.

Brief FAQ section about child abuse.

Toll-free number for reporting abuse.

Links to a small number of related sites.

HUSBAND BATTERING

http://www.vix.com/pub/men/battery/battery.html

Sponsor: Vixie Enterprises.

Articles, statistics, and bibliography on domestic violence toward men.

INTERNATIONAL SOCIETY FOR THE PREVENTION OF CHILD ABUSE AND NEGLECT

http://www.ispcan.org

Sponsor: International Society for the Prevention of Child Abuse and Neglect.

Information about the Society's conferences and training programs.

Worldwide links for professional associations dealing with abuse and neglect.

Ψ NATIONAL CLEARINGHOUSE ON CHILD ABUSE AND NEGLECT INFORMATION

http://www.calib.com/nccanch

Sponsor: National Clearinghouse on Child Abuse and Neglect Information, U.S. Department of Health and Human Services.

FAQs and statistical information about child abuse and child protective services.

Bibliographies about abuse and neglect.

Information about preventing abuse.

Annotated links to Web sites of agencies and professional societies dealing with abuse and neglect.

National Clearinghouse on Child Abuse and Neglect Information

The Clearinghouse is a national resource for professionals seeking information on the prevention, identification, and treatment of child abuse and neglect and related child welfare issues. Go to "Services" for more information in these areas. Also, see our Highlights area for weekly updates!

Ψ NATIONAL COUNCIL ON ELDER ABUSE

http://www.gwjapan.com/NCEA

Sponsor: National Council on Elder Abuse, a partnership of six agencies.

Fact sheet about elder abuse.

Links to hotline numbers for reporting abuse and to adult protective services agencies in every state.

Information about ordering pamphlets on elder abuse.

Directory of relevant Web sites.

Lists upcoming conferences.

NATIONAL DOMESTIC VIOLENCE HOTLINE

http://www.ndvh.org

Sponsor: National Domestic Violence Hotline.

Information about the hotline.

Links to sites dealing with domestic violence.

PARENTS ANONYMOUS, INC.

http://www.parentsanonymous-natl.org

Sponsor: Parents Anonymous, a nonprofit organization offering free parental support groups to prevent child abuse.

Web site contains information about Parents Anonymous, with contact information for finding a local support group.

SEXUAL ASSAULT INFORMATION PAGE

http://www.cs.utk.edu/~bartley/saInfoPage.html

Sponsor: Unknown.

Directory of Web sites dealing with rape, abuse, and sexual harassment. Does not appear to be updated frequently.

Sexual Assault Information Page

About SAIP	Frequently Asked Questions	Search	Usage Statistics
Newsletter	Announcements/Requests	Add URL	Awards

Acquaintance Rape	Prevention
Awareness	Professional Abuse
Child Sexual Abuse	Rape
Counseling	Rape Crisis Centers
Crime Victims Compensation	Rape Trauma Syndrome
Date Rape	Related WWW Resources
Dissociative Disorder	Ritual Abuse
Domestic Violence	Rohypnol
Incest	Secondary Victims
Law	Self Defense
Literature	Sexual Assault
Media	Sexual Assault Crisis Centers
Memory	Sexual Harassment
Men's Activism	Survivors
Men's Resources	University Resources
Offenders	Usenet Newsgroups and IRC
Poetry	Victims
Post-Traumatic Stress Disorder	Women's Resources

SURVIVORSHIP

https://www.ctsserver.com/~svship

Sponsors: Caryn StarDancer; Survivorship, a nonprofit organization dealing with "sadistic sexual abuse, ritualistic abuse, mind control, and torture."

FAQs about ritualistic abuse.

Tips for managing "triggers" (i.e., stimuli that elicit memories of abuse).

"Self-Reprogramming Worksheet" that uses cognitive therapy questioning techniques to alter dysfunctional cognitions resulting from abuse.

Message boards for paying members.

V. ADDITIONAL CONDITIONS: BEREAVEMENT

See also the Web sites on death and dying that we have included in chapter 4.

AIRCRAFT CASUALTY EMOTIONAL SUPPORT SERVICES (ACCESS)

http://www.aircrashsupport.com

Sponsor: AirCraft Casualty Emotional Support Services, a volunteer organization providing support to family members of those who died in airplane crashes.

Links to Web sites of relevant organizations.

Bibliography of self-help books that deal with grief.

ASSOCIATION FOR PET LOSS AND BEREAVEMENT, INC.

http://www.aplb.org

Sponsor: Association for Pet Loss and Bereavement.

Lists support organizations, support groups, and pet cemeteries.

Bibliography on pet loss and bereavement.

COMPASSIONATE FRIENDS

http://www.compassionatefriends.org

Sponsor: Compassionate Friends, an organization that supports adults who have lost a child.

Information about the organization's local support groups.

Links to other Web sites dealing with grief.

JULIE'S PLACE

http://www.juliesplace.com

Sponsor: Debra Nelson.

Support resources for children or teens who have lost a sibling.

Links to relevant Web sites.

Personal narratives.

MOTHERS IN SYMPATHY AND SUPPORT

http://www.misschildren.org

Sponsor: Mothers in Sympathy and Support, a nonprofit organization providing support to parents after the death of their baby.

Links to Web sites and other resources.

Lists Web resources for helping professionals deal with death, including ethical concerns.

NATIONAL ORGANIZATION OF PARENTS OF MURDERED CHILDREN, INC.

http://www.pomc.com

Sponsor: National Organization of Parents of Murdered Children.

Information about the organization's support of antiviolence programs.

Tips for professionals dealing with parents whose child has been killed.

Click on "Legal Issues" for a detailed description of the path through the justice system taken by a criminal case.

CHAPTER 2
Mental Health Metasites and Search Engines

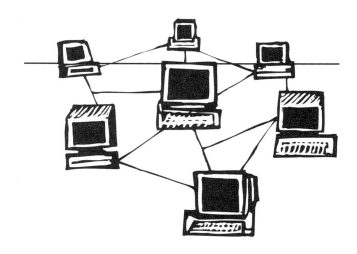

Section 1
Sites That Link to Other Mental Health–Related Web Sites

Ψ ABOUT.COM MENTAL HEALTH RESOURCES
http://mentalhealth.about.com/health/mentalhealth

Sponsor: Leonard Holmes, Ph.D., a psychologist in private practice. Dr. Holmes acts as a "guide," furnishing brief annotations of the sites he lists.

Well-organized, selective lists of disorders and resources.

Self-help oriented, rather than professional.

AMERICAN PSYCHOLOGICAL SOCIETY PSYCHOLOGY L!NKS
http://www.psychologicalscience.org/links.html

Sponsor: American Psychological Society.

Links to associations of research and academic psychology.

Ψ AMOEBAWEB

http://www.vanguard.edu/psychology/amoebaweb.html

Sponsor: Douglas Degelman, Ph.D., Professor of Psychology at Vanguard University of Southern California.

Well-organized links to research psychology resources.

Has considerable depth of information; surprisingly, other psychology sites seem to have left this one off their lists of resources.

Graphically clean and spare; it gets you quickly to the resources you seek.

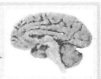

AmoebaWeb
Psychology resources on the Web!
AmoebaWeb is maintained by Douglas Degelman, Ph.D.
Professor of Psychology at Vanguard University of Southern California.
This page was last updated Tue, May 16, 2000.

General References	Applied Psychology	Health Psychology	Psychology and Religion
Professional Organizations	Biopsychology	History of Psychology	School Psychology
Full Text Journals	Cognitive Psychology	Intelligence	Sensation and Perception
Online Tests	Cross-Cultural Psychology	Language	Social Psychology
Career Preparation	Developmental Psychology	Learning	Sport Psychology
Graduate Study	Disorders	Marriage and Family	States of Consciousness
Research and APA Style	Emotion and Motivation	Memory	Statistics and Testing
Parenting	Gender and Sexuality	Personality	Therapy

Ψ ASK NOAH ABOUT: MENTAL HEALTH

http://www.noah.cuny.edu/mentalhealth/mental.html

Sponsor: New York Online Access to Health, a partnership of City University of New York, New York Public Library, and others.

Directory of fact sheets for many common mental disorders and their generally accepted treatments.

Resources referenced on this site appear to have been chosen from authoritative sources.

ATHABASCA UNIVERSITY PSYCHOLOGY RESOURCES

http://server.bmod.athabascau.ca/html/aupr/psycres.shtml

Sponsor: Psychology Centre at Athabasca University, Alberta, Canada.

Straightforward, no-frills, no-ads links to major clinical and research psychology resources.

BEHAVENET

http://www.behavenet.com

Sponsor: BehaveNet, Inc., an organization that publishes home pages for mental health professionals.

Professional licensing boards in the U.S., agencies and governmental organizations involved with mental health, and treatment guidelines.

"Clinical Capsules" briefly summarize the *DSM-IV* characteristics of many disorders.

Many pages list books and other media concerning the topic under discussion.

CHRIS EVANS'S BOOKMARKS

http://www.psyctc.org/bookmark.htm

Sponsor: Chris Evans.

Extremely long single page containing links to journals, associations, mailing lists.

Has a wide-ranging list of Web sites related to psychology and health.

May take a long time to load; if you plan to use it regularly, consider saving it to your hard drive.

Evans gives his personal opinion of many of the sites.

In fact, the entire Web page is extremely personalized (including a link to a discussion of Charlie Chaplin's film heroines).

Ψ COGNITIVE AND PSYCHOLOGICAL RESOURCES ON THE INTERNET

http://www-psych.stanford.edu/cogsci

Sponsors: Ruediger Oehlmann and the Stanford University Psychology Department.

Resources relevant to research in cognitive science and psychology; not aimed at the clinical practitioner.

Extensive links to academic conferences and organizations.

Cognitive and Psychological Sciences on the Internet

Sections Academic Programs | Organizations & Conferences | Journals & Magazines | Usenet Newsgroups | Discussion Lists |
Announcement/Distribution Lists | Publishers | Software | Miscellany | | **Top Level** (Verbose)

COUNSELINGNETWORK.COM

http://www.counselingnetwork.com/WCNasp/Main.asp

Sponsor: BizMarkets.com, a New Media Solutions, Inc. company.

Designed for counselors wanting to market products and services.

Has a list of "Web resources" that mixes notices of academic positions available with ads for counselors' private practices.

Marketing, rather than clinical information, takes the front seat.

THE COUNSELING WEB

http://seamonkey.ed.asu.edu/~gail/index.htm

Sponsor: Arizona State University Division of Psychology in Education.

For the counseling psychologist, including career counseling resources.

Contains links to APA-approved counseling psychology programs and predoctoral internships.

This site is not frequently updated.

CYBER-PSYCH

http://www.cyber-psych.com

Sponsor: Nicole M. Harrington, Daemon Technologies (CA).

Brief lists of links to general topics in mental health. Many are more popularly than academically oriented.

Black background makes the links difficult to read in some browsers.

CYBERPSYCHLINK

http://cctr.umkc.edu/user/dmartin/psych2.html

Sponsor: Dawn Martin, a former psychology graduate student.

One of the earliest Web resource directories for psychology.

This site is not frequently updated

DATA_PSYCH

http://www.datapsych.com

Sponsor: Eric Muller.

A few links to articles that are primarily of interest to research psychologists.

Ψ DR. BOB'S MENTAL HEALTH LINKS

http://uhs.bsd.uchicago.edu/~bhsiung/mental.html

Sponsor: Robert Hsiung, M.D., University of Chicago Department of Psychiatry.

Targets mental health professionals, especially physicians.

A good resource for biological psychiatry.

"Virtual pamphlet collection" that is useful for clients.

"Dr. Bob's Psychopharmacology Tips" contains clinical observations and lore that can't be found in drug company pamphlets.

DR. MICHAEL FENICHEL'S CURRENT TOPICS IN PSYCHOLOGY

http://www.tiac.net/biz/drmike/Current.shtml

Sponsor: Dr. Fenichel is a clinical psychologist in New York City.

The author has annotated many of the links and has written some articles himself. Many of his links are to self-help and other nonprofessional materials.

Somewhat disorganized, the screen is divided into two frames that contain different sets of links to related topics.

ENCYCLOPEDIA OF PSYCHOLOGY

http://www.psychology.org

Sponsor: Department of Psychology, Jacksonville (FL) State University.

Frequently updated links (nearly 1,700 at the time of our visit) to Web sites and articles about psychological theory and research.

Hierarchical structure makes it easy to find what you're looking for.

Contains useful references to material about behavior, cognition, and neuroscience, but is not oriented to the clinical practitioner.

Encyclopedia of Psychology

Encyclopedia of Psychology
[Home] [Add a Resource] [Modify a Resource] [New] [Popular] [Random Link] [Search]
Categories:

Career (40)
What career, why, and how to begin

Environment Behavior Relationships (978)
The Study of Psychological Phenomena

Organizations (81)
Organizations and Institutions of Psychology

Paradigms and Theories (86)
Ways of thinking about Psychology

People and History (108)
The history of Psychology, and its people

Publications (188)
Publications and Documents

Resources (200)
Resources for Information

Underlying Reductionistic Machinery (60)
The Biological Factors Underlying Behavior

FRAGMENTS—GENERAL MENTAL HEALTH SITES

http://tigerherbs.com/eclectica/fragments/respgs/generalmh.html

Sponsor: "Tracker."

About twenty links to mental health megasites, along with listings by topic for a few disorders.

Has prominent warnings on every page to survivors of abuse who might run across "material that is 'triggering' for you."

One of the few sites containing links for both sides of the recovered memory controversy (most sites provide links to only one side of the issue).

FREUDNET

http://plaza.interport.net/nypsan/network.html

*Sponsor: Abraham A. Brill Library of
the New York Psychoanalytic Institute.*

Lists databases and organizations related to clinical practice.

This site is not frequently updated.

GALAXY

http://galaxy.einet.net/galaxy/Social-Sciences/Psychology.html

Sponsor: AHN/FIT Internet, LLC.

Not particularly comprehensive list of psychology organizations and
Usenet groups.

Has slightly more depth than one sees at first glance; click on any of
the topics near the top of the page to see more resources.

Psychology < *Social Sciences* < Home

- Branches
- Diseases and Disorders
- Education

- History
- Hypnosis
- Journals
- Psychologists
- Self - Help
- Surveys and Tests

GUIDE TO THE MENTAL HEALTH INTERNET

http://www.virtualcs.com/mhi.html

*Sponsors: Internet Guides Press and Dr. David Luboff,
Professor of Psychology at Saybrook Graduate School,
San Francisco.*

Lists a few sites in about fifteen broad areas such as diagnosis, treatment, medications, and self-help that Dr. Luboff believes would be useful to mental health professionals.

This site is not frequently updated.

INTERNET MENTAL HEALTH

http://www.mentalhealth.com

Sponsor: Phillip W. Long, M.D., who has avoided corporate sponsorship because he believes that "pharmaceutical companies distort medical education."

Lists only sites that contain more than ten pages in English of what the sponsor considers scientifically sound information.

Sites are rated by popularity.

Provides a series of online diagnostic programs for various disorders (Java-enabled browser required).

INTERNET MENTAL HEALTH RESOURCES

http://www.med.nyu.edu/Psych/src.psych.html

Sponsor: Herb Stockley.

A long single page with alphabetized links for disorders, organizations, and other aspects of mental health.

INTERNET PUBLIC LIBRARY PSYCHOLOGY REFERENCE

http://www.ipl.org/ref/RR/static/soc7000.html

Sponsor: University of Michigan School of Information.

Has about twenty annotated links to other sites, mostly megasites.

JUNG, ANALYTICAL PSYCHOLOGY, AND CULTURE

http://www.cgjungpage.com/jpresources.html

Sponsor: Donald Williams, M.A., a Jungian analyst.

A long single page with annotated links to Web sites concerning Jungian theory, publications, and training programs.

LINKS TO OVER 7,000 OF MH AND PSYCH'S GREATEST HITS!

http://www.geocities.com/HotSprings/3616/links.html

Sponsor: Unknown.

Actually has only 150 randomly organized links to other Web sites that in turn link to 7,000 to 10,000 other sites.

This site might be entertaining for the casual "Web grazer."

LINKS2GO

http://www.links2go.com/topic/Clinical_Psychology,_Psychiatry,_Mental_Health

Sponsor: Links2Go, a company that provides online directories.

Hierarchically organized in a graphical tree format, Links2Go directs the user to the links for each topic that are most highly cited by other Web pages. Top half of the page shows the hierarchy of topics in purple; bottom half shows relevant Web site links in blue.

The user can either click through the list of topics by using hyperlinks, or use the site's search engine to locate the desired topic.

Clicking on a link will cause the browser to open a new window and go to that site; the Links2Go directory window handily remains open underneath the new window.

MAGIC STREAM

http://fly.hiwaay.net/~garson

Sponsor: Regina Garson.

**Magic Stream Journal
...a guide to emotional wellness:**

Contains brief lists of categorized links for self-help and professional use.

MEDMARK PSYCHIATRY

http://www.medmark.org/psy

Sponsor: MedMark.

Selected links to professional and self-help resources for various diagnoses.

Ψ MEDSCAPE PSYCHIATRY

http://www.medscape.com/Home/Topics/psychiatry/psychiatry.html

Sponsor: Medscape, Inc.

Registration required (free). Well worth a regular visit. Although the site contains some links to other psychiatry/mental health resources, it also has its own unique content.

Can be customized to present news from various topic areas within medicine.

Detailed day-by-day summaries of several major psychiatry conferences, going far beyond the generic coverage in the newspapers.

Regularly updated articles, available only at this site, on various practical aspects of psychiatric treatment.

Abstracts of recent publications on a selected topic (e.g., panic disorder), allowing the practitioner a quick review of recent knowledge in the field.

MEDWEB

http://www.medweb.emory.edu/MedWeb

Sponsor: Robert W. Woodruff Health Sciences Center Library at Emory University, Atlanta.

Brief lists of associations, treatment centers, and journals organized by subject.

Click on "Browse by Subject." If you then click on "Mental Health, Psychiatry, Psychology," you are taken to an alphabetized list of nearly 600 links that can only be viewed 25 at a time. More conveniently, next to the link for "Mental Health, Psychiatry, Psychology" is a link labeled "Focus further" that allows you to browse by subject.

MEDWEBPLUS: PSYCHIATRY

http://www.medwebplus.com/subject/Psychiatry.html

Sponsor: MedWebPlus.Com.

267 links in psychiatry viewable alphabetically or by topic and graded according to how often MedWeb was able to access the link.

MENTAL HEALTH IN AUSTRALIA

http://www.mentalhealth.org.au

Sponsor: Mental Health Association (Queensland, Australia).

Links to Australian mental health resources and academic psychology departments.

Ψ MENTAL HEALTH INFOSOURCE

http://www.mhsource.com

Sponsor: CME, Inc.

Has an extensive "Mega-Links" page to various mental disorders that is many screenfuls long and takes a long time to load.

Promotes its own conferences for physicians, and could be improved by better coverage of services and meetings available from other vendors in addition to CME, Inc.

Contains a search engine.

"Ask the Experts" section for questions from patients and therapists.

MENTAL HEALTH MATTERS!

http://www.mental-health-matters.com

Sponsor: Judy Castelli, who describes herself as an "Artist/Survivor."

Brief list of resources for professionals, plus many sources of self-help and advocacy information for clients.

Mental Health Matters!
Mental Health and Mental Illness
Information & Resources for Mental
Health Professionals, Consumers and
Families

Ψ MENTAL HEALTH NET

http://mentalhelp.net

Sponsor: CMHC Systems. Operated by Ohio psychologist Mark Dombeck, Ph.D.

Probably the largest megasite for mental health resources.

Home page looks like a portal site, with current mental health news headlines, links to chat and support forums, and an index (site map).

One of the most basic resources for the therapist seeking practice-related information.

Breaks up what could have been lengthy pages into shorter ones that load faster.

Has a bookshop with thoughtful reviews of new books.

NATIONAL ELECTRONIC LIBRARY FOR MENTAL HEALTH

http://cebmh.warne.ox.ac.uk/cebmh/nelmh

Sponsor: National Electronic Library for Mental Health (UK).

Under development at the time of our visit. The heart of the site was reached by clicking "Library," which led to information and links concerning practice guidelines and evidence-based mental health.

 Introducing the National electronic Library for Mental Health

Ψ NATIONAL MENTAL HEALTH SERVICES KNOWLEDGE EXCHANGE NETWORK (KEN)

http://www.mentalhealth.org

Sponsor: The Center for Mental Health Services, part of Substance Abuse and Mental Health Services Administration, U.S. Department of Health and Human Services.

Includes a searchable bibliography of documents on mental health obtainable from Federal and State agencies, as well as links.

Includes mental health links for children.

Good source for statistics related to mental health treatment in the United States.

NETPSYCHOLOGY

http://www.netpsych. corn

Sponsor: Leonard Holmes, Ph.D.

Lists and reviews sites that provide online mental health services. Supported by advertisements for mental health products and services.

Ψ NON-MAINSTREAM PSYCHOTHERAPY AND COUNSELING RESOURCES ON THE INTERNET

http://ourworld. compuserve.coni/homepages/selfheal/lnonmain.htm

Sponsor: Nick Totton, a Reichian therapist.

Body-oriented, movement, and spiritual therapies, as well as various experiential therapies.

ONLINE DICTIONARY OF MENTAL HEALTH

http://human-nature.com/odmh/index.html

Sponsor: Centre for Psychotherapeutic Studies, University of Sheffield, UK.

Links, indexed by subject, for various disorders.

Parts of this site are out-of-date.

OPEN DIRECTORY PROJECT: PSYCHOLOGY

http://dmoz.org/Science/Social_Sciences/Psychology

Sponsor: Open Directory Project.

The Open Directory Project attempts to recruit knowledgeable volunteer editors to produce a selective index of Web sites organized by topic, but many of the categories lack editors.

Looks and works like more generalized Web search engines such as Yahoo! or Excite; if you are familiar with such sites, you'll be at home here.

Ψ POLICY INFORMATION EXCHANGE ONLINE

http://pie.org/mimhweb/pie/pie.asp

Sponsor: Missouri Institute of Mental Health, University of Missouri-Columbia.

Contains links to documents and Web sites concerning governmental mental health policies.

Ψ PSYCH CENTRAL: DR. GROHOL'S MENTAL HEALTH PAGE

http://psychcentral.corn

Sponsor: John Grohol, Psy.D., one of the pioneers of online psychology resources.

Click on "Mental Health & Psychology Resources Online" to see an annotated, well-organized, and rated list of URIs concerning various disorders.

FAQs about symptoms and treatments.

An easy way to subscribe to mailing lists for professionals: Go to http://psychcentral.com/resources/Psychology/Mailing_Lists.

Live chats and forums.

Book reviews.

PSYCH SITE

http://www.stange. simplenet.com/psycsite

Sponsor: Ken Stange, The Department of Psychology, Nipissing University Ontario, Canada.

Concise and well-organized list of major online resources in both research and clinical psychology. Ten to fifteen Web links per topic.

PSYCH WEB

http://www.psychwww. corn

Sponsor: Russ Dewey, Ph.D.

Especially relevant to students and teachers of psychology.

Contains "Mind Tools," which are outlines of time management and goal setting skills.

Has a section on sports psychology.

Ψ PSYCHCRAWLER

http://www.psychcrawler. com

Sponsor: American Psychological Association.

A search engine only with no lists of links.

Searches scientific and professional association Web sites, yielding a high rate of useful, science-based content in its search results.

PSYCHE MATTERS

http://www.psychematters. corn

Sponsor: Cheryl Martin, RN, LPC.

Lists links related to psychoanalytic theory and practice, child development, and attachment theory.

Includes a message board.

Links to professional associations organized by discipline.
Online bibliographies and psychoanalytic papers.

PSYCHIATRY ONLINE—THE INTERNATIONAL FORUM FOR PSYCHIATRY
http://www.priory.coni/psych.htm

Sponsor: Priory Lodge Education Ltd.

Online journal containing full-text articles on biological psychiatry, such as medication effects and ECT.

Although the Web site indicates that the majority of its readers are from the U.S., much of the news and practice-directed material concerns the U.K.

PSYCHNET-UK
http://www.psychnet-uk.com

Sponsor: PsychNet-UK is "an independent private Web site."

Contains a search engine for the Web site, along with lists of links to various subject areas within psychology, but is confusingly organized, with a few links.

PsychNet-UK

The Psychology Web Directory for Mental Health Professionals, Students, those wanting assistance or seeking to know more about the areas of mental health.

PSYCHOLOGICAL SCIENCE ON THE NET
http://www.psychologicalscience.net

Sponsors: M. Kimberly MacLin, Ph.D. and Otto H. MacLin, Ph.D.

This site tries to cover everything and claims more than 8,000 links.

Sends psychology-related greeting cards (e.g., Stroop task, optical illusions) with user-selectable text.

The search engine for the site may run slowly, yielding few results. Without using it, the user can see about 15 links at a time in no apparent order (click on "Psychology Topics").

Psychological Science on the Net!

PSYCHOLOGY ONLINE RESOURCE CENTRAL

http ://www.psych-central. corn

Sponsor: Donna Stuber-McEwen, Associate Professor at Friends University.

Links of greatest relevance to psychology graduate students and their instructors, such as lists of common errors in American Psychological Association (APA) manuscript format.

Resources for prospective graduate students.

Contains a list of online journals.

PSYCHOLOGY RELATED WEB AND INTERNET INFORMATION

http://www.albany.edu/psy/other.html

Sponsor: Psychology Department at State University of New York, Albany.

A long single page of links to professional and academic resources in psychology.

Web navigators who get overwhelmed when faced with hundreds of links might prefer the thoughtfully selected choices presented here.

Department of Psychology

UNIVERSITY AT ALBANY
STATE UNIVERSITY OF NEW YORK

PSYCHOLOGY VIRTUAL LIBRARY

http://www.clas.ufl.edu/users/gthursby/psi

Sponsors: World Wide Web Virtual Library; University of Florida maintains the lists of links.

Relatively brief lists of links with a one- or two-sentence descriptions.

An unusual feature is a link to "What's New in Psychology Sites."

PSYCHWATCH.COM

http://www.psychwatch.com

Sponsors: Fritz A. Galette, Ph.D.; and Chris M. Nuesell, Ph.D., Fordham University.

Directed at the clinical practitioner, the Web site includes practical information such as how to bill insurance companies for services, conference announcements, and job listings.

Sends out a weekly e-mail newsletter with mental health-related content and conference announcements. Newsletters are also readable and searchable on the Web site. Some of the links within the site do not work. For example, clicking on "How to Deal with HMOs" on the private practice page merely led back to the site's home page.

RESOURCES FOR PSYCHOLOGY AND COGNITIVE SCIENCES ON THE INTERNET
http://www.ke. shinshu-u. ac.jp/psychlindex.html

Sponsor: Department of Kansei Engineering at Shinshu University, Nagano, Japan.

Lists of journals, conferences, and Web sites.

This site is not frequently updated.

SNAP MENTAL HEALTH RESOURCES
http ://www. nbci. com/LMOID/resource/0,566,-303,00.html

Sponsor: National Broadcasting Company, Inc.

A commercial site with links to self-help resources.

Ψ SOCIAL PSYCHOLOGY NETWORK
http://www.socialpsychology.org

Sponsor: Webmaster Scott Plous, supported by a National Science Foundation grant.

Thousands of links to resources in social psychology, including journals, job listings, rankings of doctoral programs.

An outstanding site, with many well-organized links and minimal graphic distraction. Links to a slide show and discussion by Philip Zimbardo concerning his infamous and aborted 1971 social psychology experiment in which the basement of Stanford's psychology department became a simulated prison, with students as guards and prisoners.

Social Psychology Network
— MENU — *Maintained by Scott Plous, Wesleyan University*

THEPSYCH

http://www.thepsych.com

Sponsor: Nora Blanco-Dufour.

Spotty coverage of disorders, professional organizations, and institutions. Contains a search engine.

THE ULTIMATE FORENSIC PSYCHOLOGY DATABASE

http://flash.lakeheadu. ca/~pals/forensics

Sponsor: Michael W. F. Decaire, a psychology undergraduate.

Directory of online articles and Web sites about forensic psychology.

Although this site does not appear to be frequently updated, the links are still valuable.

UNION INSTITUTE RESEARCH ENGINE

http://www.tui. edu/Research/Resources/Psych. html

Sponsor: Union Institute.

THE UNION INSTITUTE RESEARCH ENGINE

Online Research in Psychology

Lists various types of research psychology (clinical, perception, developmental, etc.) and related Web sites and organizations. Each subheading has about ten links.

UNITED KINGDOM PSYCHIATRIC PHARMACY GROUP MENTAL HEALTH LINKS
http://www.ukppg.co.uk/links.html

Sponsor: UK Psychiatric Pharmacy Group.

Lists Web sites (mostly within the Uk focused on biological psychiatry.

WEBPSYCH PARTNERSHIP
http://www.ismho.org/webpsych

Sponsor: International Society for Mental Health Online, a nonprofit corporation. long single page of about sixty resources in alphabetical order.

Webmasters for the resources listed here have agreed to abide by a set of guidelines that keep their sites up-to-date and "objective."

WHO'S WHO IN MENTAL HEALTH ON THE WEB
http:1/idealist. com/wwmhw/profiles/view. html

Sponsor: Linda Chapman.

Searchable (by geography as well as content) profiles of mental health professionals in many countries.

Includes only professionals who have chosen to post their profiles here; no charge for posting one's profile.

YAHOO! HEALTH: MENTAL HEALTH
http://dir.yahoo.com/Health/Mental_Health

Sponsor: Yahoo! Inc.

Categorized links to Web sites that have either registered themselves with Yahoo! or that have been suggested to the company by users.

Yahoo!'s links have not been evaluated by psychology professionals and therefore vary wildly in authority and accuracy of content.

Categories

- Addiction and Recovery@
- Bereavement *(52)*
- Booksellers@
- Conferences *(15)*
- Counseling and Therapy *(289)* NEW!
- Diseases and Conditions@
- Institutes *(41)*
- Libraries *(3)*
- News and Media *(19)*
- Organizations *(136)* NEW!

- Personal Growth *(43)*
- Policy and Law *(7)*
- Psychiatry@
- Psychology@
- Shopping and Services@
- Social Work@
- Stress Management *(18)*
- Suicide@
- Web Directories *(17)*

Section 2
Sites That List
Conferences, Journals,
Databases, or Libraries

BIBLIOGRAPHY OF BASIC REFERENCE SOURCES IN PSYCHOLOGY
http://www.princeton.edu/~psychlib/basicrefhtm

Sponsor: Princeton University Psychology Library.

Lists printed resources for researching psychological literature.

Ψ DOCTOR'S GUIDE TO MEDICAL CONFERENCES AND MEETINGS
http://www.pslgroup.com/dg/psychiatry.htm

Sponsor: P/S/L Consulting Group, Inc.

Chronological list of psychiatric and neuropharmacological conferences, with contact information.

GENERAL PSYCHOLOGY INTERNET GUIDE
http://www.library.miami.edu/netguides/psygate.html

Sponsor: Richter Library, University of Miami (FL).

Directory of online databases in health care, law, and social sciences. Some databases are open to paid subscribers only but many are open access.

INTELIHEALTH
http://www.intelihealth. corn

Sponsors: Aetna U.S. Healthcare; Johns Hopkins University and Health System.

Registration (free) required. To get to a short list of online databases, click on "Resources."

JOURNALS AND PUBLISHERS
http://www.nwcm.ac.uk/uwcm/infos/alljnls

Sponsor: University of Wales College of Medicine.

Alphabetical directory of home pages for many health care journals.

KNOWLEDGE EXCHANGE NETWORK CALENDAR
http://www.mentalhealth.org/calendar/searchcal.cfm

Sponsor: The Center for Mental Health Services, part of Substance Abuse and Mental Health Services Administration, U.S. Department of Health and Human Services.

Directory of conferences with detailed descriptions and contact information. Searchable by date or keyword.

LIBRARY OF THE NATIONAL MEDICAL SOCIETY
http ://www.medical-library.org

Sponsor: National Medical Society.

Full-text online journals available for a subscription fee.

Ψ LINKS TO PSYCHOLOGICAL JOURNALS

http ://pc55w3 .wiso.uni-augsburg.de

Try one of these U.S. mirror sites if the German site does not work:

http://telehealth.net/armin, http://mentalhelp.net/journals,

http://www.psychwww.com/resource/journals.htm

Sponsor: Armin Günther.

More than 1,600 links to print and online psychology and social science journals.

Probably the most comprehensive and frequently updated list of its kind.

Allows searches of the home pages of journals indexed here.

MEDICAL MATRIX: JOURNALS

http://www.medmatrix.org/_SPages/Psychiatry.asp

Sponsor: Medical Matrix Project.

Annotated directory of online health care journals, ranked by an editorial board of physicians.

MEDICAL/HEALTH SCIENCES LIBRARIES ON THE INTERNET

http://www.lib.uiowa. edu/hardin-www/hslibs.html

Sponsor: Hardin Library for the Health Sciences,
University of Iowa.

Regularly updated directory of library home pages.

Ψ MEETINGS, ORGANIZATIONS, AND RESOURCES IN BEHAVIORAL HEALTHCARE

http://www.umdnj.edu/psyevnts/psyjumps.html

Sponsor: Myron Pulier, M.D., Clinical Associate Professor of Psychiatry,
New Jersey Medical School, Newark, NJ.

Lists 3,500 mental health organizations and associations, indexed by name. Meetings and events indexed by location and date. More limited listings of other mental health Internet resources.

Extremely well-organized, with links to the organizations' Web sites as well as their phone numbers and addresses.

Frequently updated. One of the best places on the Internet to find organizations and training resources in mental health.

MENTAL HEALTH INFO SOURCE MEETINGS FOR PHYSICIANS

http://www.mhsource.com/resource/assocmeeting.html

Sponsor: CMI, Inc.

Chronological list of conferences with phone numbers.

Ψ NIMH NEWS & EVENTS

http://www.nimh.nih.gov/events/index.cfm

Sponsor: National Institute of Mental Health.

Directory of scientific meetings sponsored by NJMIH, along with summaries of past meetings.

NEWS & EVENTS

PSYCHIATRY AD REFERENDUM DATABASE

http ://www.info-med. co.uk/adref/genpsy/search.htm

Sponsor: Unknown.

Allows searches of mental health journals by keyword and author, one journal at a time; reprints may be ordered.

Ψ UNITED STATES NATIONAL LIBRARY OF MEDICINE

http://www.n/m.nih.gov

Sponsor: U.S. National Library of Medicine, National Institutes of Health.
Searchable abstracts to more than 4,000 biomedical journals.

Home of MEDLINE, probably the best place to search medical journals. Offers more than 11 million citations, often with abstracts.

Abstracts that you select can be displayed as a single Web page and then saved to your hard drive.

Full-text articles can be ordered online for a fee.

MedLinePlus offers consumer information.

UNIVERSITY OF ADELAIDE LIBRARY: JOURNAL CONTENTS

http://library.adelaide. edu.au/guide/med/menthealth/mentjnl.html

Sponsor: University of Adelaide Library, Australia.

Lists print journals in the fields of mental health and neuroscience.

Many of the journals have an additional link that brings up a reverse chronological list of all the articles in Medline's database that appeared in the journal.

Useful for accessing the tables of contents for journals to which one does not subscribe.

WHICH DATABASE TO USE?

http://www.wooster.edu/library/guides/databases/dbsubjectpsychology.html

Sponsor: College of Wooster (OH).

Directory of databases in psychology, neurosciences, and medicine.

Although many of the databases are viewable only by paid subscribers, a handy table describes the contents of each database.

YALE LIBRARY: MEDICINE: PSYCHIATRY

http://www.med.yale.edu/library/si/select.php3?prof_subject=Medicine~Psychiatry

Sponsor: Cushing-Whitney Medical Library, Yale University.

Lists associations, journals, and clinical guidelines.

Many of the full-text resources are only available to associates of Yale and its hospital.

Cushing/Whitney Medical Library
Selected Internet Resources in Biomedicine

Psychiatry

What's New

Back to...
- SIR Home
- Medical Library
- EPH Library

General...
- Consumer Health
- Databases
- Journals
- Textbooks
- Search Engines

- Associations and Organizations
- Clinical Guidelines
- Databases
- Education Resources
- Images
- Journal Tables of Contents, Abstracts, etc.
- Journals
- Mailing Lists, Discussion Groups and Newsgroups
- Patient Education Resources
- Reference Resources
- Society, Arts, and Ethics
- Subject Guides
- Tests and Measures
- Texts and Textbooks
- Yale University and Yale-New Haven Medical Center

CHAPTER 3
Non-Medical Sites of Interest

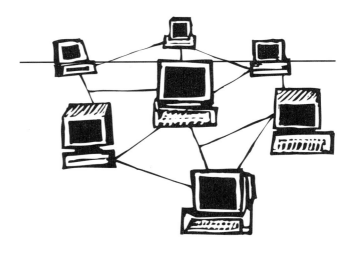

Section 1
Treatment Modalities and Orientations

We do not necessarily endorse any particular modality listed below. Therapists should make personal choices regarding treatment methods they employ.

I. ACUPUNCTURE AND ACUPRESSURE

ACUPRESSURE.ORG
http://www.acupressure.org

Sponsor: Techcoop-Trading SA (Switzerland).

Quotes the definitions of acupressure used on other Web sites and looks for commonalities.

Links to a few other sites.

AMERICAN ACADEMY OF MEDICAL ACUPUNCTURE

http://www.medicalacupuncture.org

Sponsor: American Academy of Medical Acupuncture.

FAQs on acupuncture. Abstracts of recent literature, some with comments on research design.

Has a page of links.

Use the site map to navigate.

BRITISH MEDICAL ACUPUNCTURE SOCIETY

http://www.medical-acupuncture.co.uk

Sponsor: British Medical Acupuncture Society.

Information for professionals and patients.

Complete issues of the Society's journal *Acupuncture in Medicine* available for download.

HIGH TOUCH® JIN SHIN

http://www.hightouchnet.com

Sponsor: High Touch®, a registered trademark of Betsy Ruth Dayton.

Describes a gentle touch technique to "release blockages in the body's energy flows." Describes how to self-administer the technique.

II. ALEXANDER TECHNIQUE

ALEXANDER TECHNIQUE

http://alexandertech.org

Sponsor: American Society for the Alexander Technique.

FAQs, listing of classes and workshops in the U.S., directory of Alexander Technique teachers in the U.S.

Links to related sites.

Ψ ATI

http://www.ati-net.com

Sponsor: Alexander Technique International, an international professional organization.

Extensive online articles from ATI's journal.

Many links to other Internet resources, videos, and books.

Welcome to
ALEXANDER TECHNIQUE INTERNATIONAL ™

The World-wide Professional Organization for the F. M. Alexander Technique

COMPLETE GUIDE TO THE ALEXANDER TECHNIQUE

http://alexandertechnique.com

Sponsor: Two centers that practice the Alexander Technique.

FAQs on the Alexander Technique, help in finding a teacher, and a directory of links about the Alexander Technique.

Summarizes recent and older scientific research.

SOCIETY OF TEACHERS OF THE ALEXANDER TECHNIQUE

http://www.stat.org.uk

Sponsor: Society of Teachers of the Alexander Technique (UK).

Accredits Alexander Technique instructors. Lists courses and approved training resources.

III. ANIMAL-ASSISTED THERAPY

DELTA SOCIETY

http://www.deltasociety.org

Sponsor: Delta Society, an organization promoting "mutually beneficial" animal-human interactions.

Describes Society's programs and publications.

Click on "Table of Contents" to see a directory of other animal-human interaction and animal therapy Web sites.

DOG-PLAY

http://www.dog-play.com/therapyl.html

Sponsor: Diane Blackman.

Extensive directory of pet therapy Web sites.

NATIONAL CENTER FOR EQUINE-FACILITATED THERAPY

http://www.nceft.com

Sponsor: National Center for Equine-Facilitated Therapy.

Brief description of this facility's hippotherapy program.

SUPER DOG ANIMAL-ASSISTED THERAPY

http://www.superdog.com/therapy.htm

Sponsor: Superdog Training (CA).

Contact information for regional pet therapy associations.

Book list with brief reviews.

THERAPET

http://www.therapet.com

Sponsor: Therapet, a nonprofit organization.

Brief descriptions of the benefits of animal-assisted therapy.

IV. ART THERAPY

AMERICAN ART THERAPY ASSOCIATION

http://www.arttherapy.org

Sponsor: American Art Therapy Association, Inc.

News of the AATA, its ethics code, links to other art therapy Web sites, and a brief FAQ section.

AMERICAN ART THERAPY ASSOCIATION, INC.

ART THERAPY CREDENTIALS BOARD

http://www.atcb.org

Sponsor: Art Therapy Credentials Board.

Information about obtaining ATR credentials.

ART THERAPY IN CANADA

http://home.ican.net/~phansen

Sponsor: Petrea Hansen-Adamidis, Hons B.A., Dipl.AT.

Links page for international art therapy resources.

Bibliographies of published articles on art therapy.

Directory of art therapy forums and e-mail discussion lists.

ART THERAPY ON THE WEB

http://www.sofer.com/art-therapy

Sponsor: Danny Sofer, a Web site designer.

Directory of art therapy sites.

ART THERAPY RESEARCH

http://www.arttherapyresearch.homestead.com

Sponsor: Donna J. Betts, M.A., art therapist.

Bibliography of art therapy research, with tips for conducting art therapy research studies.

V. PSYCHOLOGICAL ASTROLOGY

CENTRE FOR PSYCHOLOGICAL ASTROLOGY

http://www.astrologer.com/cpa

Sponsor: Centre for Psychological Astrology (UK).

Operates a workshop and training program to link humanistic psychology with astrology.

Web site has act information and tables of contents from the Centre's past journal issues.

VI. BIBLICAL THERAPY, CHRISTIAN AND PASTORAL COUNSELING

AMERICAN ASSOCIATION OF PASTORAL COUNSELORS

http://www.aapc.org

Sponsor: American Association of Pastoral Counselors (VA), an association of mental health professionals with additional training in pastoral counseling.

Directory of relevant Web sites, membership directory, and their ethics code.

BIBLICAL CHRISTIAN COUNSELING MINISTRIES, INC.

http://www.bccm.org

Sponsor: Biblical Christian Counseling Ministries, Inc. (MO).

The organization establishes "Biblically based, Christian counseling ministries" in churches. Offers courses in "Cognitive Biblical Therapy."

BIBLICAL COUNSELING ASSOCIATION

http://www.biblical-counsel.org

Sponsor: Biblical Counseling Association, "an Internet ministry" (IN).

FAQs concerning the association's fundamentalist perspective on parenting and emotional difficulties.

CHRISTIAN COUNSELING CENTER REFERRAL NETWORK

http://www.hope-healing.com

Sponsor: Center for Christian Therapy, Inc.

Lists Christian counselors and treatment centers in the U.S. that have paid a fee to be listed here.

CHRISTIAN COUNSELING INTERNATIONAL

http://www.cciworld.org

Sponsor: Christian Counseling International (CA).

CCI is a school offering training in "theotherapy," which is an attempt to integrate psychology, theology, and medicine.

FOCUS ON THE FAMILY WITH DR. JAMES DOBSON
http://www.family.org

Sponsor: Focus on the Family, a nonprofit organization headed by Dr. James Dobson, psychologist and broadcaster.

Describes publications and other media available from this organization.

Online articles for the public by Dobson and others.

VII. BIOENERGETICS

Ψ INTERNATIONAL ACADEMY OF BIONETIC PRACTITIONERS
http://www.iabp.net

Sponsor: International Academy of Bionetic Practitioners (CO).

Offers training in bionetics. Streaming video of a bionetic session (free viewer software required).

INTERNATIONAL INSTITUTE FOR BIOENERGETIC ANALYSIS
http://www.bioenergetic-therapy.com

Sponsor: International Institute for Bioenergetic Analysis (NY).

FAQs on Lowen's approach.

Links to online scientific papers.

Directory of therapists in the U.S. and other countries.

Abstracts of recent articles.

Conference information.

VIII. BIOFEEDBACK

Ψ ASSOCIATION FOR APPLIED PSYCHOPHYSIOLOGY AND BIOFEEDBACK
http://www.aapb.org

Sponsor: Association for Applied Psychophysiology and Biofeedback, an association of professionals that disseminates information on clinical practice and research.

FAQs on biofeedback that explain how it works and what conditions it helps.

Well-selected and annotated page of related Web sites.

Searchable list of members in the U.S.

BIOFEEDBACK CERTIFICATION INSTITUTE OF AMERICA

http://www.bcia.org

Sponsor: Biofeedback Certification Institute of America.

Allows a geographical search of practitioners accredited by BCIA. Lists accredited providers of biofeedback training.

Ψ BIOFEEDBACK FOUNDATION OF EUROPE

http://www.bfe.org

Sponsor: Biofeedback Foundation of Europe.

Offers workshops on biofeedback.

Click on "Library" to read detailed protocols for biofeedback treatment of specific conditions.

BIOFEEDBACK NETWORK

http://www.biofeedback.net

Sponsor: Biofeedback Network.

Paid listings for biofeedback providers and professional associations.

BIOFEEDBACK WEBZINE

http://webideas.com/biofeedback

Sponsor: Unknown.

Original research articles, online biofeedback equipment sales, and an international list of biofeedback conferences.

Ψ EEG SPECTRUM

http://www.eegspectrum.com

Sponsor: EEG Spectrum Mental Fitness Training (CA).

Offers training in EEG biofeedback.

Web site features well-organized bibliographies, case histories, and full-text articles on using biofeedback with various emotional disorders, learning disabilities, and other conditions.

IX. BREATH WORK AND REBIRTHING

OPTIMAL BREATHING

http://www.breathing.com

Sponsor: Michael Grant White.

Describes the importance of good breathing for a healthy life.
Sells a relaxation tape.

ASSOCIATION FOR HOLOTROPIC BREATHWORK INTERNATIONAL

http://www.breathwork.com

Sponsor: Association for Holotropic Breathwork International.

Directory of links related to Grof's holotropic breathwork and transpersonal psychology.
Lists workshops for holotropic facilitators.

REBIRTHING: THE MOST ORIGINAL BREATHWORK

http://www.rebirthing.com

Sponsor: Peter Kane, "Certified Rebirther."

Describes rebirthing as a breathing process that enhances a person's connection with feelings.
Describes "Voice Dialogue," an approach to increasing communication and connection between "disowned selves."

www.rebirthing.com

rebirthing the most original breathwork

BREATH AWARENESS CENTER FOR REBIRTHING

http://www.breathaware.com

Sponsor: Breath Awareness Center for Rebirthing (NJ).

Describes breathing techniques as a way to resolve birth trauma.

Instructions for several breathing techniques.

X. BRIEF AND SOLUTION-ORIENTED THERAPY

Ψ BILL O'HANLON

http://www.brieftherapy.com

Sponsor: Bill O'Hanlon, M.S.

O'Hanlon, who was influenced by Milton Erickson (and for a time served as his gardener), describes his "solution-oriented" therapy approach as "less formulaic" than the more well-known Brief Therapy Center (Milwaukee) approach.

Offers some tips for getting unstuck during problem solving.

Much valuable content may be accessed by clicking the "Bill's Attic" link at the bottom of the page. Especially note the bibliographies on solution-based therapy.

Start at "Bill's Attic" and click "Free Handouts." You will arrive at a list of very specific suggestions and assessment questions for use in solution-based therapy.

Ψ BRIEF THERAPY CENTER

http://www.brief-therapy.org

Sponsor: Brief Therapy Center (WI).

Lists the publications of some of the pioneers of solution-focused brief therapy.

Each staff member contributes an article of clinical tips concerning the application of the Center's brief therapy approach.

Books and multimedia materials are available for purchase.

BRIEF THERAPY INSTITUTE OF DENVER

http://www.btid.com

Sponsor: Brief Therapy Institute of Denver, Inc.

Describes services offered by this group practice.

A few FAQs about brief therapy.

MENTAL RESEARCH INSTITUTE

http://www.mri.org

Sponsor: Mental Research Institute, a nonprofit research and clinical institute in Palo Alto, CA.

MRI pioneered strategic therapy beginning in the 1960s. The Web site describes MRI's history, current research projects, and training opportunities.

Don Jackson, MRI's first director, detailed his proposal for MRI in an historic memo, found at http://www.dondjackson.com/probtc.htm.

XI. CO-COUNSELING AND RE-EVALUATION COUNSELING

Ψ CO-COUNSELLING INTERNATIONAL

http://www.dpets.demon.co.uk/cciuk

Sponsor: Co-Counselling International (UK), a network of therapists.

FAQs on co-counseling.

Online manuals for co-counseling teachers.

Directory of relevant Web sites.

RE-EVALUATION COUNSELING

http://www.rc.org

Sponsor: The Re-Evaluation Counseling Committees (WA).

Describes re-evaluation counseling, which is a mutual peer counseling approach.

Online articles from back issues of this organization's journal.

XII. CHIROLOGY

PSYCHODIAGNOSTIC CHIROLOGY

http://www.pdc.co.il

Sponsor: Arnold Holtzman, Ph.D. (Israel).

Articles and case studies on the use of hand reading for psychological diagnosis.

XIII. CLIENT-CENTERED THERAPY

Ψ ALLAN TURNER'S PERSON-CENTRED COUNSELLING HOME PAGE

http://users.powernet.co.uk/pctmk

Sponsor: Allan Turner, a counselor in the UK.

The best Web site we found concerning client-centered approaches.

Links to full-text articles.

Annotated directory of relevant Web sites.

Training and educational resources.

CLIENT-CENTERED THERAPY

http://world.std.com/~mbr2/cct.html

Sponsor: Matt Ryan.

Very brief description of client-centered therapy and a few links.

THE FOCUSING INSTITUTE

http://www.focusing.org

Sponsor: The Focusing Institute.

Describes philosophical and clinical roots of Focusing, a client-centered technique invented by Eugene Gendlin, Ph.D., that helps people learn to identify and work with a "felt sense" of their life space.

Full-text articles about focusing, bibliographies of print materials, literature review of the research on Focusing.

Directory of relevant links.

XIV. COGNITIVE-BEHAVIORAL THERAPY

ASSOCIATION FOR ADVANCEMENT OF BEHAVIOR THERAPY

http://www.aabt.org

Sponsor: Association for Advancement of Behavior Therapy, an organization promoting behavior therapy and cognitive therapy.

Describes the organization, its mission, and its annual conference.

Directory of AABT members.

Fact sheets on various disorders may be obtained from AABT by mail.

BECK INSTITUTE FOR COGNITIVE THERAPY AND RESEARCH

http://www.beckinstitute.org

Sponsor: Beck Institute for Cognitive Therapy and Research (PA).

Describes training programs in cognitive therapy.

Newsletter and lists of publications by the Institute's clinical faculty.

INTERNATIONAL ASSOCIATION OF COGNITIVE PSYCHOTHERAPY

http://iacp.asu.edu

Sponsor: International Association of Cognitive Psychotherapy (MS).

Searchable abstracts of *Journal of Cognitive Psychotherapy*.

Links to other cognitive therapy sites.

NATIONAL ASSOCIATION OF COGNITIVE BEHAVIORAL THERAPISTS

http://www.nacbt.org

Sponsor: National Association of Cognitive Behavioral Therapists, a professional society that accredits cognitive therapists and promotes the teaching of CBT.

Referral database of therapists credentialed by this organization.

Information about the Association's annual conference.

SCHEMA THERAPY

http://www.schematherapy.com

Sponsor: Jeffrey Young, Ph.D., Columbia University Department of Psychiatry.

Describes Schema Therapy, an approach related to cognitive therapy.

Includes slide shows on theory, clinical and research forums, a bibliography, and information on training.

XV. COLOR THERAPY (CHROMOTHERAPY)

COLOR THERAPY & COLOR SYMBOLOGY

http://www.nursehealer.com/Color.htm

Sponsor: NurseHealer.com.

Annotated Web links about color therapy, crystals, psychic healing.

At the bottom of the page are links that produce search results on the term "color therapy" from major Internet search engines.

XVI. DANCE THERAPY

AMERICAN DANCE THERAPY ASSOCIATION

http://www.adta.org

Sponsor: American Dance Therapy Association.

Describes ADTA, which is a professional organization of dance therapists.

Links to related Web sites.

DANCE/MOVEMENT THERAPY LINKS

http://users.erols.com/leopold/DanceMovement.htm

Sponsor: Daniel Leopold.

Links to dance and movement therapy articles, organizations, and individual dance therapists' pages.

XVII. DRAMATHERAPY AND PSYCHODRAMA

AMERICAN SOCIETY OF GROUP PSYCHOTHERAPY AND PSYCHODRAMA

http://www.asgpp.org

Sponsor: American Society of Group Psychotherapy and Psychodrama.

Links to regional chapters, training programs, and the Society's annual conference.

DAVID PRATT, DRAMATHERAPY CONSULTANT

http://freespace.virgin.net/david.pratt3/dramatherapy.htm

Sponsor: David Pratt, a nurse and dramatherapist (UK).

Links to Web sites about dramatherapy and other creative arts therapies.

NATIONAL ASSOCIATION FOR DRAMA THERAPY

http://www.nadt.org

Sponsor: National Association for Drama Therapy.

Describes the association. Lists conferences and workshops.

Click on "Government Affairs" to find links for other creative therapy Web sites.

PSYCHODRAMA SECTION, INTERNATIONAL ASSOCIATION OF GROUP PSYCHOTHERAPY

http://members.tripod.com/~portaroma/iagp_pd.htm

Sponsor: International Association of Group Psychotherapy.

Extensive bibliography of published articles and books on psychodrama.

Directory of relevant Web sites.

Links for psychodrama journals and mailing lists.

PSYCHODRAMA TRAINING INSTITUTE

http://www.psychodramanyc.com

Sponsor: Psychodrama Training Institute (NY).

Offers training in psychodrama.

**Psychodrama
Training Institute**

PSYCHODRAMA: WORLDWIDE COMMUNITY

http://www.psychodrama.ch

Sponsor: Swedish Moreno Institute.

Lists Web sites of psychodrama organizations and training programs; directory of other links about psychodrama.

XVIII. ECOPSYCHOLOGY

ECOPSYCHOLOGY ONLINE

http://isis.csuhayward.edu/ALSS/ECO

Sponsor: The Ecopsychology Institute, California State University at Hayward.

Online magazine, with the most recent issue dated 1998.

GREEN EARTH FOUNDATION

http://www.rmetzner-greenearth.org

Sponsors: Green Earth Foundation (CA); Ralph Metzner, Ph.D.

Articles and links focusing on the "healing and harmonizing of the relationships between humanity and the Earth."

Directory of Web sites related to hallucinogenic drug experiences.

 Green Earth Foundation

PROJECT NATURECONNECT

http://www.ecopsych.com

Sponsor: Institute of Global Education (WA).

Offers online courses (for a fee) and interactive online experiences that aim to reconnect people with nature.

XIX. EYE MOVEMENT DESENSITIZATION AND REPROCESSING (EMDR)

EMDR INTERNATIONAL ASSOCIATION

http://www.emdria.org/main.html

Sponsor: EMDR International Association.

FAQs on EMDR.

Information about the Association's certification programs.

Directory of certified members.

Links to other EMDR Web sites.

Ψ EMDR INSTITUTE

http://www.emdr.com

Sponsor: EMDR Institute, Inc. (CA).

FAQs about EMDR for professionals and the general public.

Extensive and well-referenced reviews of research on EMDR and its efficacy.

Information about EMDR training programs.

EYE MOVEMENT DESENSITIZATION AND REPROCESSING

Ψ EMDR PORTAL

http://www.emdrportal.com

Sponsor: Tom Cloyd, M.S., M.A.

Articles, questionnaires, forms, and treatment protocols.

Links to related Web sites and EMDR practitioners.

The site is frequently updated.

EMDR PRACTITIONER

http://www.emdr-practitioner.net

Sponsor: EMDR Association of Europe.

An electronic online journal.

Book and multimedia reviews.

Full-text articles.

Country-specific links to news and contact persons in a number of European countries.

THE STRATEGIC DEVELOPMENTAL MODEL FOR EMDR

http://www.kitchur.org

Sponsor: Maureen Kitchur, M.S.W, R.S.W.

Describes Kitchur's model for developing a rapid, focused EMDR treatment plan that she claims will produce "comprehensive healing."

XX. FENG SHUI

FENG SHUI DIRECTORY OF CONSULTANTS

http://www.fengshuidirectory.com

Sponsor: Art Restoration Services (VA).

Online articles and bibliography of print materials.

Discussion board.

Lists feng shui consultants and training programs.

FENG SHUI GUILD

http://www.fengshuiguild.com

Sponsor: Feng Shui Guild.

Web site for an international organization promoting the teaching of feng shui.

Lists educational programs and local feng shui chapter meetings.

Online articles.

GEOMANCY.NET

http://www.geomancy.net

Sponsor: Geomancy.Net.

Offers free and fee-based feng shui information and planning tools.

XXI. GESTALT THERAPY

GESTALT!

http://www.g-g.org/gestalt!

Sponsor: Gestalt!, *an online journal on Gestalt therapy.*

Full-text articles on Gestalt theory.

Directory of Web sites about Gestalt theory and Gestalt therapy.

GESTALT THERAPY PAGE

http://www.gestalt.org

Sponsor: International Gestalt Therapy Association.

Click on "contents page" to find historical articles, documents, and old photographs relating to the origins of Gestalt therapy.

Lists upcoming workshops and training seminars.

Worldwide directory of Gestalt therapists.

Ψ INTERNATIONAL SOCIETY FOR GESTALT THEORY AND ITS APPLICATIONS

http://www.enabling.org/ia/gestalt/gerhards/gtax.html

Sponsor: International Society for Gestalt Theory and Its Applications.

Many resources concerning Gestalt Theory, including full-text articles, bibliographies, and conference information.

Links to Web sites about Gestalt therapy.

International directory of Gestalt therapy training institutes.

XXII. GROUP THERAPY

AMERICAN GROUP PSYCHOTHERAPY ASSOCIATION

http://www.groupsinc.org

Sponsor: American Group Psychotherapy Association.

Describes the Association.

Brief FAQ section about group psychotherapy.

GROUP PSYCHOTHERAPY HOME PAGE

http://www.group-psychotherapy.com

Sponsor: Haim Weinberg, psychologist and chair of the Israel Group Psychotherapy Association.

Directory of upcoming conferences.

Directory of group psychotherapy and group dynamics institutes and training centers.

Brief FAQ section about group therapy.

INTERNATIONAL ASSOCIATION OF GROUP PSYCHOTHERAPY

http://www.psych.mcgill.ca/labs/iagp/IAGP.html

Sponsor: International Association of Group Psychotherapy.

Click on "Electronic Forum" for a list of Web sites about group therapy and related subjects.

XXIII. HAKOMI

HAKOMI

http://www.hakomi.com

Sponsor: Ron Kurtz Training, Inc. (OR).

Links to other Web sites about Hakomi, which is "the integrative use of mindfulness, the body, and nonviolence in psychotherapy."

Click on either "Hakomi Institute" or "Hakomi Institute of San Francisco" to see Web sites with detailed FAQs about Hakomi.

XXIV. HUMANISTIC PSYCHOLOGY

A. H. MASLOW PUBLICATIONS

http://www.maslow.com

Sponsor: A. H. Maslow Publications.

Bibliography of Maslow's publications.

ASSOCIATION FOR HUMANISTIC PSYCHOLOGY

http://www.ahpweb.org

Sponsor: Association for Humanistic Psychology.

Selected full-text articles from AHP's magazine and journal.

Click on "Internet Connections" to see an annotated directory of Web sites about humanistic psychology.

Lists AHP professional members and their Web sites.

XXV. HYPNOSIS

AMERICAN SOCIETY OF CLINICAL HYPNOSIS

http://www.asch.net

Sponsor: American Society of Clinical Hypnosis.

Describes workshops, conferences, and the certification program of the society.

Brief FAQ section about hypnosis.

Links page to conferences and other hypnosis associations.

HYPNOSIS ONLINE IN THE UK

http://www.hypnosis.org.uk

Sponsor: Charles Barr, Ph.D., Hertford (UK).

FAQs on hypnosis (although many authorities would disagree with some of the information).

Good list of links to other hypnosis Web sites.

MILTON H. ERICKSON FOUNDATION

http://www.erickson-foundation.org

Sponsor: Milton H. Erickson Foundation, a nonprofit corporation with the mission of promoting Erickson's contributions to clinical hypnosis and psychotherapy.

Describes the Foundation's conferences and publications.

Links to full-text articles about Milton Erickson, hypnosis, and strategic therapies.

Ψ SCIENTIFIC HYPNOSIS HOME PAGE

http://www.hypnosis-research.org/hypnosis/index.html

Sponsors: Jean Holroyd, Ph.D.; Susan King Obarski, M.F.A.; Society for Clinical and Experimental Hypnosis.

Excellent searchable database of more than 11,000 articles from the hypnosis literature.

Scientifically based FAQs concerning hypnosis.

Links to hypnosis associations.

Bulletin board for discussion of hypnosis research designs ("Researchers Talk Shop").

SOCIETY FOR CLINICAL AND EXPERIMENTAL HYPNOSIS

http://sunsite.utk.edu/IJCEH/scehframe.htm

Sponsor: Society for Clinical and Experimental Hypnosis.

Abstracts from *International Journal of Clinical and Experimental Hypnosis.*

Information about the Society's annual conference and workshops.

XXVI. KINESIOLOGY

AMERICAN ACADEMY OF KINESIOLOGY AND PHYSICAL EDUCATION

http://www.aakpe.org

Sponsor: American Academy of Kinesiology and Physical Education.

Online membership directory and newsletters.

HEALTH KINESIOLOGY UK

http://www.healthk.co.uk

Sponsor: Health Kinesiology UK.

FAQs, self-help techniques, case histories, and directories of practitioners.

KINESIOLOGY NETWORK

http://www.kinesiology.net

Sponsor: Kinesiology Network (Sweden).

FAQs and links about kinesiology and muscle testing.

TOUCH FOR HEALTH KINESIOLOGY ASSOCIATION

http://www.tfh.org

Sponsor: Touch for Health Kinesiology Association.

Describes a system of muscle testing and balancing; lists certified instructors.

XXVII. MARRIAGE AND FAMILY THERAPY

AMERICAN ASSOCIATION FOR MARRIAGE AND FAMILY THERAPY

http://www.aamft.org

Sponsor: American Association for Marriage and Family Therapy.

FAQs about brief marriage and family therapy.

Online articles for the general public about parenting and family issues.

Information about AAMFT's conferences and publications.

COALITION FOR MARRIAGE, FAMILY, AND COUPLES EDUCATION

http://www.smartmarriages.com

Sponsor: The Coalition for Marriage, Family, and Couples Education, LLC (DC).

Extensive links to full-text articles about teaching people marriage skills.

Books and tapes for sale.

The Coalition for Marriage, Family and Couples Education, LLC

DON JACKSON OFFICIAL WEB SITE

http://www.dondjackson.com

Sponsor: Mental Research Institute, a nonprofit research and clinical institute in Palo Alto, CA.

Biography and historical documents of one of the founders of family therapy.

MFT INFOLINK

http://www.enol.com/~sherman/MFT/MFT.html

Sponsor: Jonathan D. Sherman, M.S., a marriage and family therapist in Utah.

Links to Web sites on various theoretical orientations within family therapy.

Includes full-text articles about marriage and family therapy as a career and links to graduate educational programs in MFT.

This site is not frequently updated.

Ψ MFT RESOURCES ON THE WORLD WIDE WEB

http://www.nova.edu/ssss/FT/web.html

Sponsors: Ron Chenail, Ph.D.; and Cody W. Smith; Nova Southeastern University (FL).

Directory of family therapy organization home pages, journals, online articles, mailing lists, and other Internet resources.

XXVIII. MUSIC THERAPY

AMERICAN MUSIC THERAPY ASSOCIATION

http://www.musictherapy.org

Sponsor: American Music Therapy Association.

FAQs about music therapy. Information about AMTA publications and conferences and about careers in music therapy.

MUSIC THERAPY INFO LINK

http://members.aol.com/kathysl

Sponsor: Katherine A. Lindberg, MT-BC.

FAQs on music therapy.

Directory of Web sites on music therapy which is not frequently updated.

Ψ PRELUDE MUSIC THERAPY

http://preludetherapy.home.att.net

Sponsor: Prelude Music Therapy.

Good FAQs on music therapy by an online store that sells music therapy materials for children with special needs. Good directory of other music therapy sites.

XXIX. MYERS-BRIGGS/KEIRSEY TYPOLOGY

THE CULT OF PERSONALITIES

http://elvis.rowan.edu/~cusumano/MBPerson.html

Sponsor: Cusumano Computing Solutions.

Links for the Keirsey Temperament Sorter, an instrument that calculates personality types.

This Web site is not frequently updated.

KEIRSEY TEMPERAMENT AND CHARACTER WEB SITE

http://www.keirsey.com

Sponsor: David Keirsey, Ph.D., a computer scientist.

Home page for Keirsey's personality typing instruments, which can be taken online.

Ψ MYERS-BRIGGS PERSONALITY TYPE ON THE WEB

http://www.mbtypeguide.com/Type

Sponsor: Mary D. Hoerr, a Web designer.

Extensive reviewed links for Web sites on the Myers-Briggs Type Indicator and similar instruments that aim to identify personality types based on Jungian concepts.

XXX. NARRATIVE THERAPY

Ψ NARRATIVE PSYCHOLOGY INTERNET AND RESOURCE GUIDE

http://maple.lemoyne.edu/~hevern/narpsych.html

Sponsor: Vincent W. Hevern, SJ, Ph.D.

Extensive and well-organized directory of Web sites on narrative therapy and psychology.

NARRATIVE THERAPY BIBLIOGRAPHY

http://www.possibilitycenter.com/bt/docs/attic/narrative.htm

Sponsor: Bill O'Hanlon, M.S.

Lists published articles on narrative therapy.

NARRATIVE THERAPY BIBLIOGRAPHY

Ψ NARRATIVEAPPROACHES.COM

http://www.narrativeapproaches.com

Sponsors: Jennifer Freeman, David Epston, Dean Lobovits.

Full-text articles about narrative therapy with children.

Many links to other Web sites and bibliographies.

Click on the circular graphic at the top of the page for a handy table of contents for this site.

XXXI. NEUROLINGUISTIC PROGRAMMING (NLP)

ASSOCIATION FOR NEUROLINGUISTIC PROGRAMMING

http://www.anlp.org

Sponsor: Association for Neurolinguistic Programming (UK).

Lists NLP practice groups in the UK.

Brief list of NLP Web sites.

INSTITUTE OF NEURO-SEMANTICS

http://www.neurosemantics.com

Sponsors: Bobby G. Bodenhamer, DMin; Michael Hall, Ph.D.

Extensive online articles about NLP and extensions of the original NLP framework.

Links to other NLP resources.

Ψ NEURO-LINGUISTIC PROGRAMMING RESEARCH DATABASE

http://www.nlp.de/research

Sponsor: Dr. Franz-Josef Hücker (Germany).

Searchable abstracts of empirical investigations of NLP, including dissertations and published articles.

Ψ NLP INFORMATION CENTER

http://www.nlpinfo.com

Sponsor: Advanced Neuro Dynamics (HI).

FAQs about NLP.

Extensive and annotated directory of NLP Web sites.

NLP RESOURCES

http://www.nlpresources.com

Sponsor: Andrew Peacock.

Articles by Andrew Peacock on various aspects of NLP. Categorized links to other NLP sites.

NLP *Resources*

Dedicated to providing you with NLP tools, techniques and contacts for you to improve the quality of your life.

XXXII. ORGONOMY AND NEO-REICHIAN THERAPIES

AMERICAN COLLEGE OF ORGONOMY

http://www.orgonomy.org

Sponsor: American College of Orgonomy.

FAQs and online articles about orgonomy. Case histories.

THE ERTH (EMBODIED RELATIONAL THERAPY) PAGE

http://ourworld.compuserve.com/homepages/selfheal

Sponsor: Nick Totten.

Describes ErTh, an offshoot of Reichian bodywork.

INSTITUTE FOR ORGONOMIC SCIENCE

http://www.orgonomicscience.org

Sponsor: Institute for Orgonomic Science (NJ).

Offers training for physicians in orgone therapy.

ORGONE BIOPHYSICAL RESEARCH LABORATORY

http://www.orgonelab.org

Sponsor: Orgone Biophysical Research Laboratory, Inc. (OR).

Articles on orgone therapy by the Laboratory's director.

Directory of links criticizing the idea that HIV / AIDS is communicated by infection.

Links to other orgonomy Internet resources.

XXXIII. ORTHOMOLECULAR PSYCHIATRY

Ψ ORTHOMOLECULAR MEDICINE

http://www.orthomed.com

Sponsor: Robert F. Cathcart, M.D., an orthomolecular practitioner.

Extensive directory of links to full-text articles and other Web sites on relevant topics.

Includes links that criticize orthomolecular medicine, which are annotated with Dr. Cathcart's critique of their bias or methodological flaws.

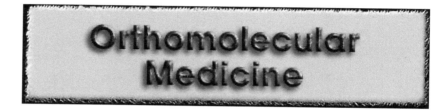

Ψ ORTHOMOLECULAR MEDICINE ONLINE

http://www.orthomed.org

Sponsor: International Society for Orthomolecular Medicine.

Describes the Society and its mission.

Full-text articles from *Journal of Orthomolecular Medicine.*

Current news of the field.

Links to Web resources.

XXXIV. PAST LIFE REGRESSION THERAPY

INTERNATIONAL ASSOCIATION FOR REGRESSION RESEARCH AND THERAPIES, INC.

http://www.aprt.org

Sponsor: International Association for Regression Research and Therapies, Inc.

Describes the mission, activities, and publications of IARRT, which claims over 1,000 members around the world.

Annotated tables of contents for IARRT's journal through 1999.

Lists upcoming workshops.

PAST LIVES REGRESSION THERAPY

http://www.pastlives.org

Sponsor: Ann C. Barham, M.A (CA).

FAQs about using hypnosis to elicit traumatic experiences from past lives and thereby relieve the effects of those experiences on the present.

Links to other relevant Web sites.

XXXV. PLAY THERAPY

ASSOCIATION FOR PLAY THERAPY, INC.

http://www.iapt.org

Sponsor: Association for Play Therapy, Inc., an international professional association.

Describes the Association's goals, publications, and conferences.

Summarizes the research on play therapy and filial play therapy.

FAMILY ENHANCEMENT AND PLAY THERAPY CENTER

http://www.play-therapy.com

Sponsor: Risë Van Fleet, Ph.D., RPT-S (PA).

Good FAQs on play therapy and filial play therapy (in which parents learn to hold play therapy sessions with their own children).

Schedule of training workshops.

Brief online articles about play therapy techniques (click on "Play Therapy Ideas").

INTERNATIONAL SOCIETY FOR CHILD AND PLAY THERAPY/ PLAY THERAPY INTERNATIONAL

http://www.playtherapy.org

Sponsors: International Society for Child and Play Therapy/Play Therapy International and Canadian Play Therapy Institute.

Lists print resources on play therapy.

Describes certification and training programs offered by the Society.

INTERNATIONAL SOCIETY FOR SANDPLAY THERAPY

http://www.sandplay.org

Sponsor: International Society for Sandplay Therapy.

Full-text articles about sandplay therapy.

Lists Web sites about sandplay, Jungian concepts, and symbolism.

Offers classes on conducting sandplay therapy.

TRANSPERSONAL SANDPLAY THERAPY CENTER

http://www.sandplay.net

Sponsor: Transpersonal Sandplay Therapy Center (CT).

Historical information about the use of sandplay for diagnosis and treatment.

Compares different schools.

Bibliography of printed books and articles.

XXXVI. POLARITY THERAPY

AMERICAN POLARITY THERAPY ASSOCIATION

http://www.polaritytherapy.org

Sponsor: American Polarity Therapy Association.

FAQs about aspects of polarity therapy.

Past issues of APTA's newsletters, including case studies, available in PDF format.

XXXVII. PRIMAL AND REGRESSIVE THERAPIES

DR. ARTHUR JANOV'S PRIMAL THERAPY CENTER

http://www.primaltherapy.com

Sponsor: Primal Treatment Training and Research Center, the Primal Foundation (CA).

Information about primal therapy, with lists of available publications and videos.

Describes Dr. Janov's treatment program and also notes the available of "long-distance therapy" via live videoconferencing.

 *DR. ARTHUR JANOV's PRIMAL CENTER*

Ψ THE REGRESSION THERAPY PAGE

http://www.geocities.com/HotSprings/Spa/7173

Sponsor: Unknown.

Extensive links to full-text articles and other Web sites about primal therapy and other regression therapies.

XXXVIII. PSYCHOANALYSIS

AMERICAN ACADEMY OF PSYCHOANALYSIS

http://www.aapsa.org

Sponsor: American Academy of Psychoanalysis.

Describes the Academy's meetings and publications.

Full-text articles from recent issues of the Academy's newsletter and tables of contents from its journal.

Ψ AMERICAN PSYCHOANALYTIC ASSOCIATION

http://www.apsa.org

Sponsor: American Psychoanalytic Association.

Officers, meetings, and activities of APSA.

Links to other psychoanalytic Web sites.

Searchable database of more than 30,000 psychoanalytic articles and books.

Full-text articles from the Association's newsletter.

Abstracts from current and back issues of *Journal of the American Psychoanalytic Association.*

AMERICAN SOCIETY OF PSYCHOANALYTIC PHYSICIANS

http://pubweb.acns.nwu.edu/~chessick/aspp.htm

Sponsor: American Society of Psychoanalytic Physicians.

Describes the Society and provides contact information.

THE ANNA FREUD CENTRE

http://www.annafreudcentre.org

Sponsor: The Anna Freud Centre (UK).

Describes training and treatment services offered at this center for child psychoanalysis.

Full-text articles describing research done at the Centre.

Links to other Web sites on psychoanalysis and parenting.

Ψ INTERNATIONAL PSYCHOANALYTICAL ASSOCIATION

http://www.ipa.org.uk

Sponsor: International Psychoanalytical Association.

Links to component psychoanalytic societies and to other professional associations in many countries.

The server is sometimes slow, requiring a wait before the site loads.

An outstanding Web-only resource is an "open door" review of outcome studies concerning psychoanalytic treatment, found at http://www.ipa.org.uk/R-outcome.htm.

Full-text articles from IPA's journal (*International Psychoanalysis*) and newsletter.

MEDWEB PLUS: PSYCHOANALYSIS

http://www.medwebplus.com/subject/Psychoanalysis.html

Sponsor: y-DNA, Inc.

Directory of Web sites for journals and psychoanalytic associations.

NATIONAL PSYCHOLOGICAL ASSOCIATION FOR PSYCHOANALYSIS

http://www.npap.org

Sponsor: National Psychological Association for Psychoanalysis, an organization that trains nonmedical psychoanalysts.

Training programs and workshops offered by NPAP.

FAQs about psychoanalysis and psychotherapy.

NEW ENGLAND INSTITUTE FOR PSYCHOANALYTIC STUDIES ONLINE CAMPUS LIBRARY

http://www.neips.org./campus/resources/library/index.htm

Sponsor: New England Institute for Psychoanalytic Studies.

Links to Web sites and full-text articles about psychoanalysis, its founders, and current journals and publishers.

Ψ PSYCHOANALYSE ONLINE

http://www.crosswinds.net/~muhs/engl.htm

Sponsor: Dr. Aribert Muhs (Karlsruhe, Germany).

Well-organized links to over 300 Web sites for psychoanalytic training institutes, journals, museums in the U.S., Europe, and South America.

Ψ SELF PSYCHOLOGY PAGE

http://www.selfpsychology.org

Sponsor: International Council for Psychoanalytic Self Psychology.

Focus is the Self Psychology approach of Heinz Kohut.

Original papers and conference abstracts.

Many articles and lectures by well-known advocates of self psychology can only be found here.

Links to other Web sites offering training in self psychology and psychoanalysis.

SIGMUND FREUD AND THE FREUD ARCHIVES

http://plaza.interport.net/nypsan/freudarc.html

Sponsor: New York Psychoanalytic Institute and Society.

Links to archival materials about Freud, public domain translations of some of Freud's writings, and a few articles about Freud.

WORLD ASSOCIATION OF PSYCHOANALYSIS

http://www.wapol.org

Sponsor: World Association of Psychoanalysis, an association with the mission of disseminating the ideas of Jacques Lacan.

Links to publications and Web sites concerning Lacanian psychoanalysis.

Some of the Web site and most of the links are in non-English languages (especially French, Spanish, and Portuguese).

XXXIX. RATIONAL EMOTIVE BEHAVIOR THERAPY

ALBERT ELLIS INSTITUTE

http://www.rebt.org

Sponsor: Albert Ellis Institute.

Training in REBT, full-text articles about REBT, and a selected bibliography of publications.

Click on "Professionals" for "Essay of the Month Index," with most articles written by Ellis.

CENTRE FOR RATIONAL EMOTIVE BEHAVIOUR THERAPY

http://members.tripod.co.uk/Stress_Centre

Sponsor: Centre for Rational Emotive Behaviour Therapy (UK).

Describes the Centre's courses in REBT.

Selected bibliography of published self-help and professional materials on RET and cognitive therapy.

A few links to relevant organizations.

RATIONAL EMOTIVE SPIRITUAL THERAPY

http://www.restcounseling.com

Sponsor: T.R.E.T.ment Christian Counseling Services, an organization that trains pastors and lay persons as Certified Christian Counselors to operate group therapy programs in churches.

Features a general description of this organization's approach and programs. Under construction at the time of our visit.

XL. REIKI

INTERNATIONAL CENTER FOR REIKI TRAINING
http://www.reiki.org

Sponsor: International Center for Reiki Training.

FAQs about Reiki.

Lists Reiki classes and describes levels of training.

More than 100 full-text articles about Reiki.

Information on developing a Reiki practice.

THE REIKI CAFE
http://www.whitefire.com/reiki

Sponsor: The Reiki Cafe.

Reiki chat area and bulletin board.

Links to other sites about Reiki.

Ψ REIKI PAGES BY LIGHT AND ADONEA
http://www.angelfire.com/az/SpiritMatters/index.html

Sponsor: Light and Adonea, Reiki teachers (AZ).

The most extensive list of Reiki links.

Numerous FAQs and original articles about Reiki, detailing specific techniques.

Reiki mailing lists and chat areas on the Internet.

REIKI, REIKI 4 ALL

http://www.reikicentrum.nl/reiki4all

Sponsor: Remy Williams.

A few general FAQs about Reiki.

XLI. ROLFING

GUILD FOR STRUCTURAL INTEGRATION

http://www.rolfguild.org

Sponsor: Guild for Structural Integration (CO).

Offers training in "the traditional Ida P. Rolf Method of Structural Integration," which is "a process of re-education of the body through movement and touch [that] systematically releases patterns of stress and impaired function."

FAQs and schedule of classes.

ROLF INSTITUTE OF STRUCTURAL INTEGRATION

http://www.rolf.org

Sponsor: Rolf Institute of Structural Integration (CO).

Describes principles of Rolfing, "a holistic system of soft tissue manipulation and movement education that organized the whole body in gravity."

FAQs about Rolfing.

Directory of Institute-certified practitioners.

XLII. SOMATIC TRAUMA THERAPY

Ψ SOMATIC TRAUMA THERAPY

http://www.nwc.net/personal/babette/somatic.htm

Sponsor: Babette Rothschild, M.S.W., L.C.S.W. (CA).

Full-text articles by Rothschild that describe how to help reduce somatic hyperarousal in clients with PTSD.

Although the site is not extensive, the material is an important aspect of PTSD treatment that has generally gotten short shrift in print.

XLIII. SUFI PSYCHOLOGY

LIST OF SUFI-RELATED RESOURCES ON THE INTERNET

http://world.std.com/~habib/sufi.html

Sponsor: Steve Habib Rose.

Discussion groups, Usenet newsgroups, and Web sites about Sufism and related topics.

SUFI PSYCHOLOGY ASSOCIATION

http://sufi-psychology.org

Sponsor: Sufi Psychology Association.

Brief description of the Association and its conferences, with contact information.

XLIV. THOUGHT FIELD THERAPY

CALLAHAN TECHNIQUES THOUGHT FIELD THERAPY

http://www.tftrx.com

Sponsor: Dr. Roger Callahan, founder of Thought Field Therapy (CA).

Describes Callahan's approach.

A few online articles about TFT and its applications; testimonials from professionals.

THOUGHT FIELD THERAPY IN THE UK

http://www.thoughtfield.co.uk

Sponsors: Robin and Mary Ellis (UK).

Brief description of TFT and contact information for the Ellises.

THOUGHT FIELD THERAPY TRAINING CENTER OF LA JOLLA

http://www.thoughtfield.com

Sponsor: Thought Field Therapy Training Center of La Jolla (CA).

FAQs about Thought Field Therapy.

Lists the Center's training program in TFT.

XLV. TRANSACTIONAL ANALYSIS

THE BERNE INSTITUTE

http://www.theberne.com

Sponsor: The Berne Institute (UK).

Offers training in TA.

Brief directory of Web sites for TA organizations and training institutes.

INSTITUTE OF TRANSACTIONAL ANALYSIS

http://www.ita.org.uk

Sponsor: Institute of Transactional Analysis (UK).

FAQs about TA and its applications.

Lists TA practitioners in the UK.

INTERNATIONAL TRANSACTIONAL ANALYSIS ASSOCIATION

http://www.itaa-net.org

Sponsor: International Transactional Analysis Association.

Describes the association.

Lists TA publications and resources.

Historical material about TA, the ITAA, and a biography of its founder, Eric Berne.

Click on "Transactional Analysis" to see a directory of relevant Web sites.

XLVI. TRANSPERSONAL PSYCHOLOGY

ASSOCIATION FOR TRANSPERSONAL PSYCHOLOGY

http://www.atpweb.org

Sponsor: Association for Transpersonal Psychology.

Describes the Association.

Lists training programs in transpersonal psychology.

Tables of contents for *Journal of Transpersonal Psychology.*

INSTITUTE OF TRANSPERSONAL PSYCHOLOGY

http://www.itp.edu

Sponsor: Institute of Transpersonal Psychology (CA).

Describes ITP's training program and facilities.

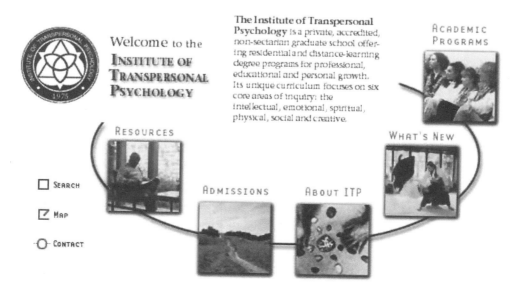

TRANSPERSONAL PSYCHOLOGY LINKS

http://www.mdani.demon.co.uk/trans/tranlink.htm

Sponsor: Michael Daniels, Centre for Applied Psychology, John Moores University (Liverpool, UK).

Organizations, publications, and Web sites about transpersonal psychology.

Ψ WORLD WIDE WEB VIRTUAL LIBRARY: TRANSPERSONAL PSYCHOLOGY

http://www.clas.ufl.edu/users/gthursby/psi/trperson.htm

Sponsor: Gene R. Thursby, Ph.D., University of Florida.

Annotated directory of transpersonal psychology Web sites.

XLVII. VIDEO THERAPY

VIDEO IMPROVEMENT PROGRAM

http://www.videoimprovement.com

Sponsor: Robert F. Stamps.

Video Improvement (VIP) is a video-based counseling program for young people, and it includes an optional Internet-based client discussion room.

VIP can be done by all types of counselors.

XLVIII. YOGA

Ψ SPIRITWEB: YOGA PATHS

http://www.spiritweb.org/Spirit/yoga.html

Sponsor: SpiritWeb.

Describes different schools of yoga.

Extensive links to other yoga Web sites.

THE YOGA SITE

http://www.yogasite.com

Sponsor: Yoga Site.

Online articles and FAQs about yoga.
Lists yoga organizations and mailing lists.
Describes different styles of yoga practice.

YOGAFINDER.COM

http://www.yogafinder.com

Sponsor: Terry Ryan.

Lists yoga teachers by geographical area.
Links to yoga-related Web sites.

Section 2
Computers and Mental
Health

Ψ COMPUTERS AND MENTAL HEALTH

http://mentalhealth.about.com/health/mentalhealth/msub36.htm

Sponsor: Leonard Holmes, Ph.D.

Surveys the various ways that mental health consumers and practitioners can use computers, Internet resources, and software.

The links on this page lead to thoughtful discussions of topics such as chat communities, software, virtual reality treatment for phobias, Web rings, and online psychological tests. Each discussion has its own relevant links.

COMPUTERS IN MENTAL HEALTH

http://www.ex.ac.uk/cimh/welcome.htm

Sponsor: Department of Mental Health, University of Exeter (UK).

Megasite focusing on the use of computers by mental health professionals.

Database of mental health software—tests, statistics, scheduling, billing—with some detailed reviews.

Extensive links to full-text articles about computer applications in mental health.

CTI PSYCHOLOGY

http://www.york.ac.uk/inst/ctipsych

Sponsor: A consortium within the UK supporting the use of information technologies in higher education.

Extensive megasite of computer applications of psychology, such as software that conducts experiments, software reviews, and case studies of information technology use within academic psychology departments.

PSYCHOLOGY OF PROGRAMMING INTEREST GROUP

http://www.ppig.org

Sponsor: Psychology of Programming Interest Group (UK).
Newsletters of PPIG, workshops, and other events.

PSYCLINK

http://www.plattsburgh.edu/psyclink

Sponsor: PsycLink Software Information Service, State University of New York, Plattsburgh.

Free downloadable software for clinicians and researchers.

Directory of software available for purchase from smaller companies and individual programmers.

SHRINKTAB WEB

http://www.shrinktank.com

Sponsor: Robert Bischoff.

Includes older software related to mental health, such as Eliza "therapy simulators," quizzes, and rating scales.

SIBYL HOME PAGE

http://www.gamma.rug.nl/sibyl.html

Sponsor: Software Information Bank of iec ProGamma.

Searchable descriptions of software, with contact information. Database was under renovation at the time of our visit.

SOCIETY FOR COMPUTERS IN PSYCHOLOGY

http://ww2.lafayette.edu/~allanr/scip.html

Sponsor: Society for Computers in Psychology.

Describes the Society's mission—to advance the use of computers in psychological research and instruction—and the Society's conferences.

The Society for Computers in Psychology

Section 3
Criminal Justice,
Forensics, Mental Health
Law, and Assorted Legal
Issues

I. GENERAL CRIMINAL JUSTICE

CRIMINAL JUSTICE DATABASE OF WWW RESOURCES
http://www2.una.edu/soccrimjust/cjdb.htm

Sponsor: Department of Sociology/Criminal Justice, University of North Alabama.

Lists URLs for Federal law enforcement and prison agencies. This site is not frequently updated.

CRIMINAL JUSTICE LINKS
http://www.criminology.fsu.edu/cj.html

Sponsor: Cecil Greek, Florida State University College of Criminology and Criminal Justice.

Thousands of links to criminal justice agencies, police and court sites, and educational resources in forensic science and criminal justice.

Not updated frequently.

CRIMINAL JUSTICE SYSTEM

http://www.criminal-justice-system.gov.uk

Sponsor: Police and prison systems in England and Wales.

Describes the various law enforcement and prison agencies within the UK.

Ψ LEGAL INFORMATION INSTITUTE

http://www.law.cornell.edu/focus/liieye.htm

Sponsor: Cornell University Law School.

Extensive links to State constitutions, codes, and court decisions.

Click on "Current Awareness: Eye on the Court" for searchable information about recent Supreme Court and other appellate decisions.

NATIONAL ARCHIVE OF CRIMINAL JUSTICE DATA

http://www.icpsr.umich.edu/NACJD

Sponsor: Inter-university Consortium for Political and Social Research, U.S. Department of Justice.

Downloadable raw data on national and international crime.

Gives examples of SAS and SPSS command files for manipulating the data; one of these programs is necessary for summarizing and interpreting the data files.

Ψ SOURCEBOOK OF CRIMINAL JUSTICE STATISTICS

http://www.albany.edu/sourcebook

Sponsor: Utilization of Criminal Justice Statistics Project, University of Albany (NY).

In Adobe Acrobat .PDF format, the Web site provides tables of U.S. data on public attitudes towards crime and the justice system, numbers of offenses and characteristics of arrested persons, and the prison population.

II. JUVENILE DELINQUENCY

NATIONAL CENTER FOR JUVENILE JUSTICE

http://www.ncjj.org

Sponsor: Research Division, National Council of Juvenile and Family Court Judges.

Statistics on juveniles as offenders and victims, in the form of FAQs.

Profiles the juvenile justice system in each U.S. state.

Ψ OFFICE OF JUVENILE JUSTICE AND DELINQUENCY PREVENTION

http://ojjdp.ncjrs.org

Sponsor: U.S. Department of Justice.

Information about this agency and its programs.

Extensive links to other Web sites about youth violence and the juvenile justice system.

III. MENTAL HEALTH LAW

INSTITUTE OF LAW, PSYCHIATRY, AND PUBLIC POLICY

http://ness.sys.virginia.edu/ilppp

Sponsor: University of Virginia.

Describes research projects and findings conducted at the Institute.

Click on "MacArthur" for downloadable research instruments and manuals dealing with forensic psychiatry.

IV. FORENSIC PSYCHOLOGY AND PSYCHIATRY

AMERICAN BOARD OF FORENSIC PSYCHOLOGY

http://www.abfp.com

Sponsor: American Board of Forensic Psychology.

Grants Diplomate status in forensic psychology.

Offers workshops on forensic psychology.

Lists Diplomates.

AMERICAN COLLEGE OF FORENSIC PSYCHIATRY

http://www.forensicpsychonline.com

Sponsor: American College of Forensic Psychiatry.

Describes the College's function as an accrediting body for forensic psychiatrists. List of members.

Abstracts from recent issues of *American Journal of Forensic Psychiatry.*

DAVID WILLSHIRE'S FORENSIC PSYCHOLOGY & PSYCHIATRY LINKS

http://www.ozemail.com.au/~dwillsh/forensic.htm

Sponsor: David Willshire.

Links, with brief descriptions, to relevant Web sites.

FORENSIC PSYCHOLOGY AND FORENSIC PSYCHIATRY

http://wwwscience.murdoch.edu.au/teaching/m235/forensicpsych.htm

Sponsor: Allan Barton, Murdoch University (Australia).

Directory of Web links on forensic psychology and criminal profiling.

This Web site is not frequently updated.

Ψ PSYCHIATRY & THE LAW FORENSIC PSYCHIATRY RESOURCE PAGE

http://ua1vm.ua.edu/~jhooper

Sponsor: James F. Hooper, M.D., FAPA (AL).

Statistics on forensic psychiatry hospitals in the U.S. and elsewhere, with descriptions of the status of forensic psychiatry in various countries.

Links to other forensic/mental health sites.

ULTIMATE FORENSIC PSYCHOLOGY DATABASE

http://flash.lakeheadu.ca/~pals/forensics

Sponsor: Michael W. F. Decaire, an undergraduate student at Lakehead University (Ontario, Canada).

The most useful part of the site is a collection of links to online articles about forensic psychology. This Web site is not frequently updated.

V. MISCELLANEOUS

Ψ ANTISTALKING WEB SITE

http://www.antistalking.com

Sponsor: Unknown, but the home page indicates that most of the information on the site comes from a book by Doreen Orion, M.D.

FAQs about stalking and stalkers. What you can do if you are stalked.

Bibliography of research on stalking.

Directory of resources concerning stalking.

NATIONAL CENTER FOR MISSING AND EXPLOITED CHILDREN

http://www.missingkids.com

Sponsor: National Center for Missing and Exploited Children.

Safety tips for preventing abduction and exploitation of children.

Searchable database of photos of missing children.

NATIONAL CENTER FOR VICTIMS OF CRIME

http://www.nvc.org

Sponsor: National Center for Victims of Crime, an advocacy organization.

Links to sites about victim services and relevant Federal and state legislation.

Current news and press releases about crime.

Ψ SUPPORT NETWORK FOR BATTERED WOMEN

http://www.snbw.org

Sponsor: Support Network for Battered Women (CA).

FAQs, for example, 'How do I know if I am a battered woman?"

Web links and full-text articles about domestic violence.

TASH—DISABILITY ADVOCACY WORLDWIDE

http://tash.org

Sponsor: TASH, a civil rights and advocacy organization for people with disabilities, their families, and other interested parties.

Includes a description of the organization's civil rights mission.

Lists disability advocacy organizations, university programs that develop or provide resources to the disabled, and links to support information for parents of the disabled.

VI. PATIENT'S RIGHTS

ADA INFORMATION CENTER

http://www.adainfo.org

Sponsor: The ADA Information Center for the Mid-Atlantic Region, which provides training concerning the Americans with Disabilities Act.

Has a succinct page of links concerning ADA.

Ψ THE DISABILITY RIGHTS ACTIVIST

http://www.disrights.org

Sponsor: Adrienne Rubin Barhydt.

Links to current news about disability rights, Web sites on relevant topics, and articles on how activists can lobby and raise money.

ELECTRONIC PRIVACY INFORMATION CENTER: MEDICAL RECORD PRIVACY
http://www.epic.org/privacy/medical

Sponsor: Electronic Privacy Information Center, part of The Fund for Constitutional Government.

Tracks legislation concerning medical record privacy.

ELECTRONIC PRIVACY INFORMATION CENTER

Medical Record Privacy

NATIONAL COALITION FOR PATIENT RIGHTS
http://www.nationalcpr.org

Sponsor: National Coalition for Patient Rights, which is "dedicated to restoring confidentiality to health care."

Describes the need for legislation protecting confidentiality of health records. Case histories of confidentiality violations.

Links to Web sites about privacy rights.

Section 4
Associations,
Organizations, and
Institutes

Home pages of associations and organizations generally include information about membership and its benefits, how to contact the organization, the organization's current officers, links to their conferences and publications, articles from recent newsletters, ethics codes (if any), and links to related organizations. Many of these home pages have additional material that is only available to members. Unless we found significant original content on an organization's Web site that nonmembers could access, we only include the association's name and URL for its home page.

I. GENERAL, PSYCHOLOGY AND COUNSELING

ACADEMY OF COUNSELING PSYCHOLOGY
http://academyofabpps.org

AMERICAN ASSOCIATION FOR THERAPEUTIC HUMOR

http://aath.org

Full-text articles on humor in psychotherapy. Bibliography of print materials on therapeutic uses of humor.

Click on "Stuff We Do," then "Humor Resources Online," to get to the jokes.

AMERICAN BOARD OF PROFESSIONAL PSYCHOLOGY

http://www.abpp.org

AMERICAN COUNSELING ASSOCIATION

http://www.counseling.org

AMERICAN MENTAL HEALTH COUNSELORS ASSOCIATION

http://www.amhca.org

Ψ AMERICAN PSYCHOLOGICAL ASSOCIATION

http://www.apa.org

APA's monthly newsletter is available in its entirety to anyone.

Many news releases summarizing recent research findings.

FAQs about various disorders and treatment approaches that make excellent patient handouts.

AMERICAN PSYCHOLOGICAL SOCIETY

http://www.psychologicalscience.org

AMERICAN SCHOOL COUNSELOR ASSOCIATION

http://www.schoolcounselor.org

Has information for parents on helping children deal with their academic problems.

American School Counselor Association

ASSOCIATION FOR ADVANCED TRAINING IN THE BEHAVIORAL SCIENCES

http://www.aatbs.com

AATBS sells independent study materials to help prepare therapists of various disciplines for their licensing exams.

ASSOCIATION FOR ASSESSMENT IN COUNSELING

http://www.aac.uc.edu/aac

ASSOCIATION FOR COUNSELOR EDUCATION AND SUPERVISION

http://www.siu.edu/~epse1/aces

ASSOCIATION FOR DEATH EDUCATION AND COUNSELING

http://www.adec.org

ASSOCIATION FOR GAY, LESBIAN, AND BISEXUAL ISSUES IN COUNSELING

http://www.aglbic.org

Association for Gay, Lesbian, and Bisexual Issues in Counseling

ASSOCIATION FOR PSYCHOLOGICAL TYPE

http://www.aptcentral.org

ASSOCIATION OF BLACK PSYCHOLOGISTS

http://www.abpsi.org

ASSOCIATION OF STATE AND PROVINCIAL PSYCHOLOGY BOARDS

http://www.asppb.org

Lists contact information for psychology boards and describes the psychology licensing examination and scoring procedure.

BRITISH PSYCHOLOGICAL SOCIETY
http://www.bps.org.uk

THE BRUNSWIK SOCIETY
http://www.albany.edu/cpr/brunswik

CANADIAN COUNSELLING ASSOCIATION
http://www.ccacc.ca

CANADIAN PSYCHOLOGICAL ASSOCIATION
http://www.cpa.ca

EUROPEAN FEDERATION OF PROFESSIONAL PSYCHOLOGISTS' ASSOCIATIONS
http://www.efppa.org

THE MENTAL HEALTH FOUNDATION
http://www.mentalhealth.org.uk
FAQs about specific mental disorders.
News about advocacy in the UK for the mentally ill.

NATIONAL ALLIANCE FOR THE MENTALLY ILL
http://www.nami.org

NATIONAL ASSOCIATION OF SCHOOL PSYCHOLOGISTS

http://www.naspweb.org

NATIONAL MENTAL HEALTH ASSOCIATION

http://www.nmha.org

NATIONAL REGISTER OF HEALTH SERVICE PROVIDERS IN PSYCHOLOGY

http://www.nationalregister.com

SOCIETY FOR THE PSYCHOLOGICAL STUDY OF SOCIAL ISSUES

http://www.spssi.org

WORLD FEDERATION OF THERAPEUTIC COMMUNITIES

http://www.echonyc.com/~wftc

II. PSYCHIATRIC AND MEDICAL

ACADEMY OF ORGANIZATIONAL AND OCCUPATIONAL PSYCHIATRY

http://www.mcn.com/aoop.htm

ACADEMY OF PSYCHOSOMATIC MEDICINE

http://www.apm.org

AMERICAN ACADEMY OF CHILD AND ADOLESCENT PSYCHIATRY
http://www.aacap.org

Fact sheets and glossaries concerning emotional disorders and psychiatric terminology commonly used in discussions of child and adolescent treatment.

AMERICAN ASSOCIATION FOR GERIATRIC PSYCHIATRY
http://www.aagpgpa.org

Ψ AMERICAN MEDICAL ASSOCIATION
http://www.ama-assn.org

Tables of contents for *Journal of the American Medical Association, Archives of General Psychiatry,* and other AMA journals. Full-text access available to members or subscribers.

Medicare payment schedules.

FAQs on many illnesses and health issues.

AMERICAN ORTHOPSYCHIATRIC ASSOCIATION
http://www.amerortho.org

AMERICAN PSYCHIATRIC ASSOCIATION

http://www.psych.org

Pamphlets and fact sheets for patients concerning psychiatric
disorders and treatments.

AMERICAN PSYCHIATRIC NURSES ASSOCIATION

http://www.apna.org

PHYSICIANS FOR A NATIONAL HEALTH PROGRAM

http://www.pnhp.org

WORLD PSYCHIATRIC ASSOCIATION

http://www.wpanet.org

III. SOCIAL WORK

BRITISH ORGANIZATION OF SOCIAL WORKERS

http://www.basw.co.uk

Has an extensive page of links to social work and social agency
resources in the UK.

COUNCIL ON SOCIAL WORK EDUCATION

http://www.cswe.org

INTERNATIONAL FEDERATION OF SOCIAL WORK

http://www.ifsw.org

international federation of social workers
fédération internationale des assistants sociaux
federación internacional de trabajadores sociales

LATINO SOCIAL WORKERS ORGANIZATION

http://www.lswo.org

NATIONAL ASSOCIATION OF SOCIAL WORKERS

http://www.socialworkers.org

NATIONAL INSTITUTE FOR SOCIAL WORK UK

http://www.nisw.org.uk

Offers abstracts of UK social service research; full-text access to the abstracted materials is available for a fee.

Lists contents of an assortment of international social work journals.

Directory of UK social service agencies.

NATIONAL ORGANIZATION OF FORENSIC SOCIAL WORK

http://www.nofsw.org

NATIONAL ORGANIZATION OF SOCIAL WORKERS

http://www.socialworkers.org

SOCIAL WORK STUDENT RESOURCE PAGE

http://www.atfloydian.u-net.com/vic/resource.htm

Links (usually in the UK) relevant to social work practice.

IV. MARRIAGE AND FAMILY THERAPISTS

AMERICAN ASSOCIATION FOR MARRIAGE AND FAMILY THERAPY

http://www.aamft.org

Useful FAQs for patients concerning marital and family therapy

CHAPTER 4
Medical, Pharmacological, and Neuroscience Sites

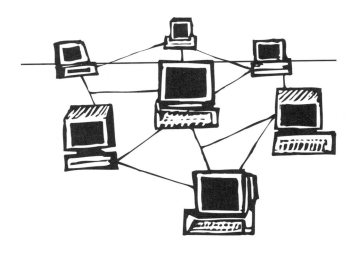

 ## Section 1
Neuropsychology and Behavioral Neuroscience

AMERICAN ACADEMY OF NEUROLOGY

http://www.aan.com

Sponsor: American Academy of Neurology.

Find a board certified neurologist and read news releases about neurology.

AMERICAN BOARD OF CLINICAL NEUROPSYCHOLOGY
http://www.med.umich.edu/abcn

Sponsor: American Board of Clinical Neuropsychology.

Grants Diplomate status by examination.

Diplomates are then eligible for membership in the American Academy of Clinical Neuropsychology (http://www.med.umich.edu/abcn/aacn.html).

Lists Diplomates.

This site is not frequently updated.

AMERICAN BOARD OF PROFESSIONAL NEUROPSYCHOLOGY
http://abpn.net

Sponsor: American Board of Professional Neuropsychology.

Grants Diplomate status by examination.

This site is not frequently updated.

BRAINSOURCE CLINICAL NEUROPSYCHOLOGY
http://www.brainsource.com/neuropsy.htm

Sponsor: Dennis P. Swiercinsky, a San Francisco clinical neuropsychologist.

Brief online articles about neuropsych assessment and a table describing common assessment instruments.

CENTER FOR COGNITIVE BRAIN IMAGING
http://www.ccbi.cmu.edu

Sponsors: A joint project of Carnegie-Mellon University and University of Pittsburgh.

Current research projects, faculty, and courses at the Center.

COGNITIVE NEUROPSYCHOLOGY LAB
http://www.wjh.harvard.edu/~caram

Sponsor: Cognitive Neuropsychology Lab at Harvard University.

Research at the lab and links to other resources.

Under construction at the time of our visit.

Cognitive
Neuropsychology
Laboratory

The Cognitive Neuropsychology Laboratory at Harvard University is one of the country's leading centers of research on cognitive processes from a neuropsychological perspective. Our research is aimed at gaining a better understanding of normal cognitive processes, as well as that of acquired neuropsychological disorders of cognition, such as aphasia, dysgraphia, neglect dyslexia, etc. Currently, our main research projects focus on the study of language production, language perception, reading, writing, and bilingualism. We are comprised of a diverse group of researchers, from varied educational and ethnic backgrounds.

Ψ COGNITIVE-NEUROSCIENCE RESOURCES

http://www.cnbc.cmu.edu/other/other-neuro.html

Sponsor: Center for the Neural Basis of Cognition, a joint project of Carnegie-Mellon University and University of Pittsburgh.

Extensive list of home pages in cognitive and neurosciences, publications, and related products.

A good starting place for exploring neuroscience research centers, but you're on your own because the links
aren't annotated.

DIVISION 40 OF THE AMERICAN PSYCHOLOGICAL ASSOCIATION— CLINICAL NEUROPSYCHOLOGY

http://www.div40.org

Sponsor: Division 40 of the American Psychological Association.

Has links to neuropsychology information sites and professional associations. Lists bylaws and other information about Division 40.

The Division's most recent newsletter can be viewed in Adobe Acrobat format.

EUROPEAN COLLEGE OF NEUROPSYCHOPHARMACOLOGY

http://www.ecnp.nl

Sponsor: European College of Neuropsychopharmacology.

Sponsors conferences and grant research awards. The Web site does not appear to contain any scientific material, but it describes upcoming conferences.

THE INSTITUTE OF COGNITIVE STUDIES

http://garnet.berkeley.edu:4247

Sponsor: Institute of Cognitive Studies, University of California at Berkeley.

Research projects, faculty, and conferences connected with ICS, which is a multidisciplinary research and training center.

LABORATORY OF NEUROPSYCHOLOGY, NIMH

http://ln.nimh.nih.gov/index.html

Sponsor: National Institute of Mental Health.

Current research interests and projects of a lab that conducts basic research on brain mechanisms.

MCCONNELL BRAIN IMAGING CENTRE

http://www.bic.mni.mcgill.ca

Sponsor: Montreal Neurological Institute, McGill University.

MPEG movies and images of real and simulated brain imaging. Software useful for brain imaging research. Describes current research at BIC.

McConnell Brain Imaging Centre

Montréal Neurological Institute, McGill University

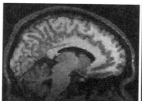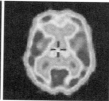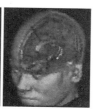

MIND/BRAIN RESOURCES

http://mind.phil.vt.edu/www/mind.html

Sponsor: Virginia Grey Hardcastle, Ph.D., Virginia Tech Department of Philosophy.

Brief lists of links in philosophy and cognitive sciences. This site is not frequently updated.

NATIONAL ACADEMY OF NEUROPSYCHOLOGY

http://nanonline.org

Sponsor: National Academy of Neuropsychology, a professional association of clinicians and researchers.

Some useful content of its own, such as a flowchart on how to respond to requests for release of raw test data when compliance would put the psychologist in coflict with professional standards concerning test security.

Hyperlinks to other professional associations.

NATIONAL INSTITUTE OF NEUROLOGICAL DISORDERS AND STROKE

http://www.ninds.nih.gov

Sponsor: National Institutes of Health.

Information for patients, clinicians, and researchers about ongoing research projects and training opportunities at NIH.

NEUROCASE ONLINE

http://neucas.oupjournals.org/contents-by-date.0.shtml

Sponsor: Oxford University Press.

Studies of interesting neuropsychological cases. Tables of contents and abstracts are free, but full-text access requires a paid subscription.

Ψ NEUROGUIDE.COM: NEUROSCIENCES ON THE INTERNET

http://www.neuroguide.com

Sponsor: Neil A. Busis, M.D.

Extensive resource list of journals, diseases, brain images, organizations, and academic departments in neurology and neurosciences.

Some original content posted here, including summaries of grand rounds and job notices.

Click on "Best Bets" for an annotated list of Web sites the author has found to be useful.

Has a useful search engine.

NEUROPSYCHOLOGY ASSOCIATION

http://fnpa.freeservers.com

Sponsor: Fordham University.

Links for online articles and a few other neuroscience sites.

NEUROPSYCHOLOGY CENTRAL

http://www.neuropsychologycentral.com

Sponsor: Telepsychology Solution, Inc.

Descriptions of assessment instruments, a few articles, and links to vendors.

FAQs concerning neuropsychology and professional associations.

NORMATIVEDATA.COM RELATED LINKS

http://www.normativedata.com/links/linksmain.html

Sponsor: NormativeData.Com.

Lists professional associations, disease support organizations, and neuropsychology journals.

ONLINE NEUROPSYCHOLOGY PROJECT

http://www.premier.net/~cogito/project/onp.html

Sponsor: J. N. Browndyke, MA, Louisiana State University Department of Psychology.

Conducts online research in neuropsychology using visitors to the Web site as participants. Contains results from the author's previous studies.

Online Neuropsychology Project

PSY 507 NEUROPSYCHOLOGY

http://home.epix.net/~tcannon1/Neuropsychology.htm

Sponsor: Brooke J. Cannon, Ph.D., Clinical Neuropsychologist, Marywood University (PA).

Neurological disorders, and links to neuroscience journals and relevant professional associations.

SEROTONIN CLUB

http://146.9.4.210

Sponsor: The Serotonin Club, an association of scientists interested in serotonin research.

Has a nontechnical explanation of what serotonin is and why it is important.

SCHEDULES FOR CLINICAL ASSESSMENT IN NEUROPSYCHIATRY

http://www.psy.med.rug.nl/0018

Sponsor: Groningen Department of Social Psychiatry (Netherlands).

Describes a structured psychiatric interview (SCAN) developed under auspices of the World Health Organization. Those who have taken a one-week training course may download the interview.

TRAINING PROGRAMS IN CLINICAL NEUROPSYCHOLOGY

http://www.swets.nl/sps/ntp/ntphome.html

Sponsor: Swets & Zeitlinger, publishers; for Division 40, American Psychological Association.

Training programs, internships, and postdocs, with contact and application information.

TBIDOC.COM

http://www.tbidoc.com

Sponsor: Antoinette Appel, Ph.D., a neuropsychologist practicing in Florida.

Describes the discipline of neuropsychology.

Click on "The Medicine of Brain Injury" to find links to other Internet resources on neuropsychology.

Under construction at the time of our visit.

Ψ WHOLE BRAIN ATLAS

http://www.med.harvard.edu/AANLIB/home.html

Sponsors: Departments of Radiology and Neurology, Brigham and Women's Hospital (Boston), Harvard Medical School, Countway Library of Medicine, American Academy of Neurology.

Beautifully clear CT and MRI images of normal and diseased brains, with a brief primer on neuroimaging.

The viewer can change the slice or orientation of the image on display. An alternative navigator uses Java to allow selection of various clinical cases and brain images.

Some of the images contain explanations to help novices understand what they are seeing (for example, a time lapse movie of changes in the brain of a multiple sclerosis patient).

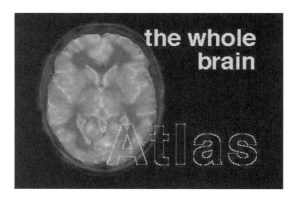

Section 2
Psychopharmacology and Pharmacology

I. PHARMACOLOGY MEGASITES

ABOUT.COM PHARMACOLOGY AND LEGAL DRUGS
http://pharmacology.about.com/health/pharmacology

Sponsor: About.com and "expert guide" Mary Ann Elchisak, Ph.D., retired Associate Professor of Pharmacology at Purdue University.

Drug manufacturers' sites, topics (e.g., analgesia, immune system, anticancer drugs), and recent topical news.

Handy FAQs on how to find drug information.

Instructions on finding clinical trials.

AMERICAN COLLEGE OF CLINICAL PHARMACOLOGY
http://www.accp1.org

Sponsor: American College of Clinical Pharmacology.

Professional organization that accredits clinical pharmacologists.

BRITISH ASSOCIATION FOR PSYCHOPHARMACOLOGY

http://www.bap.org.uk

Sponsor: British Association for Psychopharmacology.

Activities and conferences sponsored by BAP.

Has a brief page of links to other resources in biological psychiatry and psychopharmacology.

DR. BOB'S PSYCHOPHARMACOLOGY TIPS

http://uhs.bsd.uchicago.edu/dr-bob/tips/tips.html

Sponsor: Robert Hsiung, M.D., Assistant Professor of Clinical Psychiatry.

Anecdotal reports and opinions concerning biological psychiatry that were previously posted to a mailing list.

Ψ DRUG INFONET

http://www.druginfonet.com

Sponsor: Drug InfoNet, Inc.

Prescribing information and patient drug information handouts.

Visitors may submit a question to "Ask the Doctor"; past questions and answers appear as FAQs.

Links to hospitals, health care organizations, and other sources of disease and drug information.

DRUGBASE

http://www.drugbase.co.za

Sponsor: Candor Webtech.

Information from package inserts of prescription and OTC medications available in South Africa.

HEALTHSQUARE PRESCRIPTION DRUGS REFERENCE PAGE

http://www.healthsquare.com/drugmain.html

Sponsor: A "woman's health information center," operated by New Media Systems LLC.

Consumer information about medications.

Medically oriented articles about various conditions from *PDR Guide to Prescription Drugs*.

HEALTH-CENTER PHARMACY PAGES

http://site.health-center.com/pharmacy/default.htm

Sponsor: Health-Center, Inc.

Consumer information about medications, classified by type of illness.

INTERNATIONAL PSYCHOPHARMACOLOGY ALGORITHM PROJECT

http://www.ipap.org

Sponsor: Kenneth O. Jobson, M.D.

Proposes to "bring together experts...for the systematic treatment of major Axis I psychiatric disorders."

Under construction at the time of our visit.

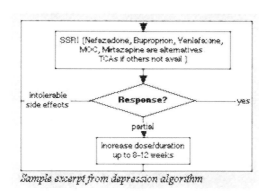

Sample excerpt from depression algorithm

Ψ PHARMINFONET

http://pharminfo.com

Sponsor: Mediconsult.com, Inc. Has an editorial board and expert panel.

Easy to locate a drug, either by the name of the drug or by the condition it treats.

Much of the information here is for technical rather than consumer use.

Scientific articles and FAQs about specific drugs.

Glossary of drug-related and medical terms.

Ψ PSYCHOPHARMACOLOGY LINKS

http://www.baltimorepsych.com/psychopharm.htm

Sponsor: Northern County Psychiatric Associates (MD).

Concise and well-chosen annotated links to many of the most important Web sites for this topic.

PSYCHOPHARMACOTEK

http://redrival.com/pptek

Sponsor: Cenk Tek, M.D., a resident at University of Maryland Department of Psychiatry.

Links to more than thirty journals, with Dr. Tek's summaries and comments on the methodology and significance of recently published articles.

RXLIST—THE INTERNET DRUG INDEX

http://www.rxlist.com

Sponsor: HealthCentral.com.

Patient information on specific medications and categories of medications. Search engine is effective even when an approximate spelling of the drug's name has been entered.

RXMED

http://www.rxmed.com

Sponsor: RxMed, Inc.

Drug monographs for many medications available in Canada; patient handouts concerning various illnesses. At the time of our visit, a preview link showed the splash page for a much more comprehensive RxMed.

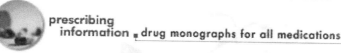

VIRTUAL DRUGSTORE

http://www.virtualdrugstore.com

Sponsor: Vimy Park Pharmacy.

Searchable database of older medications, as well as a database of newer drugs classified by application.

VIRTUAL LIBRARY: PHARMACY

http://www.pharmacy.org

Sponsor: David Bourne.

Links to drug companies, online databases, journals, and lists of conferences.

Ψ YAHOO! SPECIFIC DRUGS AND MEDICATIONS

http://dir.yahoo.com/Health/Pharmacy/Drugs_and_Medications/
Specific_Drugs_and_Medications

Sponsor: Yahoo! Inc.

Directory of medication sites, including both generic and brand name compounds.

Clicking on "Yahoo! Health: Drugs and Medications" will bring up an alphabetized list of medications, each with an information sheet similar to what pharmacists provide. An extensive list that is frequently updated.

Particularly useful for the consumer.

II. HERBAL PHARMACOLOGY AND PHARMACIES

BOTANICAL.COM

http://www.botanical.com

Sponsor: Renaissance Health and Beauty, manufacturer of herbal products.

Links to current news and articles concerning herbal remedies.

Includes a hypertext version of the 1931 book *A Modern Herbal.*

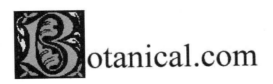

MOTHER NATURE'S HEALTHY LIVING LIBRARY

http://www.mothernature.com/library/default.asp

Sponsor: MotherNature.com, online shopping site for herbal and natural products.

Links to articles on herbal and natural remedies, organized by illness.

NBCi HEALTH: HERBAL UPDATE

http://home.nbci.com/main/page/pcp/1,3,-428,00.html?st.sn.sr.0.428

Sponsor: NBC Internet, Inc.

Directory of Web resources concerning herbal remedies, with some original articles.

PREVENTION.COM HERBAL REMEDIES

http://www.prevention.com/healing/herb

Sponsor: Women.com Networks, a publicly held company.

Fact sheets on medicinal herbs, taken from Rodale Press's *The Complete Book of Natural and Medicinal Cures.*

Ψ SOUTHWEST SCHOOL OF BOTANICAL MEDICINE

http://chili.rt66.com/hrbmoore/HOMEPAGE/HomePage.html

Sponsor: Michael Moore, Director, Southwest School of Botanical Medicine (AZ).

Manuals written by Moore on illnesses and his recommendations for herbal treatment, links to research abstracts on herbal remedies.

Alphabetized photos of many medicinal plants, with maps showing where they grow in the western United States.

Interesting historical publications, pamphlets, and illustrations. Some are in Adobe Acrobat format.

III. MISCELLANEOUS PHARMACEUTICAL SITES

Ψ BUYING MEDICAL PRODUCTS ONLINE

http://www.fda.gov/oc/buyonline

Sponsor: U.S. Food and Drug Administration.

FAQs and warnings about purchasing drugs and other medical products online.

Ψ CENTERWATCH CLINICAL TRIALS LISTING SERVICE

http://www.centerwatch.com/main.htm

Sponsor: CenterWatch, a publishing company focused on the clinical trials industry.

Patient and researcher information on current clinical trials of new medications and treatments, with detailed profiles of providers and research centers.

CLINICAL TRIALS CENTER, NAVAL HEALTH RESEARCH CENTER

http://pc176.nhrc.navy.mil/disease/clinical.htm

Sponsor: Naval Medical Center, San Diego.

Describes clinical trials on two treatments for Gulf War Syndrome. Recruits participants for the study and lists about thirty other centers around the U.S. that also recruit.

Ψ CLINICALTRIALS.COM

http://www.clinicaltrials.com

Sponsor: Pharmaceutical Research Plus, Inc.

Current clinical trials, FAQs about clinical trials, and an online form for patients desiring a clinical trial. Support groups and contact information for a number of emotional disorders.

CLINICALTRIALS.GOV

http://clinicaltrials.gov/ct/gui/c/b

Sponsor: National Institutes of Health.

Lists clinical trials that are sponsored by NIH, other Federal agencies, and pharmaceutical companies.

Specifies which trials are still recruiting patients and which ones are completed. Trials are fully searchable.

Useful FAQs, such as "Understanding Clinical Trials."

EMEA HOME

http://www.eudra.org/emea.html

Sponsor: European Agency for the Evaluation of Medical Products.

Position papers and policies concerning medicine regulation in Europe.

Has a page of links to other sites in Europe and the U.S. that deal with medicine regulation.

Ψ FOOD AND DRUG ADMINISTRATION HOME PAGE

http://www.fda.gov

Sponsor: U.S. Food and Drug Administration.

Authoritative information on policies and current news concerning food and drug regulation.

Searchable FAQs on drugs for humans, cosmetics, and food labeling and processing.

Good source of information concerning drug and food recalls.

HANDLING CYTOTOXIC DRUGS

http://www.nih.gov/od/ors/ds/pubs/cyto

Sponsor: National Institutes of Health.

Recommendations for safe preparation and administration of cytotoxic drugs.

INSTITUTE FOR SAFE MEDICATION PRACTICES

http://www.ismp.org

Sponsor: Institute for Safe Medication Practices, a nonprofit organization.

Information for consumers on medication errors and their prevention.

PHARMACOLOGY GLOSSARY

http://www.bumc.bu.edu/www/busm/pharmacology/Programmed/framedGlossary.html

Sponsor: Edward Pelikan, M.D., Boston University School of Medicine.

Dictionary of pharmacological terms. Last updated in 1998.

SEARCHING THE INTERNET FOR DRUG INFORMATION

http://www.drugs.indiana.edu/pubs/newsline/searching.html

Sponsor: William J. Bailey, M.P.H., C.P.P., Associate Professor of Applied Health Science and Executive Director, Indiana Prevention Resource Center, Indiana University.

Describes strategies and Web sites for locating authoritative drug information.

This site is not frequently updated.

U.S. PHARMACOPEIA

http://www.usp.org

Sponsor: U.S. Pharmacopeial Convention, Inc.

Sells printed products and software with drug manufacturing standards.

Brief page of links to government agencies and health care professional associations.

Section 3
General Medical Information

The authors do not endorse any of the Web sites or modalities presented below. Clinical practitioners must make individual decisions about any medical or nonmedical methods they employ.

I. Mega Medical Info Sites
- A. Conventional
- B. Alternative
    1. General Alternative Medicine Resources
    2. Specific Complementary Therapies
        - a. Aromatherapy
        - b. Ayurveda
        - c. Botanical, Herbal, and Horticultural Therapies
        - d. Chinese Medicine
        - e. Chiropractic
        - f. Homeopathy
        - g. Native American Healing
        - h. Naturopathy
        - i. Osteopathy

I. MEGA MEDICAL INFO SITES

 ## A. CONVENTIONAL

AMERICAN COUNCIL ON SCIENCE AND HEALTH

http://www.acsh.org

Sponsor: American Council on Science and Health, a nonprofit organization dedicated to consumer education; it has a large advisory board of clinicians and scientists.

Opinion and fact pieces concerning health policy issues such as tobacco use, food safety, and environmental health.

Categorized links to other sites.

CENTERS FOR DISEASE CONTROL AND PREVENTION

http://www.cdc.gov

Sponsor: Centers for Disease Control and Prevention.

Up-to-date news about current health topics, fact sheets, and statistics on diseases.

Ψ HEALTH ON THE NET FOUNDATION

http://www.hon.ch

Sponsor: Health on the Net Foundation, a nonprofit organization.

Megasite with searchable and annotated links to Web sites for many medical specialties.

Frequently updated. The search engine lists results in order of decreasing relevance.

Its editors use a code of conduct to determine which sites are authoritative.

HEALTHATOZ.COM

http://www.healthatoz.com

Sponsor: Medical Network, Inc. and its medical advisory board.

Resources on various disorders and health topics, including extensive and rated links for nonprofessionals as well as original articles.

HEALTHCENTRAL

http://www.healthcentral.com

Sponsor: HealthCentral.com, Inc.

A commercial Web site with information for consumers on many diseases.

Health columns and discussion forums.

Ψ HEALTHFINDER

http://www.healthfinder.gov

Sponsor: U.S. Department of Health and Human Services.

Handy megasite and search engine for health information, with extensively annotated links to government sites and other authoritative professional associations, academic resources, and online health media.

An easy way to find information and up-to-the-minute news.

Has special sections for teens, seniors, parents of infants, etc.

Ψ INTELIHEALTH

http://www.intelihealth.com

Sponsor: InteliHealth, Inc.

Excellent source of health care information for the consumer. Much original content.

MARTINDALE'S HEALTH SCIENCE GUIDE

http://www-sci.lib.uci.edu/HSG/HSGuide.html

Sponsor: James G. Martindale, inventor of a tongue cleaning device, whose biography states that he did not finish the third grade.

Many links to clinical cases, information for medical professionals, and multimedia presentations.

Although the pages are lengthy and take a long time to load, they contain links to many valuable resources.

Ψ MAYO CLINIC HEALTH OASIS

http://www.mayohealth.org

Sponsor: Mayo Clinic.

Original articles and current news on many health care topics.

First-aid information.

MDCHOICE.COM

http://www.mdchoice.com

Sponsor: MdChoice.com, Inc.

Physician-reviewed links to medical information for consumers and professionals.

Ψ MEDICAL MATRIX

http://www.medmatrix.org/index.asp

Sponsor: Medical Matrix.

Directory of hundreds of medical Web sites, organized by disease type, medical specialty area, and profession. Directed at health care professionals.

Free registration is required, but it is worth the time.

Web sites are annotated and ranked by Medical Matrix's editorial board of physicians.

MEDICAL WORLD SEARCH

http://www.mwsearch.com

Sponsor: Medical World Search.

Search engine for thousands of medical Web sites, with results ranked by closeness of fit to search terms.

Ψ MERCK MANUALS

http://www.merck.com/pubs

Sponsor: Merck, Inc.

Full-text versions of several Merck Manuals, which describe diseases and their recommended treatments.

U. S. MEDICINE CENTRAL

http://www.usmedicine.com

Sponsor: U. S. Medicine, a publisher of materials directed to healthcare professionals employed by the Federal government.

Recent news concerning Federal medicine and facilities.

A grab-bag of links, including several articles on Hepatitis C, links to medical schools and societies, specialized professional associations, and medical libraries.

Phone numbers and addresses of poison control centers.

VIRTUAL HOSPITAL

http://www.vh.org

Sponsor: University of Iowa.

Lectures and outlines on medical topics.

WEBMD

http://www.webmd.com

Sponsor: Healtheon/WebMD Corporation.

Fee-based service with up-to-date medical news. Since we did not pay the fee, we could not determine what other resources this site offers.

 **B. ALTERNATIVE**

1. GENERAL ALTERNATIVE MEDICAL RESOURCES

ALTERNATIVE MEDICINE

http://www.libraries.wayne.edu/shiffman/altmed

Sponsor: Shiffman Medical Library, Wayne State University (MI).

Directory of alternative therapies with relevant Web resources.

Ψ ALTERNATIVE MEDICINE HOMEPAGE

http://www.pitt.edu/~cbw/altm.html

Sponsor: Falk Health Sciences Library, University of Pittsburgh.

Well-organized directory of Internet and print resources about alternative treatments.

ASK DR. WEIL

http://www.pathfinder.com/drweil

Sponsor: Andrew Weil, M.D.

Advice on healthy diet and herbal remedies.

HOLISTIC HEALING WEB PAGE

http://www.holisticmed.com

Sponsor: Holistic Healing Web Page.

Directory of online articles and Web sites on various aspects of alternative treatments.

NATIONAL CENTER FOR COMPLEMENTARY AND ALTERNATIVE MEDICINE

http://altmed.od.nih.gov

Sponsor: The National Institutes of Health (NIH), National Center for Complementary and Alternative Medicine.

FAQs and databases concerning alternative treatments from an agency that conducts research and disseminates information to practitioners and researchers.

NATURALHEALERS.COM

http://www.naturalhealers.com

Sponsor: Net Stream.

Information about U.S. schools and training programs in alternative and complementary treatment approaches.

QUACKWATCH

http://www.quackwatch.com

Sponsor: Stephen Barrett, M.D., a retired psychiatrist.

"Quackwatch, Inc.... is a nonprofit corporation whose purpose is to combat health-related frauds, myths, fads, and fallacies." Lists and describes treatment approaches in both medicine and psychotherapy that the sponsor considers to be quackery.

Useful articles to encourage critical thinking about claims made concerning various treatments for physical and emotional disorders.

Some opinions are one-sided. Visitors to the site should look elsewhere on the Web before accepting a Quackwatch verdict as the last word on any subject.

YAHOO! HEALTH: ALTERNATIVE MEDICINE

http://dir.yahoo.com/Health/Alternative_Medicine

Sponsor: Yahoo! Inc.

Extensive directory of alternative medicine Web sites that have submitted URLs for listing.

2. SPECIFIC COMPLEMENTARY THERAPIES

a. Aromatherapy

AROMATHERAPY INTERNET RESOURCES

http://www.holisticmed.com/www/aromatherapy.html

Sponsor: Holistic Healing Web Page.

Directory of online articles, Web sites, newsgroups, and mailing lists about aromatherapy.

Ψ AROMAWEB

http://www.aromaweb.com

Sponsor: Aromaweb.

Online information about aromatherapy compounds and treatment practices. Current news about aromatherapy.

Links page.

NATIONAL ASSOCIATION FOR HOLISTIC AROMATHERAPY

http://www.naha.org

Sponsor: National Association for Holistic Aromatherapy, a nonprofit educational organization.

Describes the organization and its recent conferences.

There are a few links to aromatherapy Web sites.

b. Ayurveda

NATIONAL INSTITUTE OF AYURVEDIC MEDICINE

http://niam.com

Sponsor: National Institute of Ayurvedic Medicine (NAMI).

Describes basic principles of Ayurveda. A few links to other sites and descriptions of current research at NAMI.

AYURVEDIC INSTITUTE

http://www.ayurveda.com

Sponsor: Ayurvedic Institute (NM).

Training course in Ayurveda.

Ads for the Institute's store and spa.

c. Botanical, Herbal, and Horticultural Therapies

AHTA HOME PAGE

http://www.ahta.org

Sponsor: American Horticultural Therapy Association.

Describes horticultural therapy.

Lists Web sites, local chapters of the Association, and training sites in the field.

DR. EDWARD BACH CENTRE

http://www.bachcentre.com

Sponsor: Bach Centre (UK).

Flower remedies for anxiety, possessive love, "deep gloom for no reason," etc.

HERB SOCIETY (UK) ONLINE

http://metalab.unc.edu/herbmed/HerbSociety

Sponsor: Herb Society (UK).

Annotated directory of sites on herbal remedies. Beautiful color photographs of herbs decorate this site.

HUMAN ISSUES IN HORTICULTURE

http://www.hort.vt.edu/human/human.html

Sponsor: Diane Relf, Ph.D., Virginia Polytechnic Institute and State University.

Journal articles and Web resources on horticulture therapy.

Ψ MEDHERB.COM

http://www.medherb.com

Sponsor: Medical Herbalism, a quarterly journal.

Many links, mostly annotated, to Internet resources on medical herbs and their uses, and interactions with prescribed drugs.

Ψ UNIVERSITY OF WASHINGTON MEDICINAL HERB GARDEN HOME PAGE

http://www.nnlm.nlm.nih.gov/pnr/uwmhg

Sponsor: University of Washington Medicinal Herb Garden.

Color photos of medicinal herbs with links to other Web sites that discuss each herb.

Virtual tour of the UW herb garden.

d. Chinese Medicine

ACUPUNCTURE.COM

http://www.acupuncture.com

Sponsor: Acupuncture.com.

Online articles about traditional Chinese medicine, including Qi Gong, massage, and herbal medicine as well as acupuncture.

Describes laws regulating acupuncture in each U.S. state.

Directories of acupuncture practitioners in countries outside the U.S.

Patient testimonials.

CHINESE MEDICINE AND ACUPUNCTURE IN CANADA

http://www.medicinechinese.com

Sponsor: Maria C. W. Chan.

Links for professional associations, government regulations, and online articles concerning Acupuncture, Qi Gong, etc.

e. Chiropractic

CHIROPRACTIC INTERNET RESOURCES

http://www.holisticmed.com/www/chiropractic.html

Sponsor: Holistic Healing Web Page.

Extensive directory of Web resources.

CHIROWEB

http://www.chiroweb.com

Sponsor: Dynamic Chiropractic, a magazine for chiropractors.

FAQs about chiropractics.

Directory of other Web resources on chiropractics.

f. Homeopathy

HOMEOPATHIC EDUCATIONAL SERVICES

http://www.homeopathic.com

Sponsor: Dana Ullman, MPH.

Information on homeopathy for the general public. Lists other Web resources in the field.

Ψ HOMEOPATHY HOME

http://www.homeopathyhome.com

Sponsor: Nicholas Haworth (UK).

Directories of Web resources, a discussion board, articles, and recent news items about homeopathy.

Sites for vendors of homeopathy supplies.

Lists sites and resources in a variety of languages and geographical areas.

NATIONAL CENTER FOR HOMEOPATHY

http://www.homeopathic.org

Sponsor: National Center for Homeopathy (VA).

Promotes homeopathy to the general public, conducts training programs for practitioners, and publishes a magazine for the public.

Contains a FAQ section about homeopathy.

g. Native American Healing

NATIVE AMERICAN HEALING

http://www.healing-arts.org/mehl-madrona

Sponsor: Lewis Mehl-Madrona, M.D. Ph.D., University of Pittsburgh Medical Center.

Describes Native American healing techniques and their applications to medical illnesses. The following link is a fascinating paper summarizing the results of a meeting between Native American healers and the author that compares Native American approaches with standardized North American medical practices: http://www.healing-arts.org/mehl-madrona/mmtraditionalpaper.htm

h. Naturopathic Medicine

NATUROPATHIC MEDICINE IN THE UK

http://www.naturopathy.org.uk

Sponsor: General Council and Register of Naturopaths (UK).

Describes the philosophy and treatment techniques of naturopathic medicine. Lists registered naturopaths in the UK and elsewhere.

NATUROPATHIC MEDICINE NETWORK

http://www.pandamedicine.com

Sponsor: Pandamedicine.

A few online articles describing the practice of naturopathic medicine. No external links.

Some material is accessible only to naturopathic physicians.

Naturopathic Medicine Network

Ψ NATUROPATHIC PHYSICIANS ONLINE

http://naturopathic.org/Welcome.html

Sponsor: American Association of Naturopathic Physicians.

FAQs on naturopathic medicine.

Links to Web sites and articles about alternative medicine.

Message board.

NATUROPATHICDOC

http://naturopathicdoc.com

Sponsor: Gary Bachman, ND, a naturopathic physician in Mount Vernon, WA.

FAQs about naturopathy.

Brief directory of alternative medicine Web sites.

i. Osteopathic Medicine

AMERICAN OSTEOPATHIC ASSOCIATION

http://www.am-osteo-assn.org

Sponsor: American Osteopathic Association.

Describes the association and its mission.

FAQs about osteopathy and news articles for the general public.

Click on "Gregory's Links" for a list of nearly 300 related links. Most are Web sites of osteopathic physicians.

OSTEOPATHIC MEDICINE WEBRING

http://www.osteopathicmedicine.org/

Sponsors: Ed Delgado, DO; Lee Burnett, DO; Gregory Gulick.

Click "Members" to see a list of more than 170 osteopathy sites that are part of the webring.

This is the most extensive links page on this subject that we found.

STUDENTDOCTOR NETWORK

http://osteopathic.com/ocom.html

Sponsor: StudentDoctor Network, a collection of medical student Web sites.

FAQs about osteopathic medicine.

Section 4
Miscellaneous Medical

I. MEDICATION COMPLIANCE

IMPROVING MEDICATION COMPLIANCE

http://www.lifescapepro.com/topcomart-improvingcompliance.html

Sponsors: Jack E. Rosenblatt, M.D.; Lifespace, LLC.

Brief online article for professionals about the causes of medication non-compliance in psychiatric patients, with strategies for improving compliance.

IT'S UP TO YOU: IMPROVING MEDICATION COMPLIANCE

http://www.stadtlanders.com/general/compliant.html

Sponsors: Teri Wagner, PharmD.; Stadtlanders Pharmacy.

Online article for patients with chronic conditions.
Describes strategies and products that aid medication compliance.

II. COMPLICATIONS

DRUG-INDUCED PHOTOSENSITIVITY

http://hsc.virginia.edu/cmc/pedpharm/v4n6.htm

*Sponsor: Pediatric Pharmacotherapy, a monthly review from Children's Medical
Center, University of Virginia.*

Lengthy table of medications that induce photosensitivity, published
in 1998. Other issues of the journal are available at
http://hsc.virginia.edu/cmc/pedpharm.

GRAPEFRUIT JUICE EFFECT

http://pharminfo.com/pubs/msb/gfj_effect.html

Sponsor: PharmInfoNet.

Interactions between grapefruit juice and medications.

HARMFUL EFFECTS OF MEDICATIONS ON THE ADULT DIGESTIVE SYSTEM

http://www.niddk.nih.gov/health/digest/pubs/harmeff/harmeff.htm

Sponsor: National Digestive Diseases Clearinghouse, National Institutes of Health.

A fact sheet on drug-induced injuries to the digestive system.

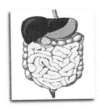

**Harmful Effects of
Medicines on the Adult
Digestive System**

◆ NIDDK *National Digestive Diseases Information Clearinghouse*

Ψ INSTITUTE FOR SAFE MEDICATION PRACTICES

http://www.ismp.org./start.html

Sponsor: Institute for Safe Medication Practices, a nonprofit organization.

FAQs for patients on how to take medication safely.

Links to the larger U.S. associations of health care professionals.

Lists medical textbook errata concerning medications.

NATIONAL COORDINATING COUNCIL FOR MEDICATION ERROR REPORTING AND PREVENTION

http://www.nccmerp.org/index.htm

Sponsor: MCC MERP, a coordinating body of 19 national organizations interested in reducing medication errors (e.g., American Association of Retired Persons, American Medical Association).

Click on "About Medication Errors" to see a taxonomy of errors and a system for tracking them.

Includes a form to report medication errors, news releases, and recommendations.

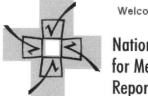

Welcome to the NCC MERP web site

National Coordinating Council for Medication Error Reporting and Prevention

III. TOXICOLOGY (INCLUDING ENVIRONMENTAL ILLNESS)

AMALGAM RELATED ILLNESSES

http://www.algonet.se/~leif/yaTITLfr.html

Sponsor: Leif Hedegard, a Swedish student of medicine and computer science.

Abstracts of articles about the medical effects of mercury amalgam dental fillings.

CHRONIC FATIGUE SYNDROME? OR CHRONIC MERCURY POISONING?

http://www.teleport.com/~ctseng/cfs_pages/index.html

Sponsor: Jeff Clark, who states that he suffers from chronic mercury poisoning.

News articles and personal narratives about the harmful effects of mercury amalgam dental fillings.

FIND YOUR POISON CENTER

http://www.aapcc.org/findyour.htm

Sponsor: American Association of Poison Control Centers.

Database of U.S. poison control centers, searchable by geographical directory or zip code.

Ψ LSU TOXICOLOGY INTERNET RESOURCES

http://www.lib.lsu.edu/sci/chem/Internet/toxicology.html

Sponsor: Louisiana State University Libraries.

Links, with brief descriptions, to toxic substances, poisons, academic departments and institutes of toxicology, and relevant publications.

Ψ MCSURVIVORS

http://www.mcsurvivors.com

Sponsors: Lynda Hamilton, a person who has multiple chemical sensitivities; and Webgoddess, a Web page designer.

Many links to articles, films, periodicals, and treatment centers concerning multiple chemical sensitivities.

MCSurvivors A Resource Web Site for Multiple Chemical Sensitivity and Environmental Illness

Articles
Books
Bulletin Boards
Centers
Films and Videos
Food
General Information
Legal Aid
On-Line Libraries
Organizations
Periodicals
Personal Home Pages

A Resource Web Site for
Multiple Chemical Sensitivity
and Environmental Illness

MULTIPLE CHEMICAL SENSITIVITY

http://www.ourlittleplace.com/mcs.html

Sponsor: Gordon and Jacki, a couple from Florida who both suffer from multiple chemical sensitivities.

Lists the health risks of perfumes, fabric softeners, and other commonly used products.

SOCIETY OF TOXICOLOGY HOME PAGE

http://www.toxicology.org

Sponsor: Society of Toxicology, a nonprofit scientific society.

In addition to information about the society and its educational efforts, there is an extensive page of links to relevant professional associations, articles concerning lab and animal testing of chemicals, and other toxicology sites.

TERATOLOGY SOCIETY

http://teratology.org

Sponsor: Teratology Society, a scientific society whose members study the causes of birth defects.

Has several pages of links to Web sites concerning specific birth defects, as well as to sites of scientific, charitable, and support organizations.

WORLD WIDE SUBJECT CATALOG: TOXICOLOGY

http://www.uky.edu/Subject/toxicology.html

Sponsor: University of Kentucky.

Many links to sources of information on toxic chemicals and hazardous substances.

IV. DEATH AND DYING

CHOICE IN DYING

http://www.choices.org

Sponsor: Choice in Dying, Inc., a nonprofit organization.

Information about living wills and advance directives (with downloadable forms for most states).

Current news about end-of-life issues and legal developments.

DEATH AND DYING GRIEF SUPPORT

http://www.death-dying.com

Sponsor: Death & Dying.

Online articles, including personal narratives and supportive articles for dying people and those close to them.

Funeral and terminal illness "planners."

DEATHNET

http://www.rights.org/deathnet/open.html

Sponsor: DeathNet, a volunteer-staffed archive.

Articles on various aspects of dealing with death, including the right to die. Extensive online library at http://www.rights.org/deathnet/lr_library.html.

The site is international in focus, with materials from Canada, South Africa, Australia, and the U.S.

ELISABETH KUBLER-ROSS, M.D.

http://www.doubleclickd.com/kubler.html

Sponsor: Daniel Redwood.

An inspiring and thought-provoking interview with Dr. Kubler-Ross, author of *Death, The Final Stage of Growth.*

Ψ GROWTH HOUSE, INC.

http://www.growthhouse.org

Sponsor: Growth House, Inc.

Extensive links to Web sites about hospice care, "death with dignity," helping children to deal with illness and death, AIDS, cancer, and bereavement.

Ψ HOSPICE NET

http://www.hospicenet.org

Sponsor: Hospice Net, an Internet-only nonprofit organization providing information and links useful to terminally ill patients and their families.

Hospice Net

For patients and families facing life-threatening illness

FAQs concerning hospice services, pain control, issues for caregivers, and bereavement.

Useful links page.

V. MEDICAL CONDITIONS WITH PSYCHIATRIC RAMIFICATIONS NOT DIRECTLY ASSOCIATED WITH AXIS I OR II DISORDERS

ADVANCED TECHNIQUES FOR OVERCOMING CFS [CHRONIC FATIGUE SYNDROME], FMS [FIBROMYALGIA SYNDROME], AND GWS [GULF WAR SYNDROME]

http://www.beatcfsandfms.org

Sponsor: Glenn Weinreb, GW Instruments.

Extensive Web links about these conditions.

Discussion of strategies for treating aspects of each condition, but without information about the authority of the sources for these recommendations.

Ψ AEGIS

http://www.aegis.com and http://www.aegis.org/hivinfoweb

Sponsor: Aegis, a nonprofit organization.

This is a very large, frequently updated database of information about HIV/AIDS.

Rapidly searches its own database and other large Internet resources on AIDS.

Lists clinical trials.

Well-organized collection of annotated links to other AIDS sites.

Ψ AIDS CLINICAL TRIALS INFORMATION SERVICE

http://www.actis.org

Sponsors: Food and Drug Administration, Centers for Disease Control and Prevention, National Library of Medicine, National Institute of Allergy and Infectious Diseases.

Searchable database of clinical trials for AIDS treatment.

Lists drug information.

AIDS Clinical Trials Information Service

AIDS KNOWLEDGE BASE

http://hivinsite.ucsf.edu/akb/1997/index.html

Sponsor: University of California San Francisco, San Francisco General Hospital.

A highly technical textbook on AIDS, its prevention and treatment, and associated legal issues.

AMERICAN ASSOCIATION FOR CHRONIC FATIGUE SYNDROME

http://www.aacfs.org

Sponsor: American Association for Chronic Fatigue Syndrome.

Links to many sites about Chronic Fatigue Syndrome.

Bibliographies of the scientific literature.

Web site is not frequently updated.

AMERICAN GULF WAR VETERANS ASSOCIATION

http://www.gulfwarvets.com

Sponsor: American Gulf War Veterans Association.

Extensive collection of links to online news releases, articles, and Web sites.

AMERICAN THYROID ASSOCIATION

http://www.thyroid.org

Sponsor: American Thyroid Association, a professional association dealing with research and treatment of thyroid disorders.

Describes the association's professional activities.

Online brochures for patients concerning thyroid disorders.

Links to relevant Web sites for professionals.

THE BODY: AN AIDS AND HIV INFORMATION RESOURCE

http://www.thebody.com

Sponsor: Body Health Resources Corporation.

Well-organized document library and FAQs concerning AIDS and its treatment and prevention.

Forums in which experts answer submitted questions.

Bulletin boards on HIV-related topics.

Ψ CHRONIC FATIGUE AND IMMUNE DYSFUNCTION SYNDROME ASSOCIATION OF AMERICAN, INC.

http://www.cfids.org

Sponsor: CFIDS Association of America, Inc.

Fact sheet about CFS.

Extensive collection of articles from the Association's newsletter, intermingled with links to abstracts from scientific journals.

Research news.

CHRONIC FATIGUE SYNDROME & FIBROMYALGIA INFORMATION EXCHANGE FORUM

http://www.co-cure.org

Sponsor: Raymond Colliton.

Directory of Web sites about these conditions.

Hyperlinks to articles about CFS and FMS with summaries of their content.

Ψ DISEASES OF THE LIVER

http://cpmcnet.columbia.edu/dept/gi/disliv.html

Sponsor: Howard J. Worman, M.D., Columbia University.

FAQs about liver diseases and treatment.

Annotated summaries of recent papers.

Links to other sites on liver disease.

Ψ ENDOCRINE DISEASES

http://www.endocrineweb.com

Sponsor: YourDoctor, Inc.

Extensive FAQs concerning the various parts of the endocrine system, disorders, and treatment.

The site map is particularly useful.

EPILEPSY FOUNDATION

http://www.efa.org

Sponsor: Epilepsy Foundation, a support and advocacy group for people with seizure disorders.

FAQs for nonprofessionals about epilepsy and its treatment.

Links to local affiliates around the U.S.

EPILEPTICS.COM

http://www.epileptics.com

Sponsor: Eric Borgos.

Links to epilepsy Web sites, newsgroups, chat areas, and clinics.

FIBROMYALGIA NETWORK

http://www.fmnetnews.com

Sponsor: Fibromyalgia Network.

Fact sheets about fibromyalgia diagnosis and treatment.

Links to relevant Web sites.

Ψ FIBROMYALGIA PATIENT SUPPORT CENTER

http://fmpsc.org/info/info.htm

Sponsor: Fibromyalgia Patient Support Center.

Extensive collection of links to information about fibromyalgia and treatment options. This site is frequently updated.

HEP-C ALERT

http://www.hep-c-alert.org

Sponsor: Hep-C Alert, a nonprofit educational association.

FAQs and links about Hepatitis-C, and recent news topics.

MOTHERRISK

http://www.motherisk.org

Sponsor: Hospital for Sick Children, Toronto.

Describes the hospital's programs for supporting at-risk mothers.

Ψ NERVOUS SYSTEM DISEASES

http://www.mic.ki.se/Diseases/c10.html

Sponsor: Karolinska Institutet (Sweden).

Extensive megasite for central and peripheral nervous system diseases and their treatments.

VI. ADDITIONAL MEDICAL-RELATED WEB SITES

ANGEL FLIGHT FOR VETERANS

http://veterans-aeromedical.org

Sponsor: Angel Flight for Veterans, a charity.

Arranges free or low-cost medical transportation for veterans, active duty military personnel, and their families.

ANGEL FLIGHT FOR VETERANS
Dedicated To Helping Veterans And Their Families in Need of Medical Transportation

Mission	AF America	Giving to AFV	Contact Us
News	Aviation Charities	Health Charities	Main Page

THE MEDICINE PROGRAM

http://www.ims-1.com/~freemed/info.html

Sponsor: The Medicine Program, a volunteer organization.

For a $5.00 processing fee per medication, a patient receives applications for pharmaceutical programs that supply free medications to qualified applicants.

MEDMARKET.COM

http://www.medicom.com

Sponsor: MedMarket.Com.

A megasite for suppliers of physician's office needs and home health care products.

Ψ NEEDY MEDS

http://www.needymeds.com

Sponsors: Libby Overly, M.S.W.; Rich Sagall, M.D.

Information about pharmaceutical company programs that supply medications free or at reduced cost to people who cannot afford them. The programs are indexed by drug and manufacturer.

Details the application process for each medication.

Updated frequently.

PATIENTTRAVEL.ORG

http://www.patienttravel.org

Sponsor: Mercy Medical Airlift, a charity.

Charitable transportation for medical evaluation and treatment within the U.S.

YAHOO! NEWS: FULL COVERAGE: GULF WAR SYNDROME

http://fullcoverage.yahoo.com/Full_Coverage/Health/Gulf_War_Syndrome

Sponsor: Yahoo!

Links to Web sites and current news articles.

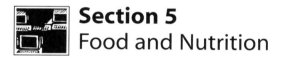

Section 5
Food and Nutrition

I. FOOD AND NUTRITION

AMERICAN DIETETIC ASSOCIATION

http://www.eatright.org

Sponsor: American Dietetic Association.

Fact sheets about proper diet and links to consumer and professional Web sites.

AMERICAN SOCIETY FOR CLINICAL NUTRITION

http://www.faseb.org/ascn

Sponsor: American Society for Clinical Nutrition.

Press releases about this professional society's meetings and activities. Some links to other organizations' Web sites.

Ψ ARBOR NUTRITION GUIDE
http://www.arborcom.com

Sponsor: Dr. Tony Helman, an Australian physician and nutritionist.

A megasite with links to sites about food science, clinical nutrition, and cooking.

Click on the icons at the top of the page to see how rich this site is.

Links are annotated, and every link category has a "Pick of the Crop."

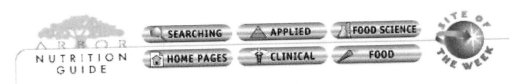

CYBERMACRO
http://www.cybermacro.com

Sponsor: Great Eastern Sun Natural Food Products.

Articles on the macrobiotic diet originating from the site's discussion forums, recipes, and links to sites about macrobiotics and "natural health."

FOOD ALLERGY NETWORK
http://www.foodallergy.org

Sponsor: Food Allergy Network, a nonprofit association that distributes information about food allergies, especially in children.

FAQs and recipes.

Summaries of a few research studies on food allergies.

Online shopping for people with food allergies is provided

The Food Allergy Network

FOOD AND NUTRITION INFORMATION CENTER

http://www.nal.usda.gov/fnic

Sponsor: United States Department of Agriculture.

Dietary guidelines and links to information about nutritional composition of foods and restaurant items.

INTERNATIONAL FOOD INFORMATION COUNCIL FOUNDATION

http://ificinfo.health.org

Sponsor: IFIC Foundation, which disseminates information about food science to consumers.

Articles about food safety and nutrition for consumers.

Ψ NUTRITION INFORMATION AND YOUR HEALTH

http://ai2.bpa.arizona.edu/~polin/nutrition

Sponsor: University of Arizona Health Sciences Center.

Megasite for professionals, with annotated links to sites about nutrition, health recipes, exercise, weight control, and alternative medicine.

Ψ NUTRITION NAVIGATOR

http://navigator.tufts.edu

Sponsor: Tufts University.

Megasite with reviews and ratings of hundreds of nutrition Web sites.

Has a handy search engine. For example, a search for "lactose intolerance" yielded more than 800 annotated and rated results.

Resources are categorized to meet the interests of parents, women, children, professionals, and people with special nutritional needs.

A Rating Guide to Nutrition Websites

Presented by the Center on Nutrition Communication, *School of Nutrition Science and Policy*

About This Site About the Ratings Visitor Feedback Submit Site Awards

Women   Focus On: Hot Topics
               Women's Health

Kids   Search

VEGSOURCE INTERACTIVE

http://www.vegsource.com

Sponsors: Medical professionals interested in health vegetarian nutrition.

Extensive discussion boards on aspects of vegetarianism, an online magazine, and a recipe directory.

Click on "VegCentral" to see categorized links that are rated by popularity.

II. FITNESS AND EXERCISE

ATOZFITNESS

http://www.atozfitness.com

Sponsor: Lewis Wolk.

Fitness and bodybuilding links.

Ψ FITNESS FIND

http://www.fitnessfind.com

Sponsor: FitnessFind.com.

Links to many resources on exercise and nutrition.

Ψ WORKOUT.COM

http://www.workout.com

Sponsor: Workout.com, Inc.

Extensive information about different exercises, categorized by fitness goal. Many of the exercises have brief how-to videos. Site requires free registration.

CHAPTER 5
Mailing Lists, E-Groups, Usenet, and Other Web Sites of Value to the Therapist

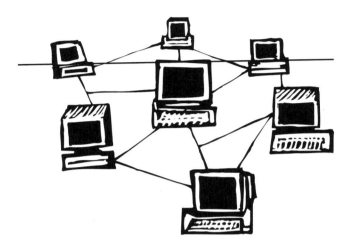

 Section 1
Mailing Lists, E-Groups, and Usenet

I. MAILING LISTS

Mailing lists, or listservs, allow subscribers to send e-mail messages to other subscribers by submitting their message to the appropriate address. Their contribution is then automatically forwarded to all members of the listserv. These discussions are constructed around individual topics and contributors are expected to stay within the confines of the chosen topic. These discussion groups usually have between a few dozen and a few hundred members; some consist of only a handful of people, while others contain several thousand. The average mean number of subscribers is probably about 50.

The vast majority of mailing lists are open, meaning that one can subscribe simply by sending an e-mail to the administrative address and entering the appropriate subscription command. There is no screening process or intermediary. A small percentage require the potential member to identify his or her credentials and reasons for wishing to participate. A select few are open only to members of a certain organization; these groups are rarely promoted on the Web. Once membership has been accepted, the user sends contributions to an e-mail address that is different from the one used to subscribe, unsubscribe, or obtain information.

Mailing lists sometimes have moderators—individuals who regularly screen messages for content and appropriateness. The moderator can often be contacted if the prospective member has any questions. Other lists are wide open, regulated only by the occasional negative comments of participants. Both open and moderated lists often have an automatic "info" message that will deliver specifics about the list upon request. This information can often be obtained by sending an "INFO" request to the administrative e-mail address. Frequently, the topic alone will give the interested participant enough information to make an informed decision about the group; the description that sometimes accompanies a mailing list does not always give any additional pertinent information.

List subscribers may expect to receive as few as five messages each month or as many as several dozen per day. It's difficult to ascertain beforehand how many messages one might receive from any given list or how helpful those messages might be; therefore, it's important to retain subscription information in case one wishes to unsubscribe from a list. Instructions on contributing or unsubscribing are often found at the bottom of individual messages. In America, the words "subscribe" and "unsubscribe" (or "signoff") are most commonly used; in the UK, the commands most frequently used are "join" and "leave."

A mailing list can be a very valuable source of information and personal contacts. It can unite interested parties from around the world in stimulating discussion and debate. It can also, unfortunately, become a constant source of irritation. There are people around the world who have little to do but pontificate all day on all sorts of issues. Etiquette is often lacking in even the most professional mailing lists, and participants should make sure that their communication is especially polite and solicitous—it is easy to misunderstand e-mail communication.

Approach mailing lists with cautious optimism. Read messages for a few days to get the layout of the land before contributing. When you have a question for an individual member, don't reply to the group as a whole—instead, respond to the individual's e-mail address, which is usually included in the communication.

Most mailing lists are found either from **Liszt**, at: http://www.liszt.com; or from the **CataList** Catalog, at: http://www.lsoft.com/lists/listref.html. There are probably about 150,000 active mailing lists at any given time; CataList has listings for more than 30,000, while Liszt maintains a listing of more than 90,000. Some mailing lists are sponsored by and available from individual Web sites; these lists may or may not be listed with a catalog. Finding mailing lists is much like using a search engine—Web sites that catalog listservs do so either by categories (Liszt has 16 major ones with more subcategories), by Web-like search features, or both.

A **Directory of Scholarly and Professional E-Conferences** is maintained at: http://n2h2.com/KOVACS, with a mirror site at: http://www.mailbase.ac.uk/kovacs. There are more than 140 categories to choose from, including psychology and psychiatry. This Web site includes approximately 4,500 lists. The **InterPsych** Web site at http://www.interpsych.org also has mailing lists. Some mailing lists maintain archives of old messages; others do not. Ask group members or write the moderator for information about archives.

Below we have included many popular mailing lists that deal with topics found elsewhere in this book. There are thousands more available; we encourage the reader to explore them.

II. E-GROUPS

E-groups are mailing lists or chat rooms that are usually more casual in tone than listservs. They are generally sponsored by professional associations or organizations, search engines, large Internet service providers (ISPs), Instant Messaging programs, or virtual communities, which are Web sites where people go to explore various issues and feel a sense of belonging. E-groups may use the mailing list format in which messages are relayed to individual members; they could also be chat rooms organized around specific topics, where participants can communicate in real time.

It is often easier to subscribe to an E-Group than to a mailing list. Participants can often make one click of the mouse at the sponsoring Web site to subscribe. The largest host of these is **eGroups** at: http://www.egroups.com. People or organizations that wish to start their own group may do so for free from this Web site; limited advertising is used to support their services. For a nominal fee, this advertising can be eliminated. This is the place to start looking for popular lists that clients and their families wish to use.

III. USENET

Usenet newsgroups are similar to mailing lists, but the reader must access the messages manually rather than scan them as they arrive in the daily e-mail. No one truly "belongs" to a Usenet newsgroup; anyone may post or read messages. Whether relevant, scurrilous, insulting, or commercial in intent, any posted message appears in the newsgroup, except in those few ("moderated") lists that screen news messages before distribution. Messages posted to a Usenet newsgroup are automatically distributed to computers known as news servers. Each ISP maintains one or more news servers for its members. ISPs receive different sets of newsgroups, so that a particular newsgroup may not be accessible from some news servers. Messages remain posted for a few days to a few weeks. Some Usenet newsgroups maintain archives at Web sites, but most do not. See http://www.deja.com/info/usenet_faq.shtml for a more detailed introduction to newsgroups and posting etiquette.

The easiest way to read Usenet groups is with news reader software that can be purchased as shareware or downloaded for free; see http://www.tucows.com for a number of fine programs. However, generally used Internet browsers (Internet Explorer and Netscape) come with news reader accessories. Without using any additional software, Usenet newsgroups may be read and easily searched at http://www.deja.com/usenet. Both the freestanding news reader software and the browser accessories (but not Deja.com) will allow messages to be marked off as already read, which makes it easier to find where one left off when the newsgroup is next accessed.

Individual newsgroups are not detailed here; there are hundreds of thousands of them, and they come and go. Although they are generally not the medium of choice for professional communication, some newsgroups are useful sources of information on a variety of subjects that may be too narrow for a mailing list. Their value should not be underestimated.

One good way to find Usenet groups is to use **Deja.com** at http://www.deja.com/usenet. There is a special section to introduce the novice user to basic concepts. The general search engine **AltaVista** at: http://www.altavista.com also has a good selection; highlight "discussion groups" on their yellow search bar. Liszt, already mentioned, has postings from more than 30,000 newsgroups.

Newsgroups have distinct and identifiable names. They are organized into hierarchies, which are categories that loosely define their content, location, or sponsor. Each newsgroup name consists of one or more words separated by periods. Each word to the right of a period narrows the topic being discussed. The hierarchy name is the word that appears all the way to the left. An updated master list of these hierarchies (and they also come and go) can be found at http://www.magmacom.com/~leisen/mlnh/mlnhtables.html.

We have included here a list of mailing lists and e-groups that are of interest to clinicians. Rather than just including subscription information, we have listed the Web site where the list is categorized. It is often necessary to visit the sponsoring Web site to subscribe anyway, and the reader may also view information regarding membership and content that is updated regularly. Listings below are alphabetical, and the primary word(s) that defines its categorization is/are placed in **bold text**.

Because Web sites that categorize mailing lists do not employ a common method of classification, we have included directions on how to access individual lists from each site:

Mailing lists categorized at **InterPsych.org** do not list specific list names (i.e. AFFECTIVE-DISORDERS); use the generic description instead to access particular lists.

Mailing lists categorized at **The Directory of Scholarly and Professional E-Conferences** at http://www.mailbase.ac.uk/kovacs are listed by list name (e.g., *AFFECTIVE-DISORDERS*). Use these names (usually but not always upper case) to access particular lists. Enter the name at the Global Search feature on the home page.

E-groups listed at http://www.**egroups.com** are categorized by their group names, and groups that deal with similar topics have slightly different names (e.g., *eating_disorders, eating-disorders, eating-disorders-support-london*).

Mailing lists at the **CataList** at: http://www.lsoft.com/lists/listref.html are initially categorized by administrative e-mail address, but using the list name (e.g., *AFFECTIVE-DISORDERS*) from their general search feature will locate that particular list.

When searching from http://www.liszt.com, use the name provided below from the main Liszt search feature (Category I) at the top of their home page. There may be an occasional duplication, but the description next to each name will lead to the appropriate list.

Mailing lists, e-groups, and Usenet newsgroups are all listed below in alphabetical order by topic.

A

Adult **ADD** (AADD-FOCUSED)
http://n2h2.com/KOVACS

Alternative and holistic healing techniques for treating **ADD** (ADD-HOLISTIC)
http://n2h2.com/KOVACS

Addiction medicine
http://www.interpsych.org

Addictions (ADDICT-L)
http://n2h2.com/KOVACS

Affective disorders (AFFECTIVE-DISORDERS)
http://n2h2.com/KOVACS

Aggression (AGGRESSION-PSYCHOLOGY)
http://n2h2.com/KOVACS

Aging (AGING-D)
http://www.lsoft.com/lists/listref.html

Psychological processes in **alcohol** consumption (ALCOHOL-PSYCHOL)
http://n2h2.com/KOVACS

Alexander technique and other movement systems ("deepgravity")
http://www.egroups.com

Alternative therapies (AlternativeAnswers)
http://www.egroups.com

Alzheimer's (ALZHEIMER)
http://n2h2.com/KOVACS

Animal assisted therapy (therapydogsusa)
http://www.egroups.com

Anxiety disorders (ANXIETY-DISORDERS)
http://n2h2.com/KOVACS

Anxiety and panic (ANXIETY)
http://n2h2.com/KOVACS/

Art therapy (ARTTHX-L)
http://n2h2.com/KOVACS

Art therapy (art_therapy)
http://www.egroups.com

Aspergers (AspergersCentral)
http://www.egroups.com

Psychological **astrology** (PSYCH)
http://n2h2.com/KOVACS

Psychological **astrology** (astropsych)
http://www.egroups.com

Attachment (ATTACHMENT)
http://n2h2.com/KOVACS

Autism (AUTINET)
http://n2h2.com/KOVACS

B

Behavior analysis (BEHAVIORANALYSIS)
http://n2h2.com/KOVACS

Behavior analytic therapy (BEHAV-AN)
http://n2h2.com/KOVACS

Behavioral disorders in children and youth (BEHAVIOR)
http://n2h2.com/KOVACS

Behavioral medicine and psychology (BEHAVIORAL)
http://www.lsoft.com/lists/listref.html

Bereavement therapy (SOCW7366)
http://www.lsoft.com/lists/listref.html

Biofeedback (biofeedback)
http://www.egroups.com

Bipolar (Bi_Polar)
http://n2h2.com/KOVACS

Bipolar I (Bipolar2)
http://www.egroups.com

John **Bowlby** (attachment issues) (Bowlby-L)
http://n2h2.com/KOVACS

Clinical psychophysiology and **biofeedback**
http://www.interpsych.org

Borderline personality disorder (BorderlinePD)
http://www.egroups.com

Traumatic **brain** injury (SCR-L)
http://n2h2.com/KOVACS

Breathwork (breathwork)
http://www.egroups.com

C

Canada mental health issues (Can-mad)
http://n2h2.com/KOVACS

Child abuse and neglect (CHILD-MALTREATMENT-RESEARCH-LSU)
http://n2h2.com/KOVACS

Child and adolescent psychiatry (CHILD-PSYCH)
http://n2h2.com/KOVACS

Child and adolescent psychology (CHILD-ADOLESCENT-PSYCH)
http://n2h2.com/KOVACS

Christian issues (HEALING-HEARTS)
http://n2h2.com/KOVACS

Clinical psychology (CLINICAL-PSYCHOLOGISTS)
http://n2h2.com/KOVACS

Codependency (Codependency)
http://www.egroups.com

Co-counseling (liberationrc)
http://www.egroups.com

Cognitive science (COGSCI)
http://n2h2.com/KOVACS

Community psychology (COMMUNITY-PSYCHOLOGY)
http://n2h2.com/KOVACS

Computers in mental health
http://www.interpsych.org

Scientific study of **consciousness** (ASSC-ANNOUNCE)
http://n2h2.com/KOVACS

International **Counselor** Network (ICN)
http://n2h2.com/KOVACS

Cross-cultural psychology (C-PSYCH)
http://n2h2.com/KOVACS

Creativity (CREA-CPS)
http://n2h2.com/KOVACS

Cultural psychology (CULTPSY-L)
http://n2h2.com/KOVACS

Current issues in psychology and psychiatry (PSYCH-CI)
http://www.lsoft.com/lists/listref.html

D

Dance therapy (dancetherapylovers)
http://www.egroups.com

Dependency (DEPEN-CR)
http://n2h2.com/KOVACS

Depression (depress)
http://www.liszt.com

Depression research (DEPRESSION-L)
http://n2h2.com/KOVACS

Deprogramming (Deprogramming)
http://www.egroups.com

Developmental disabilities (AUTISM)
http://n2h2.com/KOVACS

Developmental disabilities (PSYCH-DD)
http://n2h2.com/KOVACS

Developmental disabilities support for parents (childdevdelays)
http://www.egroups.com

DID/MPD (didcs-l)
http://n2h2.com/KOVACS

Disabled sexuality (disableSexDiscussion)
http://www.egroups.com

Disaster mental health professionals (DisastMH)
http://n2h2.com/KOVACS

Dissociative disorders (DISSOCIATIVE-DISORDERS)
http://n2h2.com/KOVACS
http://www.interpsych.org

Division 12 APA (DIV12)
http://n2h2.com/KOVACS

Division 28 APA (DIV28)
http://n2h2.com/KOVACS

Divorce support (divorce-support)
http://www.egroups.com

Drama therapy (odgroup)
http://www.egroups.com

Drug abuse research (itgforum)
http://www.liszt.com

Dual diagnosis (Dual_Diagnosis)
http://www.egroups.com

Dual diagnosis support (undefeated)
http://www.egroups.com

Dual diagnosis support (Dual-Recovery)
http://www.egroups.com

E

Eating Disorders (EATING-DISORDERS)
http://n2h2.com/KOVACS

Ecopsychology (ECOPSYCHOLOGY)
http://n2h2.com/KOVACS

Ecological psychology (COMPSY-L)
http://n2h2.com/KOVACS

EMDR (EMDR)
http://www.egroups.com
http://www.emdr.com has a mailing list available to those who have
completed EMDR training through the EMDR Institute.

Employee Assistance (EA)
http://n2h2.com/KOVACS

Enneagram (ENNEAGRAM)
http://n2h2.com/KOVACS

Examination for professional practice in psychology (EPPP_Prep)
http://n2h2.com/KOVACS

European psychology (europsych)
http://www.egroups.com

Evolutionary psychology (evolutionary-psychology)
http://www.egroups.com

Experimental generators (PSYCH-EXPTS)
http://n2h2.com/KOVACS

F

Family therapy and issues (FAMLYSCI)
http://n2h2.com/KOVACS

Father's rights (Fathers_are_Parents_too)
http://www.egroups.com

Feng Shui (AppliedFengShui)
http://www.egroups.com

Fibromyalgia (fibromyalgia-CFS)
http://www.egroups.com

Fixations (FIXATE)
http://n2h2.com/KOVACS

Food and mood (pnpdeperssion)
http://www.egroups.com

Forensic psychology/psychiatry (FORENSIC-PSYCH)
http://n2h2.com/KOVACS

Fragile X (fragilex)
http://www.egroups.com

Freud (Freud)
http://www.egroups.com

G

Gay issues in psychology (QUEERPSYCH)
http://n2h2.com/KOVACS

Geriatric neuropsychology (GERIATRIC-NEURO)
http://n2h2.com/KOVACS

Advancement of **Gestalt** therapy (AAGT)
http://n2h2.com/KOVACS

Graduate students discussion list (PSYCGRAD)
http://n2h2.com/KOVACS

Group psychotherapy (GROUP-PSYCHOTHERAPY)
http://n2h2.com/KOVACS

Guilt (GUILT)
http://n2h2.com/KOVACS

H

Health Psychology (HP-BMED)
http://www.lsoft.com/lists/listref.html

Helplessness
http://www.interpsych.org

HIV/AIDS (HIV-AIDS-PSYCHO-SOCIAL)
http://n2h2.com/KOVACS

Humanistic psychology (humanisticpsychology)
http://www.egroups.com

Human rights violations in psychiatry (DENDRITE)
http://n2h2.com/KOVACS

Hypnosis
http://www. interpsych.org
http://www.apa.org/about/division/div30.html

Hypnosis-hypnotherapy (hypnosis-hypnotherapy)
http://www.egroups.com

I

Incest survivors (incestsurvivors)
http://www.egroups.com

Industrial psychology (IOOB-L)
http://n2h2.com/KOVACS

Infant development (WAIMH)
http://n2h2.com/KOVACS

Interamerican psychologists (IAPSY-L)
http://n2h2.com/KOVACS

Intersex support (twentyfourseven)
http://www.egroups.com

Intervention outcomes (OUTCMTEN)
http://n2h2.com/KOVACS

J

Jewish psychology issues (jewish-psy)
http://www.liszt.com

Jung psychological type (TYPWRT-L)
http://www.lsoft.com/lists/listref.html

K

Kinesiology (Kinesiology)
http://www.egroups.com

L

Latin psych
http://www.interpsych.org

Psychology and **law** (PSYLAW-L)
http://n2h2.com/KOVACS

Psychology in **law enforcement** (PsyCOP)
http://n2h2.com/KOVACS

M

Managed behavioral health care (MBHC)
http://www.lsoft.com/lists/listref.html

Managed care issues (NHCTEN)
http://n2h2.com/KOVACS

Psychological **marketing** and business practice issues (PsyBUS)
http://0n2h2.com/KOVACS

Media and mental health (MENTAL-HEALTH-IN-THE-MEDIA)
http://n2h2.com/KOVACS

Meditation (meditation)
http://www.egroups.com

Methadone maintenance support (methadonemaintenancefriendly)
http://www.egroups.com

Adults **molested** as children (AMAC)
http://www.egroups.com

Multiple chemical sensitivity (mcsfn)
http://www.egroups.com

Munchausen falsely accused (Lances)
http://www.egroups.com

Music therapy (MUSTHP-L)
http://n2h2.com/KOVACS

Myers-Briggs (Myers-Briggs)
http://www.egroups.com

N

Narrative therapy (NarrativeApproach)
http://www.egroups.com

NLP (NLP)
http://www.egroups.com

NLP (NLPonline)
http://www.egroups.com

Neuropsychology (NEURO)
http://www.lsoft.com/lists/listref.html

Neuropsychology or Neuropsychiatry (NEURO-PSYCH)
http://n2h2.com/KOVACS

Neuropsychology (G-NEURO)
http://n2h2.com/KOVACS

Psychiatric **nurses**
http://www.interpsych.org

0

OCD (OCD-l)
http://n2h2.com/KOVACS

Online support and counseling (DNET)
http://n2h2.com/KOVACS

Orgonomy (orgonomy)
http://www.egroups.com

Orthomolecular (orthomolecular)
http://www.egroups.com

P

Pain (chronic_pain)
http://www.egroups.com

Paraphilias (SEXUAL-VARIANTS-AND-DISORDERS)
http://n2h2.com/KOVACS

Parapsychology (PSI-L)
http://n2h2.com/KOVACS

Parkinsons support (parkinsons)
http://www.egroups.com

Past life regression (avalone)
http://www.egroups.com

Pastoral Counseling (pastoral-counseling)
http://www.egroups.com

Pedophiles support (pedophiles-anonymous)
http://www.egroups.com

Personality assessment inventory (PAI-NET)
http://n2h2.com/KOVACS

Personality Disorders (PERSONALITY-DISORDERS)
Two lists: one for clients and one for clinicians.
http://n2h2.com/KOVACS

Pick's Disease (picks-support)
http://www.egroups.com

Play therapy (playtherapy)
http://www.egroups.com

Polarity therapy (PolarityTherapy)
http://www.egroups.com

Private **practice** issues (PSYCH_PRACT)
http://n2h2.com/KOVACS

Primal therapy (primaltherapy)
http://www.egroups.com

Primal therapy (Primal-Support-Group)
http://www.egroups.com

Psychiatry (psyche)
http://www.liszt.com

Psychiatry research (psychiatry-research)
http://www.egroups.com

Psychiatry resources (P-SOURCE)
http://www.lsoft.com/lists/listref.html

Psychiatry trainees (psytrain)
http://www.liszt.com

Psychoanalysis (psychoanalysis)
http://www.egroups.com

Psychoanalysis (psychoanalysis-and-psychotherapy)
http://www.egroups.com

Psychoanalysis (PSYCHOAN)
http://n2h2.com/KOVACS

Psychoanalysis and the public sphere
http://www.interpsych.org

Psychohistory
http://www.interpsych.org

Psychopharmacology (PSY-PHAR)
http://www.lsoft.com/lists/listref.html

Psychopharmacology in treatment (PSYCHO-PHARM)
http://n2h2.com/KOVACS

Psychology (PSYCHOLOGY)
http://n2h2.com/KOVACS

Psychometrics (ASSESS-P)
http://n2h2.com/KOVACS

Psychometry (fourtellanon)
http://www.liszt.com

Psychosomatic and behavioral medicine
http://www.interpsych.org

Psychosynthesis (PSYCHOSYNTHESIS)
http://n2h2.com/KOVACS

Psychotherapists in training (PIT-D)
http://n2h2.com/KOVACS

Psychotropic drug awareness (drugawareness)
http://www.egroups.com

PTSD (PTSD)
http://www.lsoft.com/lists/listref.html (see also "Traumatic Stress Forum")

Public mental health (APHAMH-L)
http://n2h2.com/KOVACS

R

Rape crisis support (rapecrisis)
http://www.egroups.com

Reiki (Reiki)
http://www.egroups.com

Reiki Kundalini (Reiki-kundalini)
http://www.egroups.com

Remote viewing (remote-viewing)
http://www.liszt.com

Research design
http://www.interpsych.org

Research psychologists (RESEARCH-PSYCHOLOGISTS)
http://n2h2.com/KOVACS

Research psychology (APASD-L)
http://www.liszt.com

Restless legs (restless_legs)
http://www.egroups.com

Ritual abuse (ritual_abuse)
http://www.egroups.com

Rorschach information and discussion
http://www.interpsych.org

Rural care
http://www.interpsych.org

S
Schizophrenia (SCHIZOPH)
http://n2h2.com/KOVACS

Schizophrenia research (SCHIZ-L)
http://n2h2.com/KOVACS

Self-help (SLFHLP-L)
http://n2h2.com/KOVACS

Self-help support groups (SELFHELP)
http://n2h2.com/KOVACS

Sexual abuse survivors (ripplebacktome)
http://www.egroups.com

Sexual addiction (CoAnon) (screened and moderated)
http://n2h2.com/KOVACS

Shyness (shyness)
http://n2h2.com/KOVACS

Sibling loss (adult-siblings)
http://www.egroups.com

Sleep (sleephelp)
http://www.egroups.com

Sleep disorders (sleepdisorders)
http://www.egroups.com

Smart recovery (SMARTREC)
http://n2h2.com/KOVACS

Smoking cessation cognitive (CognitiveQuitting)
http://www.egroups.com

Smoking cessation support (quitting-buddies)
http://www.egroups.com

Sobriety (LivingSober)
http://www.egroups.com

Social work (SocialWork-Issues2Go)
http://www.egroups.com

Social work (SCIOFSLW)
http://www.lsoft.com/lists/listref.html

Psychiatric **social workers**
http://www.interpsych.org

Psychology **software** (CTI-PSYCHOLOGY)
http://n2h2.com/KOVACS

Solution-focused therapy (SFT-L)
http://n2h2.com/KOVACS

Sport psychology (SPORTPSY)
http://n2h2.com/KOVACS

Step parents (AAAStep-Parents)
http://www.egroups.com

Sufi (sufi-studies)
http://www.egroups.com

T

Tantric sex (TantricSex)
http://www.egroups.com

Teaching in psychology (TIPS)
http://n2h2.com/KOVACS

Telehealth news
http://www.interpsych.org

Telehealth resource list
http://www.interpsych.org

Psychological **testing** (VALIDATA)
http://n2h2.com/KOVACS

Psychological **testing** and evaluation (EVALTEN)
http://n2h2.com/KOVACS

Psychological **theory** (CROSSTALK)
http://n2h2.com/KOVACS

Thought Field Therapy (TFT-ALGO)
http://www.egroups.com

Transactional analysis (tapsychotherapy)
http://www.egroups.com

Transcultural psychology
http://www.interpsych.org

Transgender (able-trans)
http://www.egroups.com

Traumatic stress forum
http://www.interpsych.org

Secondary **traumatic stress**
http://www.interpsych.org

V

Viagra (viagra)
http://www.egroups.com

W

Widows (young-widows)
http://www.egroups.com

Witness psychology (CAAWP)
http://www.lsoft.com/lists/listref.html

Y

Yoga (yoga-news)
http://www.egroups.com

Young women (RevivingOphelia)
http://www.egroups.com

Section 2
Web Sites of Value to the
Therapist

With the exception of Part I, the sites included in this section do not have direct clinical significance but may benefit the working clinician, researcher, or academic in other ways.

I. *DSM-IV* and *ICD-10* Codes
II. Evaluating Web Sites
III. Using APA Style
IV. Finding Information on the Web
V. Humor
VI. Managed Care
VII. Intelligence and Creativity
VIII. Media

I. *DSM-IV* AND *ICD-10* CODES

These sites are not individually reviewed because they merely list diagnostic categories and their associated numerical classifications.

http://www.fgi.net/~freud/dsm4.htm

http://uhs.bsd.uchicago.edu/~bhsiung/tips/dsm4.html

http://www.nzhis.govt.nz/projects/dsm.html

http://www.who.int/msa/mnh/ems/icd10/icd10.htm#codes

http://psy.utmb.edu/disorder/dsm4/dsmnum.htm

http://www.informatik.fh-luebeck.de/icd/Indexaz.html

II. EVALUATING WEB SITES

Ψ APA DOTCOMSENSE

http://helping.apa.org/dotcomsense

Sponsor: American Psychological Association.

A brochure on how to evaluate the credibility of health information found on the Internet. Also includes some tips on Web privacy.

Can be printed out in .PDF format or ordered in printed form for distribution to clients.

CHECKLIST FOR EVALUATING WEB SITES

http://www.canisius.edu/canhp/canlib/webcrit.htm

Sponsor: Canisius College.

A checklist for Web content and many links to other similar resources.

EVALUATING WEB SITES FOR EDUCATIONAL USES: BIBLIOGRAPHY AND CHECKLIST

http://www.unc.edu/cit/guides/irg-49.html

Sponsor: Carolyn Kotlas, University of North Carolina, Chapel Hill.

Lengthy list of online and print resources.

III. USING APA STYLE

ELECTRONIC REFERENCE FORMATS

http://www.apa.org/journals/webref.html

Sponsor: American Psychological Association.

Help on citing e-mail, Web sites, specific documents in Web sites, articles and abstracts from electronic databases, and Web citations in text.

Electronic Reference Formats
Recommended by the American
Psychological Association

PROPOSED STANDARD FOR REFERENCING ONLINE DOCUMENTS IN SCIENTIFIC PUBLICATIONS

http://www.beadsland.com/weapas

Sponsor: T. Land.

Information for referencing online documents in APA style.

IV. FINDING INFORMATION ON THE WEB

COPERNIC MULTIPLE SEARCH SOFTWARE

http://www.copernic.com

Sponsor: Copernic Technologies.

This free software lets you search many search engines at the same time with one query. A professional edition is for sale at a nominal cost, but the free version will suffice for the vast majority of people.

DOGPILE

http://www.dogpile.com

Sponsor: Dogpile.com.

Queries multiple search engines with a single request.

NORTHERN LIGHT

http://www.northernlight.com

Sponsor: Northern Light Technologies.

Northern Light categorizes material from more than 5,400 sources—not just Web sites. Their Search Alert Service…will send subscribers e-mail when new Web sites are posted or content is added to their Special Collection of materials that matches individ preferences.

Special content may be purchased for a nominal cost; this is a great place to go to locate hard-to-find subjects.

YAHOO! LIST OF SEARCH ENGINES

http://dir.yahoo.com/Computers_and_Internet/Internet/World_Wide_Web/Searching_the_Web/Search_Engines

Sponsor: Yahoo!

Probably the most comprehensive listing of search engines/portals on the Web.

V. HUMOR

HUMOR IN PSYCHOLOGY

http://www.psych.upenn.edu/humor.html

Sponsor: The Psychology Department at the University of Pennsylvania.

A long (very long) list of jokes, limericks, and bumper stickers.

THE LIGHTER SIDE OF PSYCH

http://users.erols.com/geary/psychology

Sponsor: Charlotte's Web.

Well-organized section of some pretty funny stuff. For example: What do psychologists say to each other when they meet? "You're fine, how am I?"

THE MANY FACES OF DR. KATZ

http://www.sassman.com/katz

Sponsors: Tom Snyder Productions and Comedy Central.

A complete listing of Dr. Katz episodes. Additional info on this popular series.

PROFESSION JOKES: PSYCHOLOGISTS AND PSYCHIATRISTS

http://www.geocities.com/CapeCanaveral/4661/projoke30.htm

Sponsors: David Shay and Deddi Shy.

Click on the Table of Contents at the bottom for the main directory.

VI. MANAGED CARE

MANAGED CARE ISSUES FOR DEVELOPMENTAL DISABILITIES

http://www.mcare.net/index.html

Sponsor: Institute on Disability, University of New Hampshire.

A reference guide for insurance issues.

Includes a listserv and links to other sites that deal with managed care.

RATING OF INSURANCE COMPANIES

http://www.mentalhealth-madison.com/Documents/Rate_the_Insurer.htm

Sponsors: Gordon Herz, Ph.D., Mental Health Associates (WI).

Uses the TIP (Therapists' Insurer Profiling) scale to assess insurance companies. A must visit for those in private practice.

VII. INTELLIGENCE AND CREATIVITY

CREATIVITY WEB

http://www.oze-mail.com.au/~caveman/Creative/index.html

Sponsor: Charles Cave, Sydney, Australia.

Many resources for creativity and innovation

Creativity Web

Resources for Creativity and Innovation

Welcome	The Brain	Mental Workout Center
	Models of the Brain	Problems, Visual Puzzles and Word
What's New	The Creative Process	Games
	Healthy Body, Healthy Mind	
10 Creativity Kick Starts	Sound Health (Music)	Idea and Problem Bank
	Multiple Intelligences	
Creativity Basics		Resource Center
	Idea Recording	Books
	Journals and Index Cards	Software
Techniques		Web Sites
	Your Creative Space	People and Organisations
Mind Mapping		Mailing Lists
	Humour and Cartooning	
Quotations		Drawing
	Genius Gallery	
Affirmations		Visual Thinking
	Children's Corner	

DR. HOWARD GARDNER

http://www.pz.harvard.edu/Pls/HG.htm

Sponsor: Fellows of Harvard College.

Theories of multiple intelligence.

UNCOMMONLY DIFFICULT IQ TESTS

http://www.eskimo.com/~miyaguch/hoeflin.html

Sponsor: Darryl Miyaguchi.

Lots of information on a variety of tests and links to many other sites that deal with intelligence in general.

VIII. MEDIA

SELF-HELP MAGAZINE

http://www.shpm.com

Sponsor: Pioneer Development Resources.

An online educational publication written by mental health professionals for the discussion of general psychology as applied to our everyday lives. Includes more than 95 discussion forums.

REUTERS HEALTH

http://www.reutershealth.com

Sponsor: Reuters Ltd., a global financial and news service .

Free daily news on health matters.

How to Use the CD-ROM

The enclosed CD-ROM contains active links for all of the Web sites described in the book and can be used on both Macintosh and Windows-based computers. Like the book, the CD-ROM is divided by chapter and section. There is a main index file that contains links to all of the chapters and their respective sections. If you wished to look at a site that is listed in section 2 of chapter 3, simply open the file entitled "Chapter 3 Section 2" from the index. **At the bottom of each chapter section, click on the link called "Return to Index" to return back to the main index page.**

HOW TO OPEN THE FILES:

You must first have a Web browser program (such as Netscape Navigator or Microsoft Internet Explorer) open on your computer.

1. Instructions from Netscape Navigator:
   a. Click "File" on the toolbar, then "Open Page."
   b. A small window will appear asking what page you'd like to open. Click "Choose File" on this window.
   c. Locate the drive with the CD and click on it.
   d. The HTML files will appear. Highlight the file called "Index.htm" and click "Open."
   e. The file will then open in the Netscape window. Click on whichever section you would like to explore.

2. Instructions from Microsoft Internet Explorer:
   a. Click "File" on the toolbar, then "Open."
   b. A small window will appear asking what page you'd like to open. Click "Browse" on this window.
   c. Locate the drive with the CD and click on it.
   d. The HTML files will appear. Highlight the file called "Index.htm" and click "Open."
   e. Click on whichever section you would like to explore.

3. Instructions from Netscape Communicator (Macintosh):
   a. Click "File" on the toolbar at the very top of the screen, then "Open," then "Page in Navigator."
   b. A small window will appear asking where the file is that you want to open. Navigate to the desktop and click on "HTML_Internet_Handbook."
   c. The HTML files will appear. Highlight the file called "Index.htm" and click "Open."
   d. Click on whichever section you would like to explore.

In order to bookmark a site in Internet Explorer, click "Favorites" on the menu bar, then select "Add to Favorites." In Netscape Navigator, click "Communicator" on the menu bar, then "Bookmarks," then "Add to Bookmarks."